BIRDS OF PREY

Natural History and Conservation of North American Raptors

Text and Photographs by
Noel and Helen Snyder

VOYAGEUR PRESS

Printed in Hong Kong through Bookbuilders Ltd.
91   92   93   94   95   5   4   3   2   1

Typseset by
Peregrine Publications, St. Paul, Minnesota

Library of Congress Cataloging-in-Publication Data

Snyder, Noel F. R.
    Birds of prey : natural history and conservation of North American
raptors / Noel F. R. and Helen A. Snyder.
        p.   c.m.
    Includes bibliographical references and index.
    ISBN 0-89658-131-4
        1. Birds of prey—North America.   2. Birds, Protection of—North
                            America.
    I. Snyder, Helen A. (Helen Andrus).   II. Title.
    QL696.F3S678 1991
    598.91'097—dc20   91-14719
                                                                CIP

Published by
Voyageur Press, Inc.
P.O. Box 338, 123 North Second Street
Stillwater, MN 55082 U.S.A.
From Minnesota and Canada 612-430-2210
Toll-free 800-888-9653

Voyageur Press books are also available at discounts for quantities for educational, fundraising, premium, or sales-promotion use. For details contact the marketing department. Please write or call for our free catalog of natural history publications.

Contents

– CONTINUED –

BIRDS OF PREY

An adult Golden Eagle in Alaska returns to her nest with a branch late in the nestling period.

On its roost snag in southern Florida, a particularly bold wintering Peregrine Falcon launches an attach on nearby waterfowl. Peregrines almost always capture prey in flight and usually wait until circumstances allow them the advantage of surprise before taking flight.

Introduction

SINCE THE EARLIEST of times, predatory birds have figured prominently in the art, ceremonies, and legends of most human societies. Fierce images of raptors abound in the cave paintings of primitive peoples around the world. Feathers of large birds of prey once decorated the festive costumes of many Indian tribes. Ritual sacrifices of condors and eagles were formerly a widespread custom in the native religions of both North and South America. In manifestations ranging from mummies of falcons in the pyramids of Egypt to gold and turquoise owls fashioned by ancient artisans of Peru, raptors have permeated the traditions of virtually all civilizations over many thousands of years.

The cultural importance of raptors has not diminished in more modern times. Our national bird, the Bald Eagle, is a bird of prey. The Crested Caracara reigns as Mexico's sovereign symbol. Raptors have likewise been chosen for names and logos by innumerable other organizations, from baseball teams to rock bands. Condor Helicopters, Eagle Office Products, Falcon Realty, Hawkeye Heating and Cooling—the evidence of our bewitchment with these birds can be found in strange and diverse places.

Just how this timeless veneration of the birds of prey originated is not completely certain. Perhaps the bond we perceive with these bold avian aggressors traces to deep-rooted human traditions of hunting and warfare. Perhaps it is best viewed as a reflection of our intrinsic admiration and respect for creatures that can dominate the skies and kill without remorse. Perhaps it also stems from other, more primordial fears and emotions. Whatever the major sources may be, our ties to the birds of prey are indeed powerful.

North America's birds of prey fall into two distinct groups: the nocturnal raptors—the owls—which we will not be considering in this book; and the diurnal raptors—the hawks, harriers, kites, falcons, caracaras, eagles, ospreys, vultures, and condors. Traditionally, the diurnal raptors have all been assembled into one order of birds, the Falconiformes. All members of this order are meat-eaters and possess hooked bills adapted for tearing apart food. Most are large species capable of soaring flight under the proper conditions, and most have a visual acuity far surpassing our own. Because of these and other shared characteristics, it has always seemed natural to group all the diurnal raptors together.

Yet despite the many characteristics they hold in common, it is now quite well established that the falconiform groups are not all closely related to one another. In particular, the New World vultures have only a very distant common ancestry with other diurnal birds of prey, and in fact find their closest relatives among the storks. Nevertheless, for our purposes here there is still considerable logic in treating together all the groups traditionally considered to be falconiform. This is especially true for discussions of many topics in ecology and conservation. Irrespective of their ancestral relationships, the falconiform groups share much in their reproductive and foraging habits, and in their vulnerability to stresses such as environmental pollutants.

In this book we have two major goals. First, by offering glimpses into the natural history of North America's diurnal raptors and by presenting a variety of photographs of these species carrying on their daily activities, we hope to awaken curiosity about the biology of all birds of prey worldwide. Second, by detailing some of the problems faced by the North American species and by suggesting solutions to specific threats, we hope to encourage a general interest in raptor conservation. In pursuit of these goals, we do not presume that the reader already knows a great deal about raptors or natural history, and we keep scientific jargon to a minimum. On the other hand, we do consider many current topics of debate in raptor biology, in hopes the reader will be as interested in the unknowns about raptors as in the knowns.

We have not attempted to provide encyclopedic descriptive accounts of the species under consideration, nor have we attempted to provide a thorough review of the many outstanding biological studies that have been conducted with raptors over the years. These approaches have already been ably pursued in other books, such as Brown and Amadon's *Eagles, Hawks, and Falcons of the World;* Palmer's *Handbook of North American Birds;* and Newton's *Population Ecology of Raptors.* Rather, our approach is a more limited one of providing an introduction to a range of biological and conservation issues affecting birds of prey through a primary focus on our personal experiences and through discussion of selected key studies of other biologists. For those interested in more comprehensive and detailed information, we supply at the end a list of important readings that will amplify what we present in the written accounts.

The thirty-four species of raptors considered in this book are all the falconiform species that have bred regularly in recent times within the confines of continental North America. Included are species that are limited largely to cold climates, namely the Gyrfalcon and the Rough-legged Hawk, as well as a number of species, like the Common Black Hawk and Aplomado Falcon, that are primarily tropical in distribution but do reach the United States along its southern borders. The diversity of raptors found in North America is quite remarkable, and we have long pursued a personal goal of becoming familiar with all these species in the field. The experiences and photographs presented here represent the accumulation of several decades of study and recreation. We hope that they may convey in some small measure the pleasures and excitement to be found in observing raptors interacting with their fellow creatures in nature.

In truth, there is no adequate way to communicate the values that birds of prey represent for those who have come to know them well. Words, art, and photographs are invariably feeble substitutes for actual experiences. Swirling masses of migrating Broad-winged Hawks can be described after a fashion, but the descriptions cannot bring to life the spectacle itself, just as there is no way to convey properly the unique sounds and smells of a troop of hungry Black Vultures and Crested Caracaras battling over a rotten raccoon carcass. Such vivid impressions become engraved in an observer's consciousness, and their strength provides the primary motivation for the study of these birds. If this book stimulates even a single reader to venture forth into the field to discover directly the value of such experiences, we will count our efforts successful.

Our emphasis on natural history betrays a firmly held conviction that field studies of raptors are among the most rewarding pursuits a person can undertake,

either as an amateur or professional ornithologist. And despite occasional assertions to the contrary by desk-bound theoreticians, field studies in natural history remain the essential source from which all ecological generalizations must flow if they are to have any validity. Even with the North American raptors, which have already received considerable attention from naturalists, many opportunities for new discoveries and insights still exist. For the many raptor species beyond our borders which have never had more than the most cursory study, the opportunities for original contributions are nearly unlimited.

The study of tropical birds of prey, some of which are highly vulnerable to extinction, represents an especially urgent conservation priority. Virtually nothing is yet known about the natural history or ecological requirements of many of these species. In the years ahead, a comprehensive understanding of the biology of these birds will be crucial for the development of successful measures to ensure their continued existence.

As a group, North America's diurnal raptors occupy all major habitats on the continent and interact with many of the wildlife species in these habitats, often as their predators, sometimes as their prey. Moreover, the diurnal raptors suffer from many of the same conservation problems faced by these other wildlife species. In fact, as was dramatically demonstrated during the DDT era, the sensitivity of raptors to various invisible yet pervasive forms of environmental degradation can be especially great, and they can serve as valuable "indicator species" of the overall health of ecosystems. Furthermore, because raptors require relatively large expanses of habitat and feed on a great diversity of prey species, the efforts to ensure their survival necessarily aid the survival of many other creatures within their ranges. Thus, the measures taken to preserve from extinction such species as Everglade Kites and California Condors have much wider significance than just the improved welfare of these particular species.

As the human population of our planet continues to swell, it becomes increasingly difficult to preserve the biological diversity on which our survival and quality of existence depend. Perhaps this is ultimately a hopeless battle, but to give up in the effort would be to guarantee defeat. We firmly believe it is unlikely that much can be achieved without empathy and aesthetic appreciation for the intrinsic values of wildlife. We hope that this book may contribute to that empathy in ways that may eventually lead to a more stable balance between our species and the natural world.

The Major Groups of North American Raptors

NORTH AMERICA'S FALCONIFORM raptors have been traditionally classified into four families: the Vulturidae (Cathartidae), the Accipitridae, the Pandionidae, and the Falconidae. The Accipitridae is the largest group and includes the hawks, harriers, kites, and eagles. The Falconidae includes the caracaras and falcons. The Vulturidae includes the New World vultures and condors (Old World vultures are members of the Accipitridae), while the Pandionidae includes only a single living species, the Osprey.

The division of the Falconiformes into these families is based in part on anatomical and in part on behavioral and physiological characteristics. Each family is a "natural" unit comprised of species of birds that are believed to be reasonably closely related by evolutionary descent. However, the relationships between the families remain relatively uncertain for the most part. How close the Falconidae might be to the Accipitridae has been long debated, as has the degree of relationship between the Pandionidae and the Accipitridae. In contrast, the lack of a close relationship of the Vulturidae with other falconiform raptors and the close linkage of this group with the storks (Ciconiiformes) are now widely accepted. Even so, the vulturids are still usually placed in the Falconiformes, more because ingrained traditions die slowly than for any other reasons.

Regardless of just how closely the major groups are related to one another, it is worthwhile reviewing some of their important characteristics before we move on to individual species.

VULTURIDAE

The New World vultures (Vulturidae or Cathartidae) are an obviously tightly knit group of species sharing a large number of traits. All are primarily carrion feeders and possess naked heads, an adaptation reducing the risks of feather-fouling for species that commonly in-

sert their heads into the inner recesses of rotten carcasses. All also practice a curious mode of heat regulation known as urohidrosis (cooling off by drenching the legs with excrement), and all nest in caves or other cavities, laying their eggs directly on substrata of litter rather than in definable nests built of twigs. Further, all members of this group possess only weak talons more suited to walking than to grasping, and all are essentially mute except for wheezes and snorts audible at close range.

The vulturids include the two largest living members of the Falconiformes: the California Condor and the Andean Condor, both of which commonly exceed twenty pounds in weight and sometimes exceed ten feet in wingspread. Even larger vultures in a closely related family, Teratornithidae, roamed the New World only a few thousand years ago. The largest flying bird ever known to exist on the planet, *Argentavis magnificens,* was a member of this now-extinct group. Recently described from fossils found in Argentina, *Argentavis* had a wingspread estimated at an astounding twenty-three feet and a weight estimated at about 160 to 170 pounds.

In North America at present two vulturid species occur in the wild, the Black Vulture and the Turkey Vulture. A third North American species, the California Condor, has come to exist only in captivity, although there are plans to return it to the wild in the near future. In addition, historical records leave little doubt that a fourth species, the King Vulture (*Sarcoramphus papa*), occurred in Florida up until the time of the American Revolution. The King Vulture is still widespread in Central and South America, and is commonly bred in captivity.

ACCIPITRIDAE

The Accipitridae is a more diverse assemblage of raptors with more varied and to some extent more obscure relationships with one another. This group includes the hawks of the genera *Buteo* and *Accipiter*, as well as eagles of the genus *Aquila* and harriers of the genus *Circus*. It also includes a number of raptors known as kites that possess especially buoyant flight characteristics. The kites themselves are a diverse assemblage. One subgroup, which includes the Everglade Kite (*Rostrhamus sociabilis*) and Mississippi Kite (*Ictinia mississippiensis*), exhibits a peculiar fusion of bones of the middle toe. Interestingly, this same anatomical trait is also found in sea eagles of the genus *Haliaeetus*, very likely reflecting a close ancestral relationship. Thus, the Bald Eagle (*Haliaeetus leucocephalus*) apparently is much more closely allied to the Everglade Kite and Mississippi Kite than it is to the other North American eagle, the Golden Eagle (*Aquila chrysaetos*), which it more closely resembles in size and habits.

Within the Accipitridae, the largest group of species is the buteonine hawks, an assemblage made up primarily of species in the genus *Buteo*, but also including a number of other closely related species in genera such as *Buteogallus* and *Parabuteo*. Twelve of the thirty-four species of North American raptors belong to this group, and they can be characterized as medium-sized accipitrids with broad wings and relatively short tails that feed primarily on vertebrates. Confusingly, in the Old World, members of the genus *Buteo* are generally referred to as "buzzards," while members of the genus *Accipiter* are referred to as "hawks." In North America, members of both *Buteo* and *Accipiter* are commonly referred to as hawks, while buzzard is a term applied historically to certain vulturids. Nowadays, however, the term buzzard is rarely used for any North American raptor.

Most accipitrids are active predators. Their prey range from insects and snails to birds and large mammals, depending on the raptor in question. One group, the Old World vultures, has secondarily evolved to feed on carrion and exhibits many of the anatomical adaptations, especially of the head and feet, seen in the New World vultures. Nevertheless, the Old World vultures clearly reveal their accipitrid affinities by building nests of sticks.

PANDIONIDAE

The Osprey has generally been considered to be fairly closely related to the Accipitridae, although this species possesses a number of very distinct anatomical features, especially in the structure of its talons. Most ornithologists continue to classify it in a separate family, Pandionidae. The Osprey is a specialized predator of fish, and like the accipitrids, builds substantial nests of twigs.

FALCONIDAE

The Falconidae of North America include only two genera, *Polyborus* and *Falco*. Like other genera in this family worldwide, these two genera differ from accipitrids and the osprey in a number of anatomical and behavioral respects. Both possess distinctive accessory bones attached to the base of the tailbone, for example, and both possess a tendency to attack prey with the talons and bill, rather than just with the talons. None of the species in the genus *Falco* is known to build nests, and they typically breed in old nests of other species or in caves or other natural cavities. In contrast, caracaras of the genus *Polyborus* do build twig nests that are similar to accipitrid nests.

Like the vulturids and certain accipitrids, some falconids include carrion in their diets, though most are highly specialized as active predators. Species such as the Crested Caracara, that do feed on some carrion, show the typical tendency for loss of feathers in the head region that is associated with this habit.

Altogether, some 292 falconiform raptors exist in the world today, and thirty-four have bred in continental North America in recent times. Most falconiform raptors are tropical in distribution and face the increasing threats of deforestation and habitat destruction that have characterized this region of the world in recent decades. Of the North American species, only one, the California Condor, is presently on the brink of extinction. Several others, most notably the Bald Eagle and Peregrine Falcon, suffered drastic declines during the DDT era and are now recovering. Two species, the King Vulture and the California Condor, have been lost from the wild in the United States, and a third, the Aplomado Falcon has been virtually lost. All three still exist in captivity or in the wild elsewhere, and all three are excellent candidates for reintroduction efforts. The Aplomado Falcon is already the subject of a preliminary reestablishment program in Texas.

Most other raptors of North America are sustaining themselves in reasonable numbers, and a few, particularly several species of kites, have shown major increases in recent decades. Perhaps the species most vulnerable to loss are several tropical raptors that just barely reach the United States along its southern borders. These species, the Common Black Hawk, the Zone-tailed Hawk, the Gray Hawk, the White-tailed

Hawk, the Short-tailed Hawk, the Hook-billed Kite, the Everglade Kite, and the Crested Caracara, all occur in viable populations south of the border, but their North American populations are so small that they could easily disappear unless special efforts are made to ensure their survival.

HOW RAPTORS ARE CLASSIFIED

The falconiform raptors of this book, like all other living creatures, are classified in a hierarchical scheme of categories. The most basic and well-defined category is the **SPECIES**, which represents an assemblage of organisms (in this case, birds) that interbreed with one another. Species may sometimes be divided into geographic **RACES** (or subspecies) that differ from one another in subtle ways, but the various races of a species are all part of one interbreeding assemblage.

Species do not normally interbreed with other species. However, if a species shares a great many characteristics with certain other species and is believed to be very closely related to these other species, it may be classified in the same **GENUS** as these other species. A genus is thus a group of relatively similar species believed to be derived from a close common ancestral stock.

Each species is given a unique latinized scientific name, which consists of a genus name followed by a species name. For example, the scientific name of the Red-tailed Hawk, *Buteo jamaicensis,* consists of a genus name, *Buteo,* and a distinctive species name, *jamaicensis.* Other hawks in the genus *Buteo,* for example the Broad-winged Hawk (*Buteo platypterus*) and the Short-tailed Hawk (*Buteo brachyurus*), are all relatively similar to and presumably very closely related to the Red-tailed Hawk. When geographic races of a species are recognized, the race name follows the species name in the full scientific name, as in the Mexican race of the Northern Goshawk: *Accipiter gentilis apache.*

When species are classified in different genera, they are considered less closely related to one another than when they are in the same genus. Nevertheless, genera that are believed to be relatively closely related to one another are placed in the same **FAMILY**. North America's diurnal raptors belong to one or another of four different families–the Vulturidae, the Accipitridae, the Pandionidae, and the Falconidae–and each family consists of one or more genera. For example, the family Vulturidae consists of seven living species in five genera– *Vultur* (one species), *Gymnogyps* (one species), *Cathartes* (three species), *Sarcoramphus* (one species), and *Coragyps* (one species)–while the family Pandionidae consists of only one genus and species, *Pandion haliaetus*– the Osprey. That the Osprey is the only species in its family indicates that it does not have any truly close relatives among the other diurnal raptors.

Finally, the four families of North American diurnal raptors are all classified together in one **ORDER**, the Falconiformes, which is a major division of the **CLASS** Aves, which includes all birds. There is a growing consensus that these four families are not all truly closely related, and ultimately some of these families may be reclassified into a different system of orders as new information on relationships becomes available.

As a summary example of how raptors are presently classified, we give below the full hierarchy of avian categories to which the arctic race of the Peregrine Falcon belongs:

CLASS: Aves–all birds
    ORDER: Falconiformes–all diurnal raptors
        FAMILY: Falconidae–falcons, laughing falcons, pygmy falcons and falconets, forest falcons, and caracaras
            GENUS: *Falco*–falcons
                SPECIES: *Falco peregrinus*–Peregrine Falcon
                    SUBSPECIES: *Falco peregrinus tundrius*–arctic race of the Peregrine Falcon

Vultures

Above: A mated pair of California Condors sun near their nest in Ventura County in 1983. Successful in rearing chicks in both 1981 and 1983, these birds perished over the winter of 1984–1985. Right: Some eleven thousand years ago, California Condors nested in cliffs along the Colorado River in the Grand Canyon in Arizona. Remains found by Steve Emslie in nest caves on these cliffs included bone fragments of extinct mammoths, camels, bison, horses, and mountain goats—species that appear to have been common foods for the condors of that era.

California Condor
GYMNOGYPS CALIFORNIANUS

WITH BROAD BLACK and white wings approaching ten feet in span and a weight often exceeding twenty pounds, the immense, carrion-feeding California Condor is the only North American bird that can be easily mistaken at a distance for a small airplane. It is also one of the few North American birds for which a reasonably comprehensive paleontological history can be traced back through recent geological epochs. Extensive fossil deposits indicate that California Condors once ranged over nearly the entire continent, undoubtedly feasting on carcasses of the huge mammals of the ice ages. Dying mastodons, saber-toothed cats, dire wolves, ground sloths, and many others now long extinct must frequently have had their rotting bodies ripped apart and converted into condor flesh, just as the elephants, giraffes, lions, and wildebeest dying in present-day Africa generally wind up in the bellies of the condorlike griffon vultures of that continent.

With the disappearance of many of the great Pleistocene mammals of North America about eleven thousand years ago, the condors became restricted to the Pacific Coast region. Here they still found relatively good food supplies in whale carcasses and remains of other marine mammals washed ashore, and in dead Tule elk, pronghorn, mule deer, and bighorn sheep in the inland valleys. Condors were still seen with frequency from British Columbia to Baja California when the first western explorers reached this region in the eighteenth and nineteenth centuries.

However, with the settlement of the West Coast by Europeans, the fortunes of the condor again began to worsen. Many birds were lost to indiscriminate shooting and poisoning. Others may have suffered from declines in food availability resulting from uncontrolled human destruction of herds of native ungulates. Condor populations disappeared first from Oregon and Washington,

then northern California and Baja California, and by 1940 the only remaining birds were limited to a region surrounding the southern San Joaquin Valley not far north of Los Angeles. Here the condor made its last stand in the wild.

Unfortunately, despite all efforts to reverse the decline, including the establishment of the magnificent Sespe Sanctuary in the Los Padres National Forest, the

Range of the California Condor
☐ Historic (1800)
◼ Recent (1980s)
Fossils for a Pleistocene-era condor have been found in New York, Florida, Texas, New Mexico, Arizona, California, and northern Mexico.

species continued its steady slide toward extinction. By 1985, just nine individuals remained in the wild, including but a single breeding pair. Most observers were convinced that these last few birds could not survive much longer unless they might be taken captive. With the trapping of the last wild condor in early 1987, the species has now come to exist only in captivity, though there are ambitious plans to return it to the wild within a very few years.

The enormous size and striking appearance of the condor, together with its well-known prehistoric association with the giant mammals of the Pleistocene, have given the species a largely undeserved reputation of having long outlived its proper place in the ages. At the same time, the great rarity of the species and its restriction in breeding to remote and spectacularly rugged mountains have made the condor a popular symbol of pristine wilderness, the antithesis of our civilized world. Even the name "condor" evokes visions of a mysterious regal creature existing on a plane transcending ordinary reality (an image the species might not have if its original appellation of California Vulture had endured). Perhaps more than any other North American bird, the California Condor has achieved a status of awe and reverence in our society, even among those who know and care very little about the natural world.

Unfortunately, the spiritual aura that surrounds the California Condor has probably worked more to the species' detriment than to its favor. More than a few have considered it a sacrilege to subject such an exalted creature to the kinds of intensive conservation efforts that have become necessary if the species is to survive. For some, the preservation of a pristine image of the condor has been more important than the preservation of the species itself. Besides being a victim of our many ecological excesses, the condor has been a victim of its own wilderness mystique.

When we were approached in late 1979 to lead the field research effort of the U.S. Fish and Wildlife Service in a new expanded program to prevent the condor's extinction, we were intrigued by the challenge and were naively eager to have a chance to study this awesome bird. But if we had known what a quagmire of controversy we were entering, we might well have declined the opportunity.

We began studies in early 1980, in cooperation with John Ogden of the National Audubon Society and a dedicated group of field assistants. At this time, much too little information was available to indicate clearly what the major problems of the condor might be. Despite a succession of admirable studies stretching back to the 1930s, it was still unknown whether the primary causes of the species' decline might lie in poor reproduction or in poor survival. In fact, we lacked sufficient information even to specify with any accuracy how many condors might still remain in the wild, though it appeared likely there were very few, probably less than thirty.

The obvious research needs were improved censusing techniques, comprehensive studies of the remaining nesting pairs to evaluate reproductive success, and a thorough marking program, especially with radiotelemetry, to determine survival rates and causes of mortality. At the same time, it seemed wise to initiate a captive-breeding program as a fail-safe strategy, because a good chance existed that even once the major problems of the wild population were identified, they might not yield readily to remedial measures. Surrogate studies with Andean Condors and other vulturids had indicated a good potential for captive propagation and for release of captives to the wild, and it was crucial that attempts to initiate captive breeding of California Condors not be long delayed. With continued population decline, the species could soon lose much of its potential for recovery because of genetic deterioration resulting from inbreeding.

This overall approach had received the endorsement of most major conservation organizations in the states and a prestigious panel of professional ornithologists convened by the American Ornithologists' Union and the National Audubon Society in 1977. Clearly, the relatively passive conservation measures that had been in effect since the time of Carl Koford's original condor studies in the 1930s and 1940s had failed to reverse the decline. These measures, consisting primarily of habitat protection and efforts to reduce indiscriminate molestation of the species, had to be augmented by more active measures if there was to be much hope of saving the species.

Yet as necessary as this approach seemed, it did not represent a full consensus of all interested parties. It actually took several more years of exhausting debates and negotiations, coupled with a number of false starts and diversions, before a truly effective program was finally in operation. Only then did answers to many of the crucial questions about the species begin to come in.

Our field efforts in the early 1980s were focused primarily on developing effective methods to census the wild population and on locating the last breeding pairs in the wild and studying their reproductive characteristics. Success in these efforts led ultimately to a much more intensive conservation program by 1983. Sadly, by that time the wild population had dropped below twenty individuals, and further efforts became a desperate race against the clock.

An effective condor censusing method evolved largely from the work of Eric Johnson and his students at California Polytechnic State University in San Luis Obispo. These researchers had been studying the behavior of condors in one of the principal foraging areas of the species in the ranchland foothills of the southern San Joaquin Valley. The concentration of condors in this region was due to good supplies of carrion food, particularly stillborn calves, rancher-killed coyotes, and remains of hunter-killed deer. Here the birds were often seen at close enough range to allow detection of individual peculiarities in feather patterns. From the visual records kept by Eric and his crew, it appeared that there might be enough differences in these patterns from one bird to the next to allow rigorous identification of individuals, and hence comprehensive censusing of the population. But this only seemed feasible if the records of feather patterns could be made thorough enough and reliable enough, perhaps through widespread photography of birds in the field.

In late 1981, we began an intensive cooperative effort with Eric and others to photograph condors in flight throughout the known range. Initial results looked very promising. The effort was expanded in 1982 and yielded a firm count of twenty-one condors for the late summer of that year. This was the first comprehensive count of the entire condor population ever achieved, and was an important step in convincing skeptics that the species truly was in great jeopardy and needed fast and decisive aid if it was going to survive.

Photographic counts in the following years showed an alarming decline: to nineteen birds in 1983, fifteen in 1984, and only nine in 1985, yielding an overall mortality rate in the wild population approaching 25 percent annually—far too high a mortality rate to allow population stability under even the most optimistic reproductive conditions. Meanwhile, our monitoring of breeding effort and success of the remaining wild pairs indicated that the population was still doing reasonably well from a reproductive standpoint. Clearly, the species' main problem was mortality, although the exact causes of mortality remained largely unknown.

The most significant result from the observations of nesting pairs came in 1982. In this year, a pair of condors under constant daylight surveillance chose a particularly poor nest cave for egg laying—one with a floor that sloped significantly to the outside. This also was a pair that had chronic problems in coordinating incubation duties. The adults bickered continuously over

whose turn it was to warm the egg and often left the egg untended as the male repeatedly chased the female away from the nest cave. During one dispute the egg rolled out of the nest cave, and shortly thereafter it fell over the edge of the cliff, smashing on the rocks below. At the time, this incident seemed the greatest of tragedies. But as subsequent events unfolded, it became clear that it was the most fortunate thing that could possibly have happened for the species. The detailed documentation of this event and the events that followed totally revolutionized the course of the conservation program.

Forty days after destruction of their egg, the pair proceeded to lay a replacement egg. This was the first time replacement laying had ever been proven conclusively for the species, and the discovery had profound implications. Even though the second egg was also lost—in this case to raven predation—a principle had been demonstrated that was to allow an enormous increase in reproduction of the population in the years that followed. With the solid documentation of replacement-clutching in hand, we were able to obtain approval from the state and federal permitting authorities to take and artificially incubate first eggs from all condor pairs in 1983, in the expectation that they would lay again and that reproduction might be as much as doubled as a consequence.

The success of multiple-clutching far exceeded expectations, for the total production of young condors in 1983 was six individuals, thanks in large part to the skilled incubation of eggs and rearing of young carried out by Cyndi Kuehler and Bill Toone and their staffs at the San Diego Zoo. This total should be compared with an average of two fledglings that the wild population had produced annually from 1980 through 1982. Results were even better in 1984 with seven young produced. These young, together with a nestling taken captive in late 1982 when its parents exhibited an alarming decline in feeding rates, a yearling trapped in poor health in late 1982, and Topatopa (a bird taken as a starving fledgling in 1967), formed the original nucleus of a captive population at the Los Angeles and San Diego zoos, a population that now has come to offer the only hope for ultimate survival of the species.

The tremendous increase in reproduction produced by multiple-clutching in 1983 and 1984, coupled with the good survival of breeding pairs in these years, encouraged the California Condor Recovery Team to develop a plan, later approved by the state and federal authorities. Multiple-clutching of wild pairs would continue at a near maximal rate, but once a minimum of

Above: Early morning mists envelop the low elevations of the Sespe Condor Sanctuary in the Los Padres National Forest of California. A principal nesting region for the California Condor in recent decades, this area has also been a refuge for vigorous populations of black bears and mountain lions.

Below: An adult condor rests on its roost tree atop Mount Pinos of Ventura County. Condors traditionally congregated here in mid- to late summer, perhaps attracted by the cool temperatures at high elevations.

A pair of condors mutual preen on a talus slope near their nest cliff in 1981. One of these birds, "Lady of the Lake," later nested in the 1984 sequoia nest site with a different mate.

Right: Beached blue whales, such as this seventy-foot individual on the Big Sur, once formed a significant, if irregular, portion of the diet of the California Condor, just as beached marine mammals are still fed upon by the Andean Condors of South America.

five young were produced for the captive flock by each pair, further production of young from the pairs would be channeled back into the wild flock in an early release program. We all anticipated that these releases might serve to sustain the wild flock while efforts were continued to learn the causes of mortality and reverse these causes. At that time, the mortality rate, while considerable, appeared to be low enough that the increased productivity achievable by multiple-clutching might be enough to largely counterbalance it.

Unfortunately, events of the winter of 1984–1985 revealed this strategy to be much too optimistic. Six adult condors were lost from the wild population, mostly to unknown causes, and of the five wild pairs active in 1984, only one survived to breed in 1985 – a near total collapse of the wild breeding population. No longer did a significant source of young birds exist to build up the captive flock, let alone to serve as a basis for an early release program, and by then we were becoming increasingly concerned over the genetic viability of the existing captive flock. Mortality was clearly a much larger problem than had been appreciated earlier, and it had become highly questionable that the death rate could be sufficiently reduced to allow maintenance of the wild population.

Retrenchment was in order. Releases of captives to the wild in the near term could not be expected to greatly slow the decline and would at the same time jeopardize the chances for achieving a genetically viable captive population. Further, it had become clear that the entire future of the species was now totally dependent on achieving a viable captive population, and there was no point in compromising the chances for success in this endeavor. The remaining birds in the wild population had much more to contribute to conservation of the species as captives than by being left in the wild to die one by one.

Meanwhile, the discovery of a number of dead or dying condors revealed that the wild population was being stressed by mortality factors that were largely impractical to counteract. Three of four condors found dead or dying between 1983 and 1985, in part through radiotelemetry, were suffering from lead poisoning, apparently resulting from ingestion of lead bullet-fragments present in their carrion food. The fourth bird was a victim of cyanide poisoning from a coyote trap. While it was possible to "solve" the threat of cyanide poisoning by modifying cyanide trapping procedures (this activity was then under direct control by the U.S. Fish and Wildlife Service), it is doubtful that this had been a major problem for the condor overall. Lead poisoning, on the other hand, had now emerged as a very important problem, one that in all probability had been stressing the species since the first Europeans settled the region.

Unfortunately, lead poisoning was also a nearly insoluble problem, at least in the short term, as no good alternatives to lead bullets existed for hunting species such as deer – steel bullets or shot were not acceptable substitutes. Furthermore, because hunting and predator-control activities, such as coyote shooting, were very widespread and popular activities in southern California (both legally and illegally), almost all observers agreed that a blanket prohibition of shooting in the condor range would be impossible to enforce and would almost certainly be a political disaster that would actually increase mortality risks to condors via a backlash, instead of reducing them. So strong was the agreement on this point that it was never seriously considered as a practical strategy. Finally, an intensive effort in 1985 to get the remaining wild condors to feed mainly on "safe" clean carcasses provided by the research program proved to be a failure.

Instead, after a long and bitter debate over whether the last wild condors should be taken captive, a consensus at last emerged that the best hopes for the species did indeed reside in captive breeding of all the remaining individuals in the near term, followed by later reintroductions of captive progeny into very specific regions in the wild where human threats such as shooting, lead poisoning, and collisions with powerlines (all of which are documented problems for the condor) were minimal. In late 1986 and early 1987, the last of the wild condors were trapped for the captive-breeding program at the San Diego and Los Angeles zoos, yielding a total captive population of twenty-seven individuals: fourteen females and thirteen males. Current plans do not call for the return of any of these birds to the wild. Instead, releases will be conducted with progeny of these birds as soon as a secure level of reproduction and genetic representation is achieved in the captive flock.

Encouragingly, none of the California Condors taken captive has yet died, and the first chick to be produced by a captive pair hatched successfully early in 1988. In 1989, three more pairs laid eggs with a total production of four chicks. In 1990, nine pairs laid eggs producing a total of eight surviving young, and the total captive population rose to forty birds. Hopes are high that still more pairs will initiate breeding in the years just ahead. While the condor is clearly in a severe genetic bottleneck at the present time, it appears that enough reproductive vigor still exists in the population to allow both a rapid expansion in numbers and the preservation of nearly all of the remaining genetic diversity in the species. With reasonable luck, the condor may pull through its present crisis successfully, just as the Whooping Crane has bounced back from the brink of extinction. We firmly believe we may live to see the day when healthy wild populations of condors are reestablished in many regions of the Southwest.

But where can California Condors be safely returned to the wild? Much of the recent range of the condor, at least the vast foraging range in the ranchland foothills of the southern San Joaquin Valley, is clearly lethal for the species. Nevertheless, one potentially viable region for releases is the mountainous nesting areas formerly occupied by the species, which are still relatively safe from all known threats. If an adequate food supply could be provided in the nesting regions, and if naive reintroduced condors could be encouraged to rely on such a food supply, it seems possible that the species could be reestablished successfully in this part of the recent range.

The prospects for success in this approach are currently being tested by temporary experimental releases of surrogate Andean Condors into the Sespe Condor Sanctuary. This release program, under the direction of Mike Wallace and Jim Wiley, has had outstanding success so far. In the past two years, the released Andean Condors have established movement patterns that keep them well within safe mountainous regions, and they have continued to take all their food from the provided carcass supply. When enough captive California Condors are available for release, the surrogate Andean Condors will be trapped again into captivity, while the California birds take their places in the wild. Barring unforeseen developments, the first reintroductions of California Condors into the Sespe Sanctuary may occur as soon as late 1991.

Other relatively large and apparently safe areas also exist in various other parts of California and adjacent states and could potentially support viable condor populations if introductions are done in a similar manner. Given the security and time to prepare that the captive population offers, it may also be possible to re-create wild ecosystems that are sufficiently large and safe to sustain condors on completely unmanaged food supplies. Such ecosystems could have immense value as well for many species other than the condor and remain the ultimate goal of conservation efforts.

In the heat of endless debate over the best ways to conserve the condor, the real bird has sometimes been forgotten. The species has become an abstraction, much as have other controversial species such as the grizzly bear and Whooping Crane. Our only restorative to sanity through the last turbulent years of the wild population was to get out into the field to live with the real condor on a daily basis, sharing as much as possible its perceptions of the world and directly observing its difficulties with survival and reproduction. The positive aspects of participating in the condor program all came from the field work, not from the political arena. The species is a lively, interesting bird and has occupied some outstandingly beautiful terrain. Observing the condor in this setting, as it has pursued its daily activities and interacted with companion species in the wild, has given us many extraordinary experiences. These surely are the times we will recall in years ahead, while the memories of endless bureaucratic confrontations and wars fade into well-earned oblivion.

We were especially intrigued by the daily battles of nesting condors with one of their principal natural enemies—the Common Raven. To judge from fossil deposits in the La Brea Tarpits of Los Angeles, condors and ravens have coexisted in southern California for millennia. Yet their complex interactions leave unanswered many questions as to how perfectly natural selection can hone a species' defenses against its enemies. Condors seemingly could improve their position against ravens in a number of fairly simple ways, yet they have not, and have continued to take the consequences in the form of significantly reduced reproductive output.

Ravens clearly like to eat condor eggs, and once they become aware of their presence make enthusiastic efforts to acquire them, looking for any opportunities to do so that the condors might allow. Condors, for their part, could avoid this calamity by first of all placing their eggs in sites where ravens are unlikely to discover them, and secondly by guarding their nests sufficiently closely that the ravens have no chance to get at unprotected eggs. Most condor pairs in recent years have had to deal with ravens nesting nearby, and have been highly aggressive to ravens when the latter have come close to their nests, sometimes pursuing them in dramatic aerial chases. Nevertheless, on a number of occasions we have seen condors choose to nest in very open caves near raven nests while much better-protected sites have been available farther away in the same general regions. Further, nest exchanges between adult condors are often conducted in such a way as to leave the nest cave unprotected for periods of up to a half hour or longer, although there does not appear to be any overriding need for both adults ever to leave the nest simultaneously.

The height of vulnerability was reached by a condor pair of 1984 that nested on a precarious ledge just ten feet from an active raven nest. The ravens attempted to grab the condor egg at every chance, and the dust boiled out of the site during repeated tussles between the species. Since we knew that this was a pair of condors that frequently left its nest unprotected during nest exchanges, we took the egg for artificial incubation shortly after it was laid–it had no real chance for survival in the wild.

At another nesting of this same condor pair in 1982, we watched a raven pound its bill through the egg when it was indeed left unattended. At still another nesting of the same pair several miles distant in 1983, a raven was so brazen that it actually walked into the nest cave as one of the adult condors sat incubating and then proceeded to drive blows at the egg under the sitting bird! Fortunately, in this case the adult was incubating a dummy telemetered egg, so we could watch the interactions fully without any real risks for the condors or any reason for us to intervene.

Perhaps the most worrisome raven interactions we observed were at a condor nest found one hundred feet up in a giant sequoia cavity in 1984. Ravens were nesting in a cavity in an adjacent sequoia and made repeated attempts to enter the condor nest, frequently landing right on the lip of the shallow cavity. As this nest site was very difficult to scale, attempting to remove the condor egg for artificial incubation would have been unacceptably risky. We decided the best approach was to shoot the ravens when they were safely distant from the condor nest. However, when one raven is shot out from a pair, a replacement appears almost instantaneously, as we had found out in earlier attempts to eliminate ravens harassing condor nests. In this case, it took the removal of eight ravens before we wound up with a pair, still nesting in the adjacent sequoia, that appeared to have no interest in the condor nest. Shooting operations ceased at this point, and the condor egg hatched without further incident.

Overall, ravens appear to be the most likely explanation for the relatively high rate of egg breakage known for condors through the decades. We even found condor eggshell in an ancient raven nest near a condor cave where Carl Koford had documented egg breakage in the 1940s. Why the condors have not become more adept in countering the raven threat remains a major mystery.

Other natural enemies of nesting condors include black bears and Golden Eagles. With respect to eagle predation, condors have nested in about the safest region available in their range, as eagles do not commonly forage over the brushy chaparral habitat in which condors usually breed. Nevertheless, Golden Eagles have wandered into condor nest areas on occasion, and our nest-watchers twice documented them making predation attempts on condor chicks. In both cases, adult condors were fortunately present nearby and were able to intercept the eagles, preventing loss of the chicks. However, this was extremely fortuitous, as condor chicks are generally left unprotected by adults for much of the day once they reach an age of several weeks. When adult condors are present, they chase eagles from the nest area with vigorous flapping flights. They clearly recognize this species as a threat of major importance.

Black bears were abundant in the last range of the condor, and while most condor nests were high enough up on cliffs to be inaccessible to bears, some could have been easily entered by bears had they been discovered. None of the nests we watched ever fell victim to bears, though there were two close encounters that our team of observers witnessed over the years. In one instance, a bear ambling along the base of a nest cliff obviously caught the scent of the nearly full-grown nestling about seventy-five feet over his head in a small nest cave. The bear rose on hind legs to sniff the air, made repeated unsuccessful attempts to scale the cliff, then finally climbed a tall big-cone Douglas fir that rose in front of the cliff just opposite the nest. Fortunately, the tree was separated from the cliff by just enough distance that he was not able to cross over to the nest cave, and he eventually descended the tree and went on his way empty-handed. Had the bear attempted to get to the nest from the top of the cliff, it is barely conceivable he might have been able to scramble into the site. Fortunately, he was not persistent enough to discover this alternative.

During the bear's efforts to reach the nest, one of the parent condors sat atop the tree in front of the cliff, watching his progress intently, though the bird never directly threatened the bear. At another nest tended by another pair of condors, both adult condors "escorted" an intruding bear away from the site. In this instance, there was no sign that the bear had any suspicions that the condors were guarding a nest. Though he got within one hundred fifty feet of the cave, he soon wandered off, allowing the condors to return to their chick (who apparently remained completely oblivious of what had transpired).

Few ornithologists ever have an opportunity to watch egg laying in a wild bird species, and in truth there is not always a great deal to see as many birds lay their eggs inside nest structures that quite effectively conceal what is happening. Condors, of course, do not lay eggs in well-defined nest structures, though they often lay them in caves that are difficult to see into from a distance. Nevertheless, in 1982, we were able to follow clearly the entire egg-laying process in a condor whose shallow nest site was unusually favorable for observations. From a concealed location on a ridge about a third of a mile away, we could see the full extent of the cave's interior through a telescope, and no intervening vegetation obscured the details of what happened. We had been expecting egg laying from this bird, as she had been spending increasing amounts of time in the site, patiently shaping the floor with her bill, but we had no anticipation of just how egg laying might occur as it had never been witnessed before. When it finally did happen, the actual process was quite surprising.

About two minutes before the event, the bird stood up and faced into the cave from just inside the entrance. A succession of tremors shook her body, and we knew that something important was about to happen and that we should not take our eyes from the scene. Suddenly, the egg simply came shooting out of her body to land in full view on the floor of the cave entrance. Amazingly, she laid it from a standing position, and the egg came crashing to the ground with considerable force, though it was apparently unharmed! Perhaps the cushion of loose litter she had earlier gathered at the laying position was important in softening the impact. She slowly pivoted to look at the egg, then bent down with her bill almost touching it. Within a few minutes, she had settled down to commence incubation, tucking the egg in on top of her feet in the usual position adopted by vulturids.

Hatching was something we were fortunate to see at another nest of the same female, and this process held its surprises as well. We had no good information at that point as to how long incubation lasted in the species though we guessed it might be close to sixty days, judging from information on Andean Condors breeding in zoos. By May 11, 1980, we had been watching the incubation activities of the bird and her mate for some fifty-four days, and we were fortunate to be observing a site, like the site of 1982, whose interior was visible from a distance. However, our observation blind was so distant from this site that many details of events became lost in heat shimmer during the warmer parts of the day. The egg, in any event, was rarely in view, except during brief periods when the tending adult rose to roll and turn it before settling down again with ponderous care. Aside from this, we also glimpsed the egg every few days when the adults exchanged duties at the nest.

By midafternoon of May 11, the midday heat distorted the image in the telescope to such an extent that the incubating bird dissolved at times into a headless black blob. We strained to make out the bird's profile to see whether her eyes were open and alert. Normally, she would have been dozing quietly at this time of day, but today, despite soaring temperatures, she was fully awake. So were we, as we were quite worried about the condition of the egg. A little while earlier, when the bird had stood up to stretch, we had glimpsed what we thought might be a bad break in the shell, a round cracked area about the size of a dime.

Even earlier in the day, the bird had shown difficulties in centering the egg on her toes before settling on it. In trying to slide one foot under the egg, she had accidentally kicked the egg nearly a foot across the floor. Could she have punched a toe in the shell hard enough to crack it?

The afternoon wore on, and the bird remained sitting. The heat built up and crested, then finally began to subside as shadows crept toward the nest cliff from across the canyon. One growing shadow at last began its ascent of the nest cliff, finally blanketing the nest itself by early evening. Now, at last the contrasty light was gone, and the shimmer began quickly to disappear as the rocks surrounding the cave were able to shed their burdens of heat. We wiped the eyepiece and centered the scope for the best viewing conditions of the day. Although we were a half mile from the nest, the Questar picked up details such as a bit of down stuck to the bristly face feathers of the adult, and even revealed the dark red color of her eye. She sat very still, then abruptly she rose, and the egg was finally in clear view between her excrement-whitewashed legs.

There was indeed a break in the egg, and it was now closer to the size of a quarter. Wavering back and forth across the opening was a white spot. It was the egg tooth of the young chick, an ephemeral knob on the top of his bill that he was using to break free from his calcium prison. Remarkably, he had help. The adult reached down, and ever so gently for a bird this big, nibbled at the edges of the break, slowly increasing its size in the patient process of hatching.

From first pipping of a condor egg to actual hatching takes over two days, and we did not get to observe the final moment with this egg, as it happened two nights later. Nevertheless, it was clear that in these condors, unlike in many other birds, the process was a cooperative one between adult and chick, perhaps an important feature allowing the chick to conserve energy during his entry into the world.

Once the chick had hatched, we made continuous observations of his slow development and growth

Above: The adult female of the sequoia pair stands at her cavity entrance during early summer. One of only two condor nests ever found in sequoias, this site was under heavy pressure from nearby ravens. Right: California Condors in the air have relatively short tails, immense wingspreads, and extremely steady flight. Flapping only to take off and land, they are crucially dependent on air currents over topographic features to remain airborne. Distinctive patterns of molt and feather damage allowed reliable identifications of individuals and censusing of the wild population.

through the seasons. It wasn't long before he was leaving the nest to wander about on nearby slopes, but nearly six months passed before he at last took his first flight. Many additional months passed before he was finally independent of his parents. A full condor breeding cycle from egg laying to independence of a fledgling takes longer than a year, and while we occasionally saw a pair breed successfully in consecutive years, egg laying came very late in the breeding season of the second year in these cases.

Fledging is a process we watched with three different condor chicks, and in none of the three cases were parent birds present in the nesting area at the time it occurred. First flights were not very long, nor were they highly controlled, especially in landing. The birds, as they took off, appeared to have no idea where they were headed and only ended their flights when they collided with brushy slopes that loomed unexpectedly in front of them. Then followed a period of terrestrial wandering that eventually, sometimes days later, led the fledglings to sufficiently open locations that they could again take to the air. Repeated forays into the air led fairly soon to some minimal skills in avoiding inadvertent collisions with slopes and cliffs, though landings remained an approximate procedure for a much longer time. The entire process of becoming a skilled aerial performer takes a young condor many months of solo practice.

The chick whose hatching and fledging we watched in 1980 later became a central figure in the final history of the wild population. During the early 1980s, we watched this bird slowly gain independence from his parents, then pick up associations with other condors, and gradually learn to travel the full range of the species. In 1986, he initiated his first breeding attempts as a six-year-old, pairing with an old female who had lost her mate the previous year. This firmly established for the first time the capacities of the species to breed at this age. A year later he was the only known condor left in the wild. With his trapping in early 1987, a new era of captive breeding began in the efforts to prevent the extinction of the species. With considerable hope, we look forward to the time when his progeny will be reestablished in the wild under more favorable conditions than he once enjoyed.

The discovery of condors nesting high in a cavity of a giant sequoia in the Sierra Nevadas was surely one of the most unexpected and exciting occurrences during our years in the condor program. In the days that immediately followed the finding of the site, we found ourselves sitting through a heavy snowstorm trying to make out the incubating adult through the swirling haze of feathery crystals that enveloped the grove. The incubating bird covered her egg steadfastly through this early spring storm, appearing to suffer no ill effects from the frigid temperatures and exposure. White flakes drifted in to settle and accumulate on her back, but they caused her no overt concern.

At the blind where we sat immobile, wrapped in layers of down sleeping bags, the snow depth reached over half a foot. When the storm eventually passed, it left a scene of dazzling beauty, perhaps the most magical of numerous extraordinary wilderness scenes we witnessed during the condor years. Incense cedars, giant sequoias, and other immense trees, their red trunks contrasting with the sparkling white accumulation on their branches, soon began dumping powdery charges of snow as the sun started the inevitable melting process. A Pileated Woodpecker appeared from the forest and landed boldly near the towering top of the condor nest stub to announce his ownership of the region with ringing cries. Other birds, including White-headed Woodpeckers and ravens, soon made appearances as well, and the condor in her wooden cave a hundred feet from the ground finally stirred, apparently satisfied that all was well with the world once again. This was the last storm of the season and provided a welcome infusion of moisture to sustain the forest through the long hot months ahead.

The sequoia pair included a bird we had earlier come to refer to as "Lady of the Lake." However, observations of the bird's display behavior soon revealed, rather embarrassingly, that our lady was the male of the pair. We had first studied this bird intensively when he was paired with another mate along a lakeshore cliff a hundred miles distant in 1981 and 1982. And in truth, we had never been that certain about his sex. Although he was generally on the bottom in copulation attempts with his first mate, none of the attempts was ever successful, and we had always wondered if we might be watching a homosexual pair. However, we were never able to confirm sex of his first partner, as he (she) disappeared in early 1982 before there was any way to obtain such information.

The sequoia nest was discovered because a U.S. Forest Service timbering operation ran right up to the base of the nest tree, and the birds were very conspicuous to an inspection crew checking the area of cutting. That the birds nested in the site despite all the apparent disturbance associated with a lumbering operation was consistent with what we have observed over and over again with most condors—they seem to be quite tolerant of human disturbance – perhaps much too tolerant for their own good. In fact, we had earlier photographed "Lady of the Lake" with his first mate from distances less than thirty feet and with no concealment whatsoever. Whoever started the persistent rumor that condors are incredibly wary creatures, ready to desert their nests at the slightest human disturbance, should have informed the condors.

Much of our field efforts in the years following 1982 became centered around egg-pickup operations. These were always tense and exhausting affairs. Most nest sites could be reached only by what our team of assistants termed "death marches" through brutal terrain, and there were endless opportunities for catastrophes during construction of helipads and access routes to the nests and during the actual egg-pickup operations. Fortunately, the egg-pickup team led by Rob Ramey and Dave Ledig had the stamina to persevere through some pretty unreasonable conditions, and the alert cooperation we had from Charlie McGlaughlin and other personnel of Aspen Helicopters never lapsed. The former name of Aspen Helicopters had been Condor Helicopters, and we were extremely pleased when they proceeded to donate half the costs of transport in getting the many eggs we took over the years to the San Diego Zoo.

Weather is quite changeable in the condor range in spring, and one of our recurrent nightmares was that bad conditions might set in during the midst of an egg-pickup operation, leaving us stuck with an egg already taken and no way to get it to a proper incubator. Fortunately, this never happened, although we came very close on one occasion when the wind rose to such howling intensity shortly after taking the egg that Jim Dalton could only barely land the chopper and we got off only minutes before conditions became totally impossible for flight. As we streaked out of the mountains toward more stable air along the coast, the only thoughts in our minds were ones of intense relief at having made a successful escape.

Unfortunately, our problems were not yet over. In our haste to leave the area, we had not yet fastened our seat belts, and only a half mile from the nest we hit one last turbulent downdraft that "lifted" us and the egg transport case right to the ceiling, breaking one egg case thermometer in the process. Thankfully, the descent back to seat level was reasonably gentle. The egg was unharmed and ultimately hatched successfully.

After the first year of egg pickups, the overall strategy became one of taking eggs as soon as possible after they were laid in order to maximize the numbers of replace-ment eggs that might be produced. This put a considerable burden on the nest-monitoring team, as condors often inspect many potential nest sites repeatedly before finally choosing one for laying, and the potential sites are often scattered among a number of different canyons, sometimes five or even ten miles apart. There are no reliable clues that we have been able to discover that might indicate which of the alternative caves will be used, and although we always did our best to guess which ones would wind up with the eggs, we were more often wrong than right. Apparently, breeding male condors often did not know which sites were going to be used either. Just before egg laying, they generally went off to forage alone, and on their return they sometimes found their mates again only by systematically checking all the holes they had been prospecting together in the previous weeks.

Despite the difficulties in locating condor nests right at laying time, we were nearly always able to find the actual sites within two or three days of egg laying in these years, and the efforts to proceed as fast as possible in taking eggs led to a grand total of three pairs of condors demonstrating a capacity for triple-clutching within a single breeding season. Thus under optimal conditions, a single pair subjected to egg removals is theoretically capable of producing nine young in a three-year period, an enormous increase over the apparent normal maximum of two young in three years for unmanipulated pairs. Thankfully, we were able to approach a full utilization of these capacities in two very successful years of egg pickups before the catastrophic mortality of 1984–1985.

If egg pickups had not started in 1983, the current prospects for the species would be very much worse than they are. Regrettably, it was not possible to start such efforts decades ago, after K. C. Lint and Belle Benchley of the San Diego Zoo first established that captive Andean Condors were capable of double-clutching and proposed initiation of captive breeding of California Condors as a natural conservation step. In hindsight, the protectionist protests that stymied the early efforts of this highly capable zoo to begin captive breeding of the California Condor must be viewed as one of the major factors leading to the present imperiled status of the species.

Nevertheless, the condor still exists. In fact, its total numbers are greater now than they were a decade ago. Its prospects for survival in the long term are actually not all that bad, and not just in captivity. The extreme pessimism often expressed about efforts to prevent the extinction of this species is not warranted, at least not yet.

The California Condor is truly a magnificent bird, and the intense excitement felt when one of these huge creatures sails by with the wind humming through its feathers lingers for a lifetime. A planet Earth bereft of condors would be a much diminished place, and we believe that with the proper kinds of efforts this remarkable bird can again be a viable member of wilderness communities. The condor surely will not survive without a significant assist from the very species that has been primarily responsible for its endangerment. But there is no reason to despair that either the bird or its aura will be destroyed by the steps that must be taken in the years ahead. *Gymnogyps californianus* shows no indications of wanting to fade into extinction, and it is much too powerful a creature to ever lose its capacity to capture our imagination and emotions.

Vultures

Turkey Vulture
CATHARTES AURA

ROOSTING TURKEY VULTURES usually begin the day by spreading open their wings, holding them either toward or away from the first rays of the rising sun. Their six-foot wing spans terminating in curved fingerlike primary feathers seem to clutch the air in a stylized embrace, while their reddish-purple naked heads, contrasting with their jet black bodies, glisten with reflected morning light. Basking contentedly in the warm rays, the birds give no signs of haste to launch into more energetic endeavors and commonly keep their wings fully or partially extended for many minutes before finally folding them against their bodies once again. Until the morning breezes begin to stir, they remain indolently perched, occasionally preening their feathers, while most other birds have long since plunged into their daily routines of feeding, fighting, and reproductive activities.

Although the spread-wing display of the Turkey Vulture seems to be especially frequent after rainy or misty nights and may serve primarily to dry the flight feathers prior to first foraging of the day, the exact function of the posture has been long debated. The same display is also highly developed in the other New World vultures, in the storks (which are generally acknowledged to be the closest living relatives of the New World vultures), and in the Old World vultures (which are quite unrelated to their New World counterparts). All these birds depend on soaring flight and cover long distances in their daily movements. Most are also at least moderately social in foraging and roosting behavior. In their massed spread-wing displays, they present tableaus of primeval natural splendor in a great variety of habitats around the world. In particular, a tree or cliffside roost of dozens of Turkey Vultures in various stages of the spread-wing display is one of the most impressive spectacles to be found among the birds of North America.

Alone among the New World vultures, the species of the genus *Cathartes*—including the Turkey Vulture, and the Yellow-headed and Greater Yellow-headed vultures of Central and South America—are "honest" foragers. They usually discover carrion on their own, using a refined sense of smell, only to have it taken

Left: Throughout much of North and South America, the Turkey Vulture is the most familiar of the scavenging birds. Guided by an exceedingly keen sense of smell, this species commonly forages relatively close to the ground, buoyantly sailing along with distinctive uptilted wings.

Individually distinctive patterns of warts on the faces of Turkey Vultures are believed to be a result of bacterial infections caused by skin contact with decomposing carcasses.

Roosting Turkey Vultures greet the morning sun from a ledge above the immense Grand Canyon of Arizona.

A distinctive subspecies of the Turkey Vulture in Peru exhibits rapid and dramatic changes in head color during interactions around carcasses. As they gain control of food, individuals often blanch their heads to a pale white that may signify dominance to other individuals.

Range of the Turkey Vulture
☐ Breeding
▨ Breeding and wintering

away from them by other scavengers if they do not feed quickly and discreetly enough. Condors, Black Vultures, and King Vultures show no signs of olfactory skills and appear to find food primarily by watching other scavengers, especially Turkey Vultures, but also each other and species such as caracaras, ravens, and various eagles. This is not to imply that Turkey Vultures do not watch other scavengers too, as they certainly do; or to imply that condors, Black Vultures, and King Vultures never find food on their own, as they sometimes do. But as a rule in the New World, the first scavenger to locate a carcass, especially if it is not out in the open, is going to be a *Cathartes* following its nose.

The ability of Turkey Vultures to find food by smell has been a subject of controversy since before the time of the artist and ornithologist John James Audubon. Nevertheless, recent thorough studies by Kenneth Stager and David Houston have established beyond any reasonable doubt that the species does indeed rely on olfaction to find food. Audubon, who debunked this idea in a haughty paper of 1826, had it all wrong! Houston's very fine research has shown that were it not for *Cathartes* vultures, very few carcasses would ever be found by vertebrate scavengers in the heavily wooded

regions of the American tropics. As it is, very few go undiscovered, so keen are the abilities of the genus. In contrast, the Old World tropics, which do not have any olfactory-oriented scavengers among the birds, are characteristically devoid of avian scavengers in their forested regions.

By systematic placement of chicken carcasses of known age in hidden locations, Houston was able to establish that Turkey Vultures only uncommonly find carcasses the day they are killed, almost always find them on the second or third days when they are beginning to ripen, and rarely visit them when they are four days along and in a state of full-blown putrefaction. Since captive Turkey Vultures are happy to feed on fresh meat, it appears likely that the reason Houston did not often have wild individuals find his chicken carcasses on the first day was that the carcasses were still too fresh to give off enough odor to be easily findable. By the second and third days, enough decay was taking place to make the carcasses noticeably pungent, and by the fourth day, there was no question of their giving off enough odor to be findable, but very likely the quality of the meat was by then severely compromised by the buildup of microbial toxins and was no longer highly attractive to the vultures.

During late 1980, we had a chance to confirm first-hand the olfactory capacities of Turkey vultures in Peru. Here we were working with Mike Wallace in conjunction with studies he was conducting of release methods for captive Andean Condors. The abilities of the Turkey Vultures to sniff out food were often in evidence as we attempted to hide from their discovery the carcasses we were saving for the condors. No matter how the carcasses were covered up from view with straw mats or whatever, they never were really concealed from the Turkey Vultures, who often walked right into camp in their efforts to track them down, invariably approaching the hidden bounty from downwind.

As might be expected from their abilities to subsist on half-rotted meat, Turkey Vultures and other vulturids have extraordinary tolerances for the microbial toxins that permeate such food. For example, their abilities to tolerate botulism greatly exceed the capacities of many other birds, and they are similarly relatively insensitive to certain synthetic poisons, such as compound 1080, which have commonly been used to kill mammalian species such as ground squirrels and coyotes. To other poisons, such as cyanide and strychnine, they apparently remain quite sensitive, and their sensitivity to lead poisoning may well exceed that of other raptors. In a pretechnological world, the major poisons found in carcasses were of microbial origin –

poisons to which vulturids could develop resistance by their highly developed immune systems. The modern industrial world has now thrown an array of new poisons at these species, which at least in the case of the California Condor appear to have been a major cause of population decline. The extent to which Turkey Vultures are being stressed by such poisons has as yet been studied in only a very preliminary way.

Turkey Vultures occur pretty much throughout North and South America to as far north as southern Canada. They are a familiar sight in most regions, perhaps even outranking the ubiquitous Red-tailed Hawk in conspicuousness, if not abundance, in many areas. Soaring buoyantly with their wings held tipped up above the horizontal plane, they circle endlessly in search of food and generally keep closer to the ground than many other raptors.

In the United States, the species is largely migratory, and on the wintering grounds in the southern states and into South America, congregations of hundreds or even thousands of Turkey Vultures sometimes roost together. One enormous roost of several thousand individuals assembles nightly during the winter on the dikes at the south end of Lake Okeechobee in Florida. The vultures in this roost have discovered that there is a steady supply of fire-killed rats, rabbits, and snakes in the large nearby expanses of sugar-cane fields, which are cleared for harvest by burning throughout the winter.

In California, where the Turkey Vulture is partially migratory and partially sedentary, we have paid special attention to its ecological relationships with the California Condor. Curiously, at least in recent times, these two species have largely foraged in separate regions in the southern part of the condor range, though they have come together in foraging in the northern part during summer. And except for overlap in a few localities, they have tended to nest in different regions, with the condors occupying the central parts of the mountains lying between the coast and the San Joaquin Valley, while the Turkey Vultures have nested close to the coast and close to the San Joaquin Valley. Very few Turkey Vultures can be found in the central parts of the mountains except during migration.

We suspect that the main reason why condors have nested in the central mountains has nothing to do with food supplies, since food appears to be quite limited in this region and the condors have rarely foraged here. But conspicuously absent from this region are appreciable numbers of Golden Eagles, which have constituted a strong threat to condor nesting success by their capacities to prey on nestlings. The condor's powers of flight are sufficiently strong that there has been no great penalty for this species to nest in relatively enemy-free regions and commute to distant foraging grounds. In contrast, we suspect that Turkey Vultures, with their more modest flight capacities, are denied this same opportunity—it would simply take them too long to make round trips. If this is so, the Turkey Vultures nesting in the San Joaquin Valley foothills may have no choice but to take their lumps from the abundant eagles there, and in fact, one of the two nestling Turkey Vultures we radioed there in 1981 did wind up as an eagle victim after it fledged.

More difficult to explain is the absence of significant numbers of Turkey Vultures foraging in the foothills of the southern San Joaquin Valley, where the last wild condors did much of their foraging. Significant numbers of Turkey Vultures nest in these very same foothills, and food is obviously abundant here. Yet the Turkey Vultures mostly drop down to the floor of the San Joaquin Valley to forage in agricultural areas. Possibly they do so because the food supply is as good or better there and because they have faced less competition from ravens, condors, and eagles there. The last condors did not forage on the floor of the San Joaquin Valley, very likely because this region lacks enough topographic relief to provide the consistent updrafts needed by this species to stay aloft. Turkey Vultures, with their much lighter wing loading, have no troubles maneuvering in the valley bottom.

Admittedly, these explanations are tentative, and other factors may well be involved in causing the observed nesting and foraging distributions of these species. Still, our preliminary conclusions well illustrate the complexity of factors potentially affecting foraging patterns in these scavengers and the potential interactions of foraging considerations with other important facets of the species' biology.

In coastal Peru, we watched a number of carcasses in 1980 that were attended by the local scarlet-headed form of the Turkey Vulture (*Cathartes aura jota*). As individuals switched around in controlling the carcasses, a very strange and rapid transformation in head color took place. Birds that took over carcasses often blanched their head color to a pale white as they defended the food, while individuals on the periphery were characterized by full scarlet head coloration. In other Turkey Vultures seen at the same carcasses, the head was maintained in a bicolored state, with the front half of the head scarlet, and the rear of the head white, and this appears to be the typical coloration one sees in individuals in the high Andes. The color changes seen in the scarlet-headed individuals occurred in a matter of a few seconds and may have been important in signaling emotional states of individuals to each other. By comparison, we have never noted such head-color changes in the North American form of the Turkey Vulture, which has a more purplish head color, although there were what we took to be wintering North American Turkey Vultures (purple-heads) feeding right among the Peruvian scarlet-heads on a number of occasions. With such striking differences in head color among the various Turkey Vultures, we wonder if they might actually be several different species, rather than just subspecies of a single species.

Turkey Vultures characteristically nest in caves in cliffs or in hollow logs or other sheltered locations on the ground. In Florida, they commonly use the labyrinths of palmetto thickets, while in California all nests we located were in cliffs or boulder piles, similar to the sites used by condors. The spotted egg coloration of the Turkey Vulture, however, contrasts with the plain white color of condor eggs, and suggests that either there may be a tendency for Turkey Vultures to use sites that are more open and exposed to predators than those used by condors, or that this species is more vulnerable to egg predators than the condor for other reasons.

In general, studies of both nesting and nonbreeding diet of Turkey Vultures have revealed a preponderance of relatively small prey species in their carrion food, especially when compared with the diet of California Condors and Black Vultures. In large part, this emphasis may result from the abilities of this species to find relatively small prey through its remarkable sense of smell. In part it probably results from a general inability of this species to compete with these other vulturids for spaces around larger carcasses. The Turkey Vulture does best as a solitary forager, quickly finishing off small items before being challenged by its larger cousins.

On rare occasions, Turkey Vultures have been documented taking living prey, but the animals taken have generally been near death. However, during the years we studied Everglade Kites in Florida, we once flushed a Turkey Vulture from a kite nest that had contained healthy living chicks only a few days earlier. All that was left in the nest was some freshly bloodied bones, and we wondered if this had been an instance of predation rather than scavenging. Everglade Kites often harass Turkey Vultures that come close to their colonies, and we also sometimes saw Swallow-tailed Kites driving Turkey Vultures away from their nests — observations that suggest that this vulture may not always be an innocent scavenger. Perhaps the Turkey Vulture is more of a predator than is generally recognized.

Vultures

Black Vulture
CORAGYPS ATRATUS

THE BLACK VULTURE of the New World is not to be confused with the immense Black Vulture of the Old World (*Aegypius monachus*), which ranges from Spain through the Near East to Mongolia and rivals the California Condor in size. The American Black Vulture, with a wingspread of only five feet, is not much bigger than a barnyard rooster. Moreover, its bill is quite thin and weak in comparison to the bills of many other vultures.

It is nevertheless an aggressive and opportunistic bird. Individually, it is not bulky enough to intimidate most other scavengers. But like the griffon vultures of the Old World, Black Vultures quickly gather in large groups and often manage to overwhelm competitors by massed assaults, pitching into the feeding aggregations with reckless abandon. Where Black Vultures occur with Andean Condors in South America, we have seen them repeatedly rushing in to grab scraps, even as this much larger species has had apparent full control of a carcass. Sometimes their boldness has even extended to their snatching bites from right between the legs of a condor working intently on food.

The impetuousness of the Black Vulture contrasts with the more aloof personality of the similar-sized Turkey Vulture, and Turkey Vultures often appear to simply resign themselves to losing control of carcasses once Black Vultures move in. Much apparently depends on hunger and motivation, however, and sometimes Turkey Vultures defend food very aggressively.

A relatively flexible species in behavior, the Black Vulture has adapted quite well to the many habitat changes wrought by our species, and in many areas has become a common urban and suburban commensal, feeding largely on offal and garbage discarded on the edges of rural towns and cities. In this respect, and in many features of physical appearance, especially overall size and bill shape, Black Vultures are very reminiscent of two relatively small Old World vultures, the Egyptian Vulture and the Hooded Vulture. Together, these three species form an interesting trio for ecological comparisons. Nevertheless, the two Old World species are not at all closely related to the Black Vulture, and their behavioral and physical similarities to this species are presumably due to evolutionary convergence.

Black Vultures appear to be more willing than other New World vultures to take living prey, and they have been observed capturing small turtles and preying on eggs and young of colonial waterbirds on occasion. Records also exist of groups of Black Vultures successfully attacking and dismembering live skunks and possums. In Guyana, we watched them clustering around cattle giving birth, apparently waiting for an opportunity to feed on afterbirths or on stillborn calves, or perhaps sometimes on live calves. Other foods taken include all forms of carrion and even dung from livestock. Their feeding habits bear a strong resemblance to those of Common Ravens, and it is interesting that the range of the Black Vulture is for the most part quite separate from the range of that species, possibly because of a high degree of potential competition. In California, for example, Black Vultures do not occur in the regions where the last California Condors have roamed, and ravens instead have been the common small scavenger at carrion.

In North America, the Black Vulture reaches a center of abundance in Florida and the other southeastern states, although its range has been extending northward in recent years and now includes even southern Pennsylvania. In Florida, where we have become most familiar with the species, it is abundant in the prairie

Range of the Black Vulture
■ Breeding and wintering

regions of the south-central part of the state. Here it finds favorable nest sites mainly on the ground in the tangled patches of palmettos. Elsewhere in its range, the Black Vulture commonly nests in potholes and crevices in cliffs, hollow stumps, and trees, and in deserted buildings. Its main nesting requirements, like those of the other vulturids, are relatively dark, sheltered places with elevated snag or cliff perches nearby from which the birds can monitor their surroundings effectively. Black Vultures are extremely secretive in approaching their actual nest sites and like other vulturids do no nest building other than minor rearranging of

In Florida's Everglades National Park, a Black Vulture below and Turkey Vulture above prepare to leave their overnight roost.

A Black Vulture rips apart a possum carcass in southern Florida. Primarily dependent on carrion, this species is also known to take some living prey.

With its wings spread in a sunning position, a Black Vulture sated with feeding basks on the edge of a Florida marsh.

With relatively heavy wing loading, Black Vultures normally forage only at high altitudes and find food mainly by watching the activities of other scavengers.

Black Vultures often nest in palmetto thickets in south-central Florida. This species, like other New World vultures, limits its nest building to minor rearrangements of materials already present in the site.

twigs, pebbles, and other detritus already present in the sites.

In early 1978, we had several occasions to help Mike Wallace and Eric Berg find Black Vulture nests in Florida in connection with studies they were conducting on methods of releasing captive-reared vulturids to the wild. Once pairs of Black Vultures began habitually perching on conspicuous snags in the vicinity of palmetto patches, it was safe to conclude that they would soon begin nesting activities. Egg laying was signaled by the transformation of the pairs on these habitual perches into single birds. Finding nests was then generally a process of crawling on hands and knees through the palmetto jungles and keeping our noses attuned for the unmistakable putrid carrion-stench of the species, while our ears and peripheral vision were primed for warning signs of the lunker diamondback rattlesnakes that abound in this habitat.

Ultimately, Mike and Eric were successful in locating several dozen nests. All were disgustingly odoriferous and all were in apparently vulnerable locations on the ground, yet not a single nest was lost to predation. Tracks of raccoons and other terrestrial carnivores often went right past the nest clumps, so it was clear that the nests were situated in places frequented by potential enemies. Further, it seems unlikely that terrestrial carnivores would have had difficulty finding the nests, considering the rank scent clouds in which they were imbedded. It is tempting to conclude that the young vultures were simply not the most appetizing prey for these species, a situation possibly reinforced by their eagerness to regurgitate "hot carrion" when approached by potential predators. Nevertheless, in other regions observers have found evidence of fairly frequent predation on young Black Vultures by terrestrial mammals, and it is surely a mistake to assume that our own dietary inhibitions might safely generalize to hungry coons, possums, and bobcats.

One nest we located with Eric Berg was in dense palmettos right on the edge of a cypress swamp where we later studied nesting Short-tailed Hawks. Eric had spotted the adult Black Vultures perching in the region several weeks earlier, and we eventually succeeded in locating the nest site containing two well-grown young by systematically thrashing through the cypress-palmetto border. Another site that Mike and Eric had located in high sand scrub near Archbold Biological Station held newly hatched chicks. Covered with tan-colored down, they reminded us much of newly hatched Andean Condor nestlings and were distinctly different in appearance from newly hatched Turkey Vultures and California Condors, which have pure white down.

Like other vulturids, the Black Vulture lacks vocalizations other than assorted wheezes, hisses, and snorts audible at close range. We have heard these noises emitted by birds defending their nests. Others have heard them in birds engaged in mating activities. Vocalizations are better developed in the Old World vultures, but even among these species, they tend to be grunts and hisses that are much less frequently heard than the calls of most other raptors. The suppression of vocalizations in both New and Old World vultures may be tied to a relatively great use of visual displays in communication among individuals. Nestling California Condors, for example, use conspicuous flapping of partly extended wings, rather than begging calls, to solicit food from their parents, and the conspicuousness of their flapping is accentuated by patches of white down on the upper surfaces of their wings.

The roosting behavior of Black Vultures and Turkey Vultures has been studied in great detail in North Carolina by Patty Parker Rabenold. These species commonly roost together at all seasons, but the numbers of individuals of either species using a particular roost on a particular night fluctuate greatly because individuals change roosts frequently. Evidently, these vultures may soar and course so extensively on a daily basis that they cannot always efficiently return to the same roost each evening and need several roosts spaced through their ranges to avoid excessively long commutes.

Actual roosts are generally situated in tall live trees, though the birds often use nearby dead snags for sunning purposes. Black Vultures generally leave the roosts for foraging later in the morning than do Turkey Vultures, and they likewise usually return to roosts later in the afternoon or evening than do Turkey Vultures. Not infrequently, both species circle and soar for several hours in the vicinity of their roosts before finally settling in, possibly inspecting the roost vicinity carefully for potential predators before deciding that it is safe to descend.

The late departures of Black Vultures from roosts are most likely a result of their relatively heavy-bodied physical proportions. The Black Vulture needs stronger air movements than does the Turkey Vulture to soar effectively, and such air movements normally develop relatively late in the morning. In accord with their differences in flight capacities, the foraging flights of the two species are also quite different. The Black Vulture cannot match the buoyant low-altitude coursing typical of the more light-bodied Turkey Vulture, and at low altitudes, Black Vultures are pretty much limited to labored fast-flapping to keep aloft. This sort of flight is energetically inefficient for foraging. Instead, Black Vultures mainly forage from considerable heights, where soaring conditions are better and where they are in a better position to observe the food-finding activities of other scavengers.

When a Black Vulture sailing high in the clouds first spots a feeding opportunity at a carcass, it begins a rapid descent and is immediately noticed by other Black Vultures at greater distances, who likewise begin descents converging on the food. Even more distant vultures follow as if drawn by an invisible force. The sky is soon swept clean of vultures, and a large group assembles around the carcass.

The presence of large feeding assemblages can greatly facilitate the ripping apart of prey. With their relatively weak bills, Black Vultures often have difficulty getting through the tough hides of relatively large mammals. Yet when groups collaborate on a carcass, with numerous individuals pulling in unison in a variety of directions on a point of weakness, they are often able to gain much better leverage and penetrate to what would otherwise be inaccessible soft tissues. In the absence of group feeding, individual Black Vultures are often limited to easily accessible tissues such as eyes and tongues when they attempt to feed on large carcasses.

Like other vulturids and like storks, their close relatives, Black Vultures practice an unusual method of thermoregulation known as urohidrosis. In simple terms, they deliberately void their own excretory wastes on their legs, cooling these appendages as the water portion of the waste material evaporates. The blood circulating under the evaporative surfaces of the legs is also cooled in the process, and when it is pumped through the rest of the body, it cools the entire bird as a result. During hot weather, the legs of all these species take on a conspicuous, chalky-white appearance, produced by a dried crust of uric acid crystals left plastered to the skin. An endless buildup of uric acid is in part prevented by the fact that all the species practicing urohidrosis are avid bathers. Urohidrosis presumably might have general advantages for large

species with long legs living in hot environments, yet no birds other than vulturids and storks are known to possess the trait. It apparently has evolved only once among the many lineages of living birds of the world.

The opportunistic behavior of the Black Vulture allows some optimism about this species' abilities to cope with future changes in the modern world. Nevertheless, the species has several weak points in its biology which limit its prospects. One weakness studied by Jerry Jackson in Mississippi is nest-site availability. In regions where Black Vultures nest most commonly in hollow logs or hollow trees, timber management practices that reduce the average age of trees are significantly lowering the availability of such nest sites and forcing the birds to use more vulnerable thicket nest sites as alternatives, with consequent declines in nesting success. Such timbering practices may provide at least part of the explanation for recent reported decreases in Black Vulture populations in the southeastern states. A second weakness is the strong dependency the species has come to have on our own species for its food supply. Any changes in disposal methods for livestock carcasses, garbage, or slaughterhouse wastes can have strong impacts on its welfare. A thoroughly hygienic human environment does not leave much of a food supply for Black Vultures. Third, the willingness of the Black Vulture to attack newborn livestock has led in some areas to vigorous campaigns to trap and destroy the species. Such control efforts, commonly using giant self-baiting walk-in traps, were especially prevalent in Texas and Florida during the 1940s and 1950s, and the numbers of Black Vultures destroyed apparently reached the hundreds of thousands. Finally, collisions with vehicles on high speed roads have been taking an increasing toll of those Black Vultures who are attracted to road-killed mammals for food.

In spite of these vulnerability factors, the range of the Black Vulture has been expanding in recent years and the species is still very common in many regions of North America. It also remains a common species associated with human settlements throughout much of Central and South America.

Kites

Above: Soaring overhead, Everglade Kites display conspicuous white tail bases and odd-shaped wings (narrow close to the body and wider farther out). Right: An adult female Everglade Kite performs sentry duty near her nest in the eastern Everglades. Her long, relatively straight claws are adapted for plucking snails from the water, not for killing them.

Kites

Everglade Kite
ROSTRHAMUS SOCIABILIS

THE CENTRAL REACHES of southern Florida were once dominated by a gigantic and bewildering freshwater marsh whose waters flowed imperceptibly, as a forty- to sixty-mile-wide "river," from Lake Okeechobee to the southern tip of the peninsula. Known variously as the Glades, the Never Glades, or the Everglades to early explorers, this entire region remained untraversed, unmapped, and unsettled until well into the nineteenth century. In popular view, the region was so forbidding a wilderness, it would likely remain inviolate forever.

Today, the Everglades are still a vast aquatic empire, though their area has been substantially reduced by drainage activities, and their flow of waters has been tamed by numerous dikes and canals. Their long-term survival no longer seems guaranteed by the enormity of their physical characteristics.

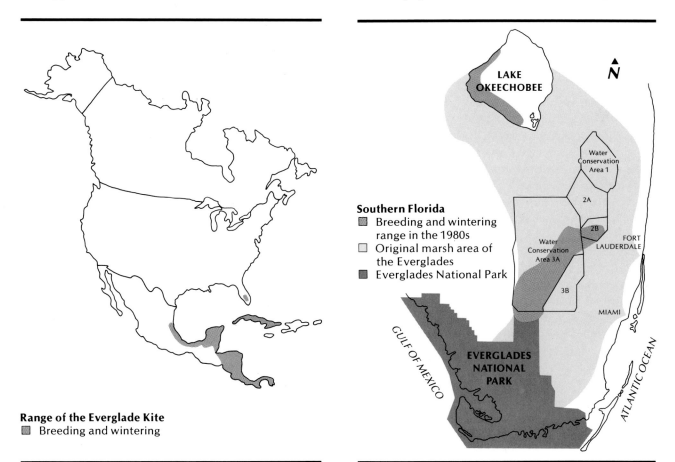

Range of the Everglade Kite
Breeding and wintering

Southern Florida
- Breeding and wintering range in the 1980s
- Original marsh area of the Everglades
- Everglades National Park

LAKE OKEECHOBEE

Water Conservation Area 1

2A

2B

Water Conservation Area 3A

FORT LAUDERDALE

3B

MIAMI

EVERGLADES NATIONAL PARK

GULF OF MEXICO

ATLANTIC OCEAN

The topography of the glades is so unrelievedly flat that dry land is virtually nonexistent, at least in years of normal rainfall. By the same token, the waters, except where canals have been dredged, are nowhere more than a few feet deep, allowing the development of endless shoals of sawgrass, cattails, and half-submerged shrubs and trees. Only a few of these plants, mainly the clumps of willows and pond apples, rise even ten feet into the air. Distinctive landmarks are rare, the horizon stretches unbroken in all directions, and one slough looks pretty much like thousands of others. It's not a place for those who panic at the possibility of getting lost.

In reality, few people have had an opportunity to face such anxieties over the years, as the Everglades have always been virtually impenetrable by conventional boats. The tangled masses of submerged and floating plants quickly foul the most weed-proof outboard motors and are much too dense to allow ready passage even of canoes. And though most parts of the glades are shallow enough and hard-bottomed enough to be explored by wading, the fatigue involved in pushing through miles of vegetation-choked marsh and the ever-present risks of encounters with cottonmouths and alligators have disheartened nearly all potential intruders.

Shielded by the inaccessibility of its primary habitat, the Florida Everglade Kite, a race of the Snail Kite of Central and South America, was the most mysterious of all our birds of prey for many years. Until the 1940s only a few hardy souls, most notably the early egg collector, Donald J. Nicholson, and his notorious outlaw guide, Henry "Gator" Redding, had made concerted efforts to fight through the swamplands to locate the species. For the great majority of naturalists, the kite continued to be known only as an extraordinarily elusive spirit they had never seen and probably never would see, a species with extremely long thin talons and a bizarrely curved bill that somehow were adapted for a strange specialized diet of aquatic snails. Beyond basic facts such as these, knowledge of the biology of the kite remained extremely fragmentary.

With the advent of airboats following World War II, the Everglades finally became easily accessible to our species. But by then, the kite population had fallen to just a few dozen individuals. Many conservationists feared that the species might soon be lost from North America. In Florida, the kite is almost completely dependent on a single species of freshwater mollusc for food: the Florida apple snail (*Pomacea paludosa*), a golf-ball-sized species with a dark brown shell. Un-

fortunately, apple snails can thrive only in regions with relatively healthy water supplies. By the 1950s, drainage activities to promote agriculture had wiped out major portions of the Everglades and had much weakened the vitality of the portions that were left. Snail populations and the kites feeding on them suffered greatly.

By the 1960s, the few surviving kites were given an inadvertent reprieve with the construction of large impoundments that compartmentalized the remaining glades – the water conservation areas. Built mainly for water storage and flood control, the conservation areas created relatively stable water levels in local areas, allowing snail populations to make a substantial recovery. The kites began to increase again as well, as was documented through the late 1960s and 1970s by Paul Sykes of the U.S. Fish and Wildlife Service.

However, because the conservation areas have caused such a massive disruption of the natural water flow of the glades, whether they may remain viable habitat for snails and kites in the long term is uncertain. Ominously, despite quite consistently favorable water levels, one of the most important conservation areas for snails and kites in the 1960s – area 2A – had by the late 1970s become a marsh virtually devoid of either species, possibly mainly because of pollution effects.

In addition, pressures are increasing to change the management of other water conservation areas in various ways. If implemented, some changes may stress the kite population severely. In particular, the desires of Everglades National Park to obtain greater water supplies from area 3A to benefit other wildlife species farther south may be difficult to reconcile with the best interests of the kite. Since the late 1970s, the kites have been mainly concentrated in area 3A, with Lake Okeechobee serving as a secondary use area. While total kite numbers have recently averaged four to five hundred individuals, if area 3A were to be lost as usable habitat, these numbers might well drop precipitously and the kite population might no longer be large enough to constitute a viable population.

Our first studies of the Everglade Kite grew out of behavioral research on the apple snail that we conducted during graduate student days at Cornell University in the mid-1960s. Our early work encouraged us to expand research into the relationships of this snail with its various predators, including the Everglade Kite, when we moved to Florida in 1967. Initial studies revealed that the apple snail occupies a central position in the food chains of the Everglades, serving as an important dietary focus for many of the region's aquatic animals, including various insects, crayfishes, fishes, turtles, and even young alligators. Three of Florida's birds feed especially heavily on the species – the Everglade Kite, the Limpkin, and the Boat-tailed Grackle – and we soon embarked on a study of the adaptations that these birds use to exploit their food supply.

The Everglade Kite's adaptations include an extremely long and thin, decurved upper bill, which cuts the columellar muscle that holds an apple snail in its shell. To aid in cutting the same muscle, the Limpkin possesses a remarkably twisted lower bill. Until our studies, the exact functions of these specialized anatomical tools had long been misunderstood. The Boat-tailed Grackle is much less dependent on apple snails for food than are the other two birds and lacks specific anatomical specializations for snail-feeding. Nevertheless, it too has developed efficient ways to extract apple snails from their shells. All three birds can commonly be found in the same regions, and we found it to be relatively uncommon for them to show signs of aggressive intolerance of one another.

Within the kite population itself, we also usually found harmonious relationships among individuals, regardless of whether they were slate-colored adult males or brown-streaked females and immatures. Consistent with its scientific name – *Rostrhamus sociabilis* – the Everglade Kite is a gregarious species, often feeding in loose assemblages and breeding in colonies of a dozen or more pairs. To be sure, solitary nesting and foraging are also quite common. But irrespective of how closely or distantly birds are associated, it is rare to see any signs of individuals excluding one another from feeding territories. Very likely, snails are usually too dispersed for defense of specific areas to offer advantages that might exceed the costs of such behavior.

Nevertheless, we once observed vigorous defense of several adjacent sections of a canal in the eastern Everglades by several nonbreeding kites. These birds had discovered an incredibly abundant food supply in a limited area. Here apple snails could be seen on nearly every submerged cattail stem, and the resident kites usually took only a few seconds to locate a victim on a given hunting foray. Intruding kites were driven away viciously and forced to forage in surrounding areas that apparently had far inferior food supplies. Under the proper circumstances, the Everglade Kite can be as aggressive as the most territorial of bird species, though ecological conditions normally do not warrant anything other than a high degree of mutual tolerance.

In 1978 and 1979, when we returned to Florida after an absence of several years, we had an opportunity to resume studies of the Everglade Kite, this time for the U.S. Fish and Wildlife Service. These proved to be two of the happiest years we have ever spent in the field. The Everglade Kite is for us the most intriguing of all the North American raptors, and we were especially delighted to be able to study the species with Rod Chandler of the National Audubon Society and two assistants supported by the National Wildlife Federation, Steve Beissinger and Gary Falxa. Unlike our efforts in the late 1960s, when we struggled to make occasional kite observations from a small skiff on the fringe of the glades, our studies in the late 1970s were aided by the full-time use of an airboat. We were able to cover the entire range of the kite in Florida, finding most nests, banding most young, and conducting intensive studies of the behavior of selected pairs.

Although Everglade Kites are often highly intolerant of blinds placed close to their nests (perhaps more so than any other North American raptor), many aspects of the breeding biology of this species are practical to study. In 1979, we watched the breeding cycles of two pairs on Lake Okeechobee from the start of nest building through to independence of young sixteen weeks later. Our observations were made mainly from a lookout platform complete with a beach-umbrella canopy that we built atop a decapitated melaleuca tree about one quarter mile from the nests. From this vantage point, we were able to see essentially all nesting and foraging activities of the birds during two full-day observation periods each week. The kites generally hunted within a mile of the nests, flapping slowly over the sloughs, and we had an unobstructed view of nearly the entire foraging range from the observation platform.

The pairs had greatly varying success in capturing snails, mostly as a result of changes in weather conditions. On days of moderate temperatures, snails frequently came to the water surface to breathe, and the kites rarely needed more than two or three minutes to locate a victim on a given foray. But on days following the passage of cold fronts, snails rarely came close enough to the surface to be vulnerable, and the kites had great difficulty finding food, sometimes taking fifteen or twenty minutes or longer to make a capture. This difficulty may explain why the kites do not commonly breed as far north in Florida as their food supply extends. Though the glowing accounts of Florida's enthusiastic tourist industry suggest otherwise, cold fronts definitely do roll down the peninsula all winter long. The intensity of these fronts decreases markedly from north to south.

Above photos: Snails are taken close to the surface only, and the birds rarely get more than their feet wet in capture attempts. A missed capture attempt yields only a cattail stalk.

A female Florida apple snail lays eggs above the water surface on a cypress trunk. Egg laying by this snail normally takes place at night, but this female did not finish until just after sunrise.

A female kite brings in a snail for her brood in the eastern Everglades. This bird was raising her young unassisted. Under good food conditions, most nests are deserted by one adult or the other at about the time young reach fledging age.

The pile of empty apple snail shells in this old kite nest in southern Florida's Everglades indicates use of the site as a feeding platform after nesting. Shells do not normally accumulate in numbers during nesting.

Nestling kites are highly cryptic (camouflaged) in coloration, unlike most other raptor nestlings.

41

Once the young kites fledged from the nests we had under close observation, we found that they very quickly became as adept as adults in grabbing snails from the water surface—perhaps not too surprising a result, as apple snails are not notably skilled in evading capture by kites. However, the fledglings took much longer to develop abilities to extract snails from their shells. Successful snail extractions demand correct orientation of the shell for removal of the operculum (the "doorway" closing off the shell's entrance) and for insertion of the bird's long curved upper bill into the snail's softparts. The young birds had special difficulties in learning how to hold a snail against a perch with the feet so that they could accomplish these tasks properly. Obviously unsure of how to proceed, they eyed their captured victims curiously, then often positioned them in orientations in which further progress was unlikely, if not impossible. Even worse, they commonly fumbled a snail in their clumsy efforts, and the snail fell from the perch to the water below, then straight to the bottom. The young kites never attempted to retrieve such snails and soon took off on renewed hunting forays to begin the whole process over again. Only after many weeks of trial and error did the fledglings become expert in snail extractions, finally taking their places as fully competent members of the population.

In our general studies of the kite population, we discovered that survival of individuals can be extremely good when food supplies are favorable. In fact, all thirteen nestlings we provided with backpack radio transmitters on Lake Okeechobee in 1979 were still alive a year to a year and a half later, the lifetime of the transmitters! To our knowledge, such high survival of nestlings after fledging (let alone radios) has never been documented in the study of any other bird.

Another important discovery was that in the late 1970s the kite population was suddenly assaulted by a totally new threat, one never before reported for any wild bird population. A full 10 percent of the nestlings found in 1979 had gruesome holes chewed in their abdomens by nest-dwelling dermestid beetle larvae. In more recent years, as documented in studies by Steve Beissinger, the frequency of attack has risen as high as 25 percent. Though most nestlings survive these attacks, some do not, and the Everglade Kite is now afflicted with a problem that it apparently did not have to face earlier.

But surely the most fascinating biological discovery of all was the finding that in good years, with favorable water conditions and abundant snails, most successful kite nests are deserted by one parent or the other at about the time young reach fledging age. Males are as likely to desert as females, and regardless of which sex leaves, the remaining parent continues to provide for the brood until they reach independence—generally about another month. Meanwhile, the deserting bird is free to start a new breeding cycle with a new partner. Under poor conditions, neither parent deserts and both struggle to raise what young they have. This desertion system is a unique nesting strategy among raptors.

Our early investigations into mate desertion raised many more questions than answers. What determines which parent deserts? What controls the precise timing of desertion? Why doesn't the species increase clutch size as an alternative to desertion? Solutions to these questions and many others have been admirably explored in more recent research by Steve Beissinger.

Rod Chandler's long-term observations of the kites on Lake Okeechobee have revealed an especially interesting movement pattern. These kites tend to abandon the lake entirely in early summer, returning in the fall. Why they leave in summer remains unclear. Their departure apparently has little, if anything, to do with simple snail abundance, as we were able to determine that snail populations remained very strong during the period of departure in 1978. However, we noticed that it was becoming increasingly painful for us to measure these snail populations with our bottom sampler scoop. The vast spike rush marshes the kites had been feeding in put forth masses of sharp-pointed stems at this season, and there was no way to reach into the water without encountering these stems. Possibly the kites did not like skewering themselves on spike rush any more than we did and left the area for this reason. Giving some support to this interpretation was the fact that before the kites left the lake entirely, they moved out of the spike rush beds and into surrounding areas of water lilies and lotuses for feeding.

In late winter of 1979, we began intensive studies of the food supplies of two kite pairs on Okeechobee. We were especially anxious to get a quantitative grasp of snail densities in the specific feeding areas used by the pairs and some measure of the impact of the pairs on their food supply. Since our bottom sampler had worked well in quantifying snail populations the year before, we anticipated similar success in this year.

It was not to be. We spent days dropping the sampler from our airboat in the very sloughs where the kites were finding snail after snail, but got nothing other than rope-burned hands for all our efforts. We captured not a single living individual. Yet the snails had to be there! The kites were locating them with maddening ease.

At this point, we concluded that the density of snails must simply be much lower than in the areas we sampled in 1978, and the obvious solution was to switch to another sampling method that would cover much more area more quickly. We began "snorkle transects"–long underwater cruises to spot snails directly, using facemasks. The logic of this approach was compelling. The water was clear, the vegetation was not too dense out in the sloughs, and we could travel many feet per minute, taking in a yard or so in width and height as we chugged along–a much, much greater area than could be covered with a bottom sampler in the same time. Wet suits took care of the cold water temperatures, and we confidently looked forward to gaining embarrassingly large volumes of informative data.

Incredibly, after hours and hours of effort, we still were unable to find a single living apple snail. Meanwhile, the kites continued their methodical harvest, yanking snail after snail out of the very same marshes we were searching. Clearly, our failure to find snails was still only a reflection of the inadequacy of our sampling methods.

Discouraged, but not yet willing to give up completely, we began a final heroic effort with "toe transects," reasoning that most of the elusive molluscs must simply be buried in detritus on the bottom. If so, by wading along barefoot, wiggling our toes through the muck, we would surely encounter them at last. While toe transects were not the most attractive method for finding snails, considering the full diversity of other creatures we might encounter in the subsurface goo, it was hard to imagine how this method could fail us, if this was where the snails really were.

Alas, despite the obvious wisdom of this approach and despite hours of exhaustive "toeing," we again found exactly zero living snails. A few old empty shells that raised fleeting hopes of victory, but nothing more.

By this time we had developed a profound respect for the abilities of Everglade Kites to breed in regions with no detectable food supply whatsoever. In fact, both pairs under study were raising vigorous large broods of three young! In terminal defeat we gave up the snail-censusing efforts as hopeless, taking consolation in the knowledge that we could still measure the "availability" of snails by timing the durations of the kites' foraging flights. Surely this was anyway much more useful than knowing the number of snails per cubic mile of marsh. No sour grapes here.

In 1978, while following the annual exodus of kites from Lake Okeechobee, we confirmed that at least one color-banded male, who had a successful spring breeding in the Moore Haven Canal area of the lake, moved nearly a hundred miles south to breed again in Conservation Area 3A during the summer. The second nesting of this bird proved to be another successful one and constituted the first conclusive evidence of multiple-brooding in the species. The fact that the kites frequently move long distances between successive broods may explain in part why the existence of multiple-brooding was previously undetected, although we now know it is a frequent occurrence closely linked with the mate-desertion phenomenon.

The discovery of multiple-brooding, coupled with a finding that kites under good water conditions often breed before they are even a year old, revealed a tremendous reproductive potential for the species, an unusual characteristic for a bird on the endangered species list. Although nesting success of the kite is characteristically low–only about 13 percent of undisturbed nests produce fledglings–the extended breeding season (sometimes continuing ten to eleven months of the year) and the numerous breeding attempts possible within a year allow the species to increase very rapidly when food supplies permit.

One important cause of the high failure rate of nesting attempts has been a relatively frequent tendency for the species to nest in structurally unsound sites. Many nests placed in flexible willow saplings, for example, were too unstable to survive collapse during the breeding cycle, yet the kites commonly chose such sites, sometimes persistently rebuilding in exactly the same locations after previous nests had fallen. The best substrates tended to be substantial shrubs and trees such as pond apples, cocoa plums, cypresses, and melaleucas. Cattails proved the worst, and nests placed in this plant rarely succeeded in fledging young. They almost always slowly tipped over as nesting progressed and eventually dumped out their contents.

Unfortunately, most kites on Lake Okeechobee have traditionally placed their nests in cattail beds and for many years produced very few young as a result. However, the problem was largely solved for the Okeechobee birds in the early 1970s, when Rod Chandler began transferring their cattail nests into specially built baskets mounted on poles in the original locations of the nests. These efforts greatly enhanced nesting success and contributed importantly to the documented increase of the species through the 1970s. Whenever we came across nests on the verge of tipping over during our studies in 1978 and 1979, we likewise improvised supports for the nests, though we found relatively few nests in cattails in these years.

Our most unusual experiences with the Everglade

Kite unfolded in 1978, when together with Paul Sykes we discovered that the major breeding colony of the species in Conservation Area 3A was immediately adjacent to a proposed commercial jetport for the Miami region of southern Florida. In fact, the proposed main runway was aimed directly at the colony from only a couple miles away! As this development represented a potentially serious disturbance for the kites, we immediately reported the situation to the U.S. Fish and Wildlife Service.

Our reward for doing so was that we soon found ourselves, together with Paul and with Herb Kale of the Florida Audubon Society, engaged in an official "section 7" evaluation of potential impacts of the jetport project on the kites. At the time, this was the last thing we wanted to be doing, as it precluded continuation of other research efforts in progress. We objected strenuously over our involvement in the evaluation, but to no avail. Fortunately, this was a battle well losing. The jetport assessment proved to be one of the most interesting and enjoyable projects we have ever participated in – far more valuable than the research we had to drop to be involved.

Our investigation quickly evolved into a direct experimental evaluation of what effects low-flying commercial aircraft would have on the behavior of the very colony in question. Eastern Airlines gave enthusiastic cooperation by rescheduling their pilot-training flights to accommodate our experimental design. And on alternate days for a period of nearly two weeks in the spring of 1978, we were soon watching the behavior of nesting pairs of kites as giant 727s roared by at frequent intervals low over the colony. The behavior of the same pairs on nonflight days served as a control.

Thankfully, the weather held favorable throughout the overflight period, and we had the good luck to avoid any airboat breakdowns or other equipment failures. Considering the complexities of getting all personnel properly deployed, things went far smoother than we had a right to expect. But what made the experiment especially enjoyable was that right from the start the results were so clear-cut. No messy ambiguous findings. No need for torturous qualifications in conclusions. The kites obviously could not have cared much less about the jets, and all aspects of their behavior that we could measure, such as copulation rates and feeding rates, remained the same irrespective of the presence or absence of nearby aircraft. About the only clear response we ever saw was that the birds (stifling yawns) would occasionally glance for a moment or two at the aircraft cruising overhead. Perhaps their lack of overt alarm was not too surprising, as on days we scheduled no 727s we also

saw fair numbers of other aircraft in the region. The kites evidently had had plenty of time to habituate to airplane disturbance, though granted the usual traffic was not nearly so close or so ear-splitting as the 727s.

As a further investigation into the abilities of Everglade Kites to tolerate such disturbance, we also made a trip to Baranquilla, Colombia, where kites were reputedly nesting in the general vicinity of the airport. Here the largest colony we could find was located in the very closest marsh to the end of the main runway – only a few hundred yards away. The decibels these birds experienced with each takeoff were far in excess of what the 727s produced in our Florida experiment. The Colombian kites, like their Florida relatives, gave no outward indications of stress or alarm.

In our summary report on the proposed jetport, we were not able to document any negative effects of low overflights on the behavior of kites. We emphasized, nevertheless, that secondary effects associated with the jetport, such as pollution and accessory developments, could represent significant hazards. On the basis of our report, the U.S. Fish and Wildlife Service rendered a "no-jeopardy" opinion on the project. Now, over ten years later, the jetport has yet to be built. But if it ever is, and if care is taken to minimize secondary effects, we doubt if it will have any appreciable impacts on the kites.

The same colony in which we watched the responses of Everglade Kites to low-flying jetliners in 1978 was the scene of another unusual occurrence a year later. We had just picked up Dave Ellis and Rich Glinski in Miami, back from a grand raptor survey across South America, and they joined us for a late-afternoon airboat trip out to check the colony before we headed up to our home near Lake Okeechobee. Rich plunged in with us, wading through the willows, as we attempted to locate and inspect the contents of nests still active in the colony. Dave remained on the airboat moored outside the colony.

We had barely started the nest checks when Dave's distinctive base voice came resonating through the willows, "You guys are not going to believe this, ho ho, but there's a California Condor coming in low over your heads."

He was right. We didn't believe it, especially knowing Dave's weakness for offbeat humor and considering the absurdity of a condor this far east of California. But to our amazement, just moments later a giant bird sailed in from the east, mobbed frantically by the nesting kites, who showed no signs of recognizing anything but evil in its approach. The bird's overall dark coloration, the immaculate white underwing triangles typical of *Gymnogyps californianus,* and an enormous wingspread – all clearly visible, all seemed fully consistent with characteristics of the condor. What other good possibilities were there? Though an aberrant immature Bald Eagle was remotely conceivable, none of us could work up any enthusiasm for this identification.

Our "condor" majestically circled the colony several times, then soared on, never beating its wings and hardly seeming to notice the slack-jawed biologists below or the kites repeatedly diving and cackling in anger. But now, with time for more sober reflection, we realized that identification of the bird as a condor was much too hasty. Although the wing color pattern was a great match for this species, the color and shape of the head and the amount of feathering on the head just did not look right. We began to suspect that the bird might really be some kind of Old World vulture that had escaped from captivity.

This supposition received considerable support when we later learned that other biologists working in the region had recently seen a very similar, if not the same, bird several dozen miles north of where we had seen it and not long before, and that there had indeed been a reported escape of captive Old World vultures still farther north in the state. By this time, our best guess at the true identity of the bird centered on an Indian White-backed Vulture, far from home and facing very questionable chances of survival in an alien environment. Unfortunately, we never saw the bird again to confirm either its survival or its identity. Its "condorhood," in any event, was only a wistful memory.

As a raptor almost totally dependent on a single variety of easy-to-catch prey, the Florida Everglade Kite enjoys a relatively uncomplicated existence under good food conditions. But when food supplies fail, this species must be prepared to move long distances and to absorb heavy mortality. Although food-stressed Everglade Kites have been seen taking unusual prey, such as small turtles and other snail species than *Pomacea paludosa,* their specialized anatomical adaptations for feeding on apple snails do not suit them well to such alternative fare. In observations by Steve Beissinger during the massive Florida drought of 1981–1982, kites that fed on turtles took hours to consume small individuals and usually did not manage to extract more than a fraction of the meat inside the shells. It is hard to imagine that the kites could long survive anywhere in the absence of apple snails, and in a sense they may be trapped forever by their anatomical specializations, facing all the risks inherent in a single-food economy.

The primary immediate threat to the Everglade Kite remains the recurrent droughts that hit the state and reduce the open-water areas to a tiny fraction of their normal extent. When the rains fail, the kites leave the main Everglades almost completely and disperse widely, attempting to find apple snails wherever they can. Ultimate survival of the species in Florida may well depend on the continued existence and good health of deep-water refugia such as Lake Okeechobee, which have traditionally served to tide the species over hard times until the rains have returned. Unfortunately, with the ceaseless growth of the human population along the coasts of southern Florida, water supplies in the Everglades are being increasingly withdrawn for alternative purposes, and pollution is beginning to affect the health of Lake Okeechobee. If the present human population increase continues, the ultimate survival of the glades and the kites will be placed in ever more direct competition with other economic priorities.

In addition to problems with water supplies, the kite now faces increasing difficulty from the invasion of the Everglades by an exotic species of tree – the melaleuca – which has been rapidly converting parts of the conservation areas and Lake Okeechobee into aquatic woodland. The melaleuca, a native of Australia, is exceedingly well adapted to conditions of long-term submersion alternating with periods of dry-downs and fires, and it is continuing to expand unchecked by natural enemies. When present in low densities, it provides excellent nest trees for the kites, but in the long term it changes open Everglades habitat into forest conditions unsuitable for the species. Unless the spread of this tree can be brought under control, the entire Everglades ecosystem may eventually be lost.

Even much more threatening to the stability of the Everglades is the long-term prospect of rising sea levels and changed climatic patterns caused by global warming trends. Current projections suggest that vast areas of the glades, which lie only a few feet above sea level, may well be inundated with salt water within the next century or two, and it is questionable that this development can be prevented even by massive construction of dikes. While the Everglade Kite population might conceivably survive such a massive disruption of its primary habitat by moving north (if global warming trends also allow apple snail populations to expand northward), can such adjustments occur smoothly enough and rapidly enough to keep pace with the projected rapidity of sea level changes? Long-term survival of the Everglade Kite in Florida is at best precarious, despite the relatively vigorous population the species has maintained in recent years.

Hook-billed Kite
CHONDROHIERAX UNCINATUS

WHILE THE EVERGLADE KITE feeds almost exclusively on aquatic snails, the Hook-billed Kite specializes on snails living in trees. But despite their similar size and common reliance on molluscan food, these two species are very different birds. In fact, the hook-bill is the oddest raptor we have ever had a chance to observe. Its repetitive calls are quite unhawklike and are reminiscent of the mellow vocalizations of the Field Sparrow. Its frail tiny nest consists of only a few twigs and looks very much like that of a dove. Stranger still, its fleshy feet are often employed like those of a parrot. Clutching a snail in one foot, either braced against the perch or up in the air, the kite works on prey much as a small child might attack an ice-cream cone held not quite upright in one hand.

In addition, the hook-bill exhibits a number of physical characteristics that set it apart from all other North American raptors. Adults have a glassy white eye coloration that gives them a distinctly demented expression. And between the eye and the bill is a peculiar greenish patch of skin topped by a yellowish patch, both of unknown significance. Lastly, the legs of the kite are so short as to look like stumps and give the species an unnatural "sawed-off" appearance in profile. A more unusual bird of prey is hard to imagine.

Could the hook-bill have evolved from some distant lineage of birds quite unrelated to other raptors? No one yet has offered a formal case for this possibility, either on anatomical, behavioral, or biochemical grounds. Still, the species has received extremely little study, and much remains to be established about its biology and ancestry.

The Hook-billed Kite is basically a Central and South American species that occurs as far north as Texas in the thorn-scrub vegetation along the Rio Grande.

Range of the Hook-billed Kite
▨ Breeding and wintering

Nesting records exist for the Santa Ana Refuge, and the birds are also sometimes seen in other locations farther upriver, but the species is erratic in distribution and is not found in these locations in all years.

In the spring of 1979, we were fortunate to spend a number of days with Tom Smith observing breeding pairs of hook-bills in northeastern Mexico. Tom, who had earlier helped us with studies of Everglade Kites

The presumed male of one pair of hook-bills studied near Tampico, Mexico, feeds an extracted snail to a recent fledgling. Feeding rates of young were at times as high as one snail every six minutes.

Many of the snails brought to the young by the presumed female hook-bill at one nest were whole. These she proceeded to extract in full view of her nestlings. Characteristically, she clutched a snail up off the perch in her left foot, then dropped the shell once she freed the softparts.

Clusters of dormant tree snails formed the entire diet of the hook-bill population near Tampico, and all kites observed in the area were the small-billed variety. Characteristically the hook-bills carried snails in their bills to the nesting area. Both adults cooperated in feeding the brood.

in Florida, was beginning an intensive study of the hook-bill in an attempt to determine the significance of a curious variability in bill size he and Stan Temple had noted for the species in museum skins. Some populations of hook-bills have bills of relatively uniform size. In other regions, two markedly different forms of the species occur—one with a very large bill and the other with a smaller, but still substantial, bill—and the two bill types do not seem to have any consistent relationships with variable characteristics of plumage coloration, body size, sex, or age of the birds. The magnitude of the dimorphism in bill size seen in some regions is sufficiently great that some observers have even proposed that more than one species of Hook-billed Kite might exist. Unfortunately, no one knows for sure if the large-billed and small-billed birds interbreed freely. For his graduate research at the University of Wisconsin, Tom was attempting to determine through field studies whether the presence or absence of the two bill sizes in different regions might be related to the sizes of snails available for food.

To help launch Tom in his research, we first joined him and his fellow graduate students, Brad Livezey and Eduardo Santana, in a search for the species in southern Texas. But although we found old nests of hook-bills and promising piles of hook-bill damaged snail shells, we found no active pairs in the area, and Tom soon headed across the border to continue the search. Several weeks later, we were delighted to hear that he had at last located a loose nesting colony of the small-billed form of the species two hundred miles south of where we had searched in Texas. Within hours we had plane reservations to join Tom in Tampico, and within a couple days we had arrived at the tract of thorn-scrub woodland in Mexico where the birds were located. At last we were going to be able to observe how the hook-bill's method of extracting snails might differ from the method used by Everglade Kites.

In the days that followed, when we weren't removing ticks and cactus spines from our legs, arms, and hair, we had a chance to watch the behavior of two pairs of hook-bills from blinds and to discover that the snail-extraction method used by this species has little of the elegance of the method used by the Everglade Kite. Rather than subtly severing the columellar muscle of the snail without damaging the shell, the hook-bill uses brute force and fractures the base of the shell with its bill, then pulls out the exposed softparts. Correspondingly, the bill of the hook-bill, even the small-billed form, is much more massive than that of the Everglade Kite and is structured to withstand the continuous wear and tear inherent in crushing dozens of shells on a daily basis. In profile the hook-bill's bill projects proportionately much farther forward from the head than the bill of most accipitrids and is reminiscent of the huge prow of a Bald Eagle.

Snails were extremely abundant in the region surrounding the hook-bill colony near Tampico—not active snails, but dormant or estivating snails clinging in a state of motionless torpor to trunks and twigs of vegetation. The snails were conspicuous and obviously were not much of a challenge to capture. The kites were taking them at a phenomenal rate. At one of the two nests observed, a nest with two young just at fledging age, we recorded substantial periods when the frequency of visits of adults to the nest was as high as one trip every six to seven minutes. We wonder if there is another large raptor anywhere in the world that might match this frequency of prey deliveries. The apple snails taken by Everglade Kites are much more massive than the snails we observed the hook-bills eating, and we have never observed Everglade Kites feeding at anything like the rate seen with the hook-bills.

Normally the hook-bills confined their movements to accipiterlike flights from tree to tree, and we never saw them circling in the sky. They brought snails to the nest vicinity quite surreptitiously and extracted them either at the nest itself or on a perch nearby. Enormous piles of shells with characteristic hook-bill damage had accumulated under some perches. The vocalizations of the adults did not carry far, and often the crunch of a snail being processed nearby was the first signal we had that an adult had returned.

The hook-bills usually transported snails in semi-extracted form still in their shells. Sometimes they carried a snail crosswise in the bill, sometimes with the upper bill inserted in the snail's aperture. Both sexes of adults fed the young independently. The presumed males were gray-backed, while their mates were brown in basic coloration. Plumage variability in this species is great, however, and some males are known to exhibit a femalelike coloration.

In accordance with Tom Smith's suspicions about the function of bill dimorphism in the Hook-billed Kite, there was only one species of tree snail of relatively uniform size for the small-billed Tampico population to exploit. Later he was able to document that in areas where the hook-bills are strongly dimorphic in bill size, a number of snail species of greatly different sizes are available as food. His hypothesis that the dimorphism might be related to availability of different-sized prey snails appears to be well supported by field data.

Sadly, when Tom Smith returned later in 1979 to again observe the hook-bills near Tampico, he found that the entire tract of thorn-scrub habitat containing the colony had been bulldozed into cropland. With the steady destruction of scrublands in northeastern Mexico, how long can hook-bills continue to exist in this region, let alone turn up in Texas farther north? Elsewhere, other populations of this species are even more vulnerable to loss. Two distinctive subspecies of the hook-bill, on Cuba and Grenada, are now exceedingly rare and considered endangered, possibly mainly because of habitat destruction. It's hard to find a following for the Hook-billed Kite among conservationists and ornithologists, in thought-provoking contrast to the fraternities of devotees who revere more spectacular species such as the California Condor or the Peregrine Falcon. But is this bizarre raptor, with its many extraordinary adaptations, any less worthy of our concern for its survival?

Kites

Black-shouldered Kite
ELANUS CAERULEUS

WITH A PURE white head, underparts, and tail, and with long black and white wings flashing conspicuously as it beats its way over open fields and meadows, the Black-shouldered Kite looks much like a wayward gull or tern. This close resemblance has sometimes led to the species being overlooked, especially in areas where gulls habitually congregate on inland prairies. Yet the kite differs sufficiently from seabirds in flight characteristics that the species can be easily identified, even from a considerable distance, if watched for any length of time.

The black-shoulder generally hunts from altitudes of fifty to one hundred feet above the ground and feeds almost exclusively on small mammals. Advancing methodically across the terrain, it periodically stalls its forward progress to stare intently at a specific area from a stationary hover. In this maneuver the bird pivots to face directly into the wind, with its body tipped upward and its wings flexing deeply and rapidly, while its feet dangle loosely underneath. After scanning the ground for a few seconds, the kite resumes slower wing beats and progresses perhaps another fifty yards, and again pulls up into a hover. The bird continues to advance and hover alternately until a prospective victim is finally sighted. Now the kite descends quickly, its wings held stiffly upward at about a 45 degree angle from horizontal, in a direct and powerful pounce.

Only a few decades ago, the Black-shouldered Kite was a relatively rare species in North America, limited largely to parts of central and western California and southern Texas. Concerned naturalists considered it a likely candidate for early extinction. Yet quite the opposite has happened. Since the mid-1960s, the species has undergone a massive population explosion, and its range has expanded to include large areas of Arizona and New Mexico, as well as most of California and Texas. There have even been sightings and breeding records for Mississippi, Louisiana, Oklahoma, Oregon, and Washington, and the bird has recently returned to Florida after a long absence.

The exact causes of the improved status of the black-shoulder are not certain, but whatever they are, they are not limited to North America. The kite has also been

Range of the Black-shouldered Kite

◻ Breeding and wintering

increasing dramatically in many other portions of its extensive range, which includes large parts of Central and South America, as well as much of Africa, southern Europe, southeast Asia, and, depending on taxonomic preferences, Australia. Some observers have attributed the worldwide increase to large-scale creation of suitable open-field habitat, resulting from clearance of forests and brushlands for pastures and croplands. Others have suggested that increased use of irrigation in agriculture and climatic change, in particular increased temperatures and rainfall, have been the most important factors, possibly because of their beneficial effects on prey populations. Overall reductions in levels of human persecution of raptors may also have played a role. Regardless of just which factors have been most important, the Black-shouldered Kite seems to have settled into a fairly comfortable relationship with modern agricultural practices, and the population expansion appears to be continuing unabated.

One region where the species has very recently become common, but where it was unknown prior to 1972, is southern Arizona. Here, in the spring of 1987, we had an opportunity to study several pairs nesting in relatively short hackberries, graythorns, and Arizona cypresses. We made especially close observations of one pair that nested in an Arizona cypress near an abandoned ranch in the Sulfur Springs Valley. The nest, only twenty-two feet from the ground, was well situated for study, and the birds proved to be vigorous and successful parents.

They were not alone. Groves of trees in open Arizona grassland-brushland habitat are magnets for nesting birds, and the cypress clump chosen by the kites had attracted an astonishing density of avian neighbors. The kites' nesting tree also hosted a pair of Greater Roadrunners building their nest only six feet under the kite nest, as well as a pair of Western Kingbirds and a pair of House Sparrows lower down. An immediately adjacent cypress snag, a primary perch tree for the kites, held a pair of Loggerhead Shrikes, a pair of Northern Mockingbirds, and another pair of Western Kingbirds, despite the fact that the snag had only a few small living branches. Another immediately adjacent tree had a pair of Cassin's Kingbirds, a pair of Bullock's Orioles, and a pair of Mourning Doves, not to mention an occasional roosting Barn Owl. Still other nearby cypresses held nesting Great-tailed Grackles and additional pairs of kingbirds, while an old hollow fence post only a hundred feet from the kite nest contained a brood of four young Ash-throated Flycatchers.

The air in the vicinity was full of birds and their cries, as they fought with one another and carried on their breeding activities. The kingbirds were the most active and found the kites, especially the young kites after they had fledged, to be irresistible targets for their abundant aggression. Still clumsy and slow in flight, the fledgling kites could not fly anywhere in the vicinity without one or more of these pugnacious passerines soon landing on their backs, yanking out feathers with their bills as they rode. These were the same kingbirds that worked unceasingly to rip apart our burlap blind for nesting material, and occasionally startled us by grabbing a beakful of hair, unfortunately still attached, through spaces in the burlap.

But as annoying as the kingbirds were, we were much more concerned by the close nesting of the roadrunners to the kites. Roadrunners are accomplished predators of vertebrates and constituted a significant threat to the kite eggs and young. Fortunately, nest attendance by the adult kites was very tight, and without any encouragement from us, the roadrunners abandoned their nest before egg laying. Moving to an alternative nest site in the rafters of an abandoned shed fifty yards away, they ultimately fledged a brood of two young, while the kites raised their three youngsters unmolested.

As has been noted by a number of biologists who have studied the black-shoulder, the species appears to be limited to regions with good populations of small mammals that are active during daylight hours. In some regions, such as much of California, the primary prey are meadow mice. However, meadow mice do not occur widely in Arizona, and in our study area, the diet of the kites proved to be virtually exclusively cotton rats. These were abundant in adjacent fields and usually necessitated no more than five to ten minutes hunting effort for the kites to locate. The kites, in fact, spent very little of the day foraging, even when food demands of their young were at a maximum in the middle to late nestling stage. Further, the adults limited almost all hunting activity to the early morning and late afternoon hours, with a long siesta of perching and preening from about 9:30 A.M. to 3:30 P.M. each day, even when weather was cloudy.

The male kite did nearly all the foraging through the nestling period, and from our tower blind we could watch many of his hunting efforts through to successful prey captures. Towing his victims back to the nesting vicinity in his talons, the male announced his return with piercing chirps very reminiscent of the calls of Ospreys. Most often he landed on a nearby stub, where he was soon joined by his mate, who immediately took the prey from his talons in her bill. Sometimes, however, we saw talon-to-talon prey transfers that took place in midair over the blind. As the pair flew side by side into the wind, the female simply moved in close enough to reach over and grab the prey in her feet, then descended to perch near the nest.

While plucking the victim, the female uttered curious *ee-gritch* calls. Then, after a minute or two, she took the prey on in to the nest, often continuing to vocalize as she ripped off portions for the young. When she finished feeding the nestlings, the female flew off from the nest to cache any uneaten portions of the prey on a nearby perch. In the early nestling period, she soon returned to brood or shade the young, occasionally flying off to collect sticks to fortify the nest. In the late nestling stage, she mainly occupied her time between feedings by guarding the nest from the top of a nearby cypress.

Between hunts, the male adult spent considerable time preening, and right through the nestling period he often mounted his mate in copulations. Mating activity late in the breeding cycle is rare in most raptors, and the overall frequency of copulations in this pair far exceeded what we have seen in observations of any other falconiform species.

Other activities occasionally observed in the nesting adults included very conspicuous fluttering flights in the vicinity of the nest tree. Both birds participated in these flights, circling low and vibrating their wings rapidly above the horizontal plane, as they simultaneously called excitedly with chirping vocalizations. The significance of these butterflylike flights was unclear.

After fledging, the young kites still focused their activities around the nest tree for several weeks, and the adults continued to bring food to the nest for transfer to the young. In time, however, transfers began to take place on other nearby perches. A month after fledging, the young were consistently flying out to meet a parent returning with food, and transfers now took place talon to talon in midair. At this stage, the fledglings mostly spent their time on high perches near the nest watching their parents hunt. Raising and lowering their conspicuous white tails in flashing displays and uttering intermittent begging screams, they appeared to be anxious to keep the adults informed of their locations and readiness to eat.

Off in the distance, the parent kites alternated hunting forays with spells of perching on mesquites and fence posts, and they now rarely returned all the way to the nest area itself. When an adult made a successful capture, off the fledglings would fly, each vying to be the first to reach the source of food. However, the first youngster to reach the parent was not always the one to wind up with the prey. We sometimes saw triple plays in which the prey passed from parent to one young to a second young in quick succession.

Black-shouldered Kites have long been known to be capable of producing more than a single brood in a breeding season. In addition, recent observations by John Mendelsohn in South Africa indicate that this species, like the Everglade Kite, sometimes practices mate desertion in the fledgling stage. In Mendelsohn's observations, however, unlike our observations of Everglade Kites, only females deserted, and desertions normally did not occur until several weeks after fledging. Very likely, mate desertion in this species, as in the Everglade Kite, allows deserters to begin new nesting attempts with new mates and thus increases their overall reproductive output.

If North American black-shoulders also practice the same sort of mate desertion as their South African relatives, the observed eagerness of males to copulate with females late in the breeding cycle may have a

A female black-shoulder prepares to brood her young in a nest in an Arizona cypress. During the early nesting stages, the male does all hunting for the pair, while the female rarely, if ever, leaves the immediate nest vicinity.

Above photos: A male black-shoulder arrives at a transfer perch with a cotton rat, calls the female off the nest, and passes her the prey.

An adult Black-shouldered Kite in flight bears a striking resemblance to a gull, but is distinguishable because of its frequent hovering.

The Sulfur Springs Valley of southeastern Arizona is one of the last places where Aplomado Falcons were known in the state. In recent years, it has become a new home for two expanding species of raptors, the Bay-winged Hawk and the Black-shouldered Kite.

definite function. It could represent an effort on their part to father at least part of the broods produced by their mates in succeeding breeding attempts with new mates. Such a genetic contribution might be advantageous to both the male and the female, but whether it actually occurs remains to be determined by careful analytical studies.

Despite its enormous and nearly worldwide range, the Black-shouldered Kite is not known to engage in well-defined seasonal migrations anywhere. However, the species tends to be at least somewhat nomadic, appearing in some regions only during outbreaks of small mammals. Normally solitary or in pairs during the day, the species occasionally congregates in overnight roosts of up to several dozen individuals during the non-breeding season. These roosts fluctuate in size and sometimes shift in location over a period of weeks or months. Most are situated in groves of trees in relatively open country, but occasionally reed beds or sugar cane fields are utilized. A tendency to roost socially is also found in many other kite species and allows comprehensive censusing of regional populations if all roosts can be located and assessed.

Kites

Mississippi Kite
ICTINIA MISSISSIPPIENSIS

LONG POINTED WINGS and a long tail give the Mississippi Kite a deceptively falconlike silhouette as it soars overhead. Nevertheless, the gregarious habits and buoyant flight of this species, coupled with its apparent reluctance to beat its wings, soon dispel any doubts as to its true identity. In size, the Mississippi Kite is similar to the Black-shouldered Kite. In coloration, it is almost uniformly a battleship gray. However, adults have a whitish patch along the trailing edge of the topsides of their wings, formed by the pale upper surfaces of their inner flight feathers. As a rule, this patch is visible only in flying individuals and only when they bank and tilt their shoulders toward the observer below.

Aloft, the Mississippi Kite is pure pleasure for the eyes. Totally at home on the winds, this species exhibits an exquisite acrobatic grace in its movements and an ease of progression that is rivaled by few other raptors. Gliding, circling, and swooping with its companions, it sails tirelessly across the skies, sometimes ascending so high above the ground that it ultimately disappears from view, lost in the clouds or lost in the glare from the sun.

The underlying reason for the Mississippi Kite's penchant for the stratosphere is a search for prey, mainly high-flying insects such as dragonflies. These it grabs in its talons after quick flapping dashes and swoops, or sometimes with nothing more than almost imperceptible slight shifts in flight direction and altitude. Occasionally, the species also takes flying birds and bats, but its overall dependence on large airborne insects is nearly 100 percent.

With such a diet and such hunting behavior, it is not surprising to find that the Mississippi Kite is a late-riser. Only with the thermal stimulation of midmorning sunlight do many of its prey species take to the air, and only with the air movements created by the sun can the kites themselves stay airborne with maximal efficiency. Until conditions are right, the kites commonly gather on conspicuous snags, preening their soft gray feathers and intermittently scanning their surroundings.

On occasion, Mississippi Kites, like kingbirds, also hunt from perches, waiting for prey to fly by, then flapping over to grab them and gliding quickly back to their perches. Such hunting behavior is sufficiently frequent that it may explain the strong tendency of the species to nest near towering trees with dead branches that can provide strategic vantage points for sighting prey.

A dependence on insects also appears to explain the relatively late breeding cycle characteristic of the species, for in most regions the greatest availability of large flying insects occurs in summer, not springtime. Unlike the many raptor species that begin breeding in March and April, Mississippi Kites do not commonly commence egg laying till late May and early June, and young are often not on the wing until August.

In addition, the Mississippi Kite's tendency to take large flying insects high in the air appears to explain its tolerance of a great variety of habitat types in its distribution across the southern United States. Such prey can be found in abundance over diverse ecological zones. In some regions, for example northern Florida, Mississippi Kites are characteristic birds of heavily forested river swamps. In other regions, as in parts of Texas and Oklahoma, they can be found coursing over endless swales of mesquite or oak scrublands. In still other regions, such as other parts of Texas and in Kansas and Oklahoma, they gather in shelter belts in the midst of open field habitats. In recent years, they have also become familiar nesting birds of the tree-lined fairways of golf courses in suburban regions of certain of the southwestern states, posing something of a nuisance, if not a hazard, to golfers by their tendencies to defend their nests with aggressive swooping dives.

Still another habitat type occupied by Mississippi Kites is one where we have become most familiar with the species—the cottonwood riparian zones of the southwestern states, for example along the San Pedro, Gila, and Verde rivers in Arizona. Here the kites have settled primarily in regions dominated by cottonwoods and salt cedar. Both tree species are primary food plants for the Apache cicadas on which the kites feed extensively.

In 1987, we observed the activities of one of Arizona's Mississippi Kite colonies along the San Pedro River for a number of days in June. Here, several dozen kites had settled along a five-mile stretch of the river that also hosted a minimum of four pairs of Gray Hawks, several pairs of Cooper's Hawks, and a pair of Common Black Hawks, as well as many Gila Woodpeckers, Bewick's Wrens, Western Kingbirds, Vermillion Flycatchers, Blue Grosbeaks, and Summer Tanagers, and uncountable numbers of Yellow-breasted Chats, Yellow Warblers, and Bell's Vireos. The population of Gray Hawks nesting in this area had increased greatly from the mid-1970s when Rich Glinski and Bob Ohmart made intensive studies of Mississippi Kites here, but the number of kites had not changed significantly.

Range of the Mississippi Kite
☐ Breeding
The Mississippi Kite winters in South America.

Many of the kites roosted in a small grove of huge cottonwoods on the west side of the river, while nests were scattered several hundred yards apart, mainly on the river's east side and mainly near the tops of tall, slender cottonwoods that defied safe ascent. Salt cedar was common in the area, though the abundance of mesquite and other woody vegetation and especially the overall abundance of mature cottonwoods were truly impressive.

The kites commonly foraged right over the crowns of the cottonwoods on the east side of the river, catching the lift of the winds deflected upward by the treetops, but at times they ascended to prodigious heights, capturing and eating endless numbers of cicadas on the

A male Mississippi Kite lands aside his mate and prepares to pass her a cicada early in the breeding season.

The Mississippi Kite in flight is among the most graceful of all birds, soaring rather than flapping most of the time. Effortless powers of flight allow a long migration to South America each fall. The kites commonly travel in flocks, circling in thermals and gliding long distances with very little expenditure of energy.

The cottonwood bottomlands of the San Pedro River in Arizona are a summer home for a population of Mississippi Kites. Cottonwoods are a favorite food tree for the cicadas on which the kites feed heavily.

An adult Mississippi Kite incubates her eggs high in a cottonwood in Texas. Mississippi Kites, like Hook-billed Kites, raise only small broods, commonly one or two young per nest, and they normally nest later than any other raptor of North America.

wing. Often it was impossible to detect any kites in the area without scanning the skies carefully with binoculars. But a few minutes later, a dozen or more birds would appear at close range, joining one another, dispersing again, then coming together again in a constantly evolving ballet of graceful movements and associations.

Prior to egg laying, the female kites often spent much of their time perched quietly on dead branches high in the cottonwoods. Their mates meanwhile worked hard to satisfy not only their own food needs, but much of the females' needs as well. Coursing the skies in the vicinity, the males brought in many of their insect victims in plummeting swoops, transferring the prey from foot to bill in the last few moments before landing aside their mates, then relinquishing the food in quick bill-to-bill passes. However, some of the swooping approaches of the males to their perched mates ended not in food transfers, but in copulations, with the males balancing on the backs of the females for episodes lasting about ten seconds.

Some of the kites did not appear to be breeders, and of these, many wore the plumage of one-year-olds: banded tails and mottled underwing coverts. Others that were associated with nests drifted in and out of the foraging groups, returning periodically to their nest locations to feed small young or to assist in incubation or in the shading or brooding of young. When we approached their nests or roosts too closely we were greeted with the characteristic *wheet-phew* vocalizations that signify alarm.

Late June temperatures along the San Pedro can reach wilting levels far over 100 degrees Fahrenheit, and our primary desires at midday were to take refuge in the shade and to swill volumes of liquids. The kites, however, remained quite active through this period, perhaps finding cooler conditions aloft. Gray Hawks also commonly made an appearance at this time, leaving the shelter of the dense cottonwood groves to land on the gravel bars at the river's edge and drink. We occasionally saw the kites do likewise. The San Pedro floodplain at this time of year is an oven, and only when the summer monsoons arrive in July, with daily thunderstorms and cloud-shelter from the sun, do conditions become more bearable.

Rich Glinski and Bob Ohmart have called attention to the curious implications of the apparent close dependence of Arizona's Mississippi Kites on mixed cottonwood and salt cedar riparian zones. Because the kites only occur commonly where both these tree species are present, and because salt cedar is an aggressive exotic species that appears to be completely replacing cottonwoods over wide areas, it is not clear whether the kites could have existed in the state in the past or whether they have a stable future here. Mississippi Kites were only first discovered in Arizona in the early 1970s when the salt cedar invasion was well underway, but should the invasion go to completion, the kites might well disappear once again.

Several other Arizona raptors, in particular Gray Hawks and Black Hawks, are likewise threatened by the continued spread of salt cedar, though unlike the kites of this region, they appear to be best adapted to uninvaded cottonwood zones. Thus vegetational changes currently taking place in the riparian zones of Arizona have profound implications, mostly negative, for a number of raptor species.

Extremely resistant to fire and capable of sprouting from small root sections, salt cedar is difficult to eradicate, even by bulldozing. In many respects, it closely resembles the melaleuca introduced into Florida's Everglades in its tenacity and encroachment capacities. It is a remarkable coincidence that both these exotic tree species presently have such importance for native kite species.

In most of its range, however, the Mississippi Kite is not in any way dependent on or threatened by salt cedar, and its overall status appears to be robust. It would be perverse to argue for the preservation of exotic salt cedar in Arizona's riparian zones for the sake of the kite, especially in view of the apparently extreme threat that this plant poses for other avian species.

Like the Swallow-tailed Kite, the Mississippi Kite is highly migratory, retiring to South America via Central America for a large fraction of the year. The migratory flights of Mississippi Kites, while not so familiar to North Americans as the migratory flights of Broad-winged Hawks and Swainson's Hawks, are sometimes impressive. In late April of 1988, we observed a dense flock of over two hundred individuals of this species heading methodically northward across the flat coastal plain of southern Texas near the Laguna Atascosa Refuge. Like many other migrating raptors, the kites alternately gained altitude by circling in columns of rising air, then coasted in long glides in their chosen direction of travel, remaining a well-integrated, closely packed assemblage till they finally faded from view in the distance.

The Mississippi Kite, like the Black-shouldered Kite, has been experiencing a recent increase in abundance and distribution, and it can now be found nearly coast to coast across the southern states during the summer months. The broad tolerances of this species for disturbed habitats and the relative security of its insect food supply from destruction by human activities allow considerable optimism for its conservation in the years ahead. Nevertheless, the biology of the Mississippi Kite is still known only imperfectly, especially on the wintering grounds in South America, so the full array of threats this raptor may face in the future cannot be safely specified. Its abilities to survive the many new ecological stresses challenging our planet, from global warming to ozone depletion, are truly *terra incognita,* just as they are for all other species.

Kites

American Swallow-tailed Kite
ELANOIDES FORFICATUS

SAILING AND CIRCLING among the treetops, with its long forked tail twisting in the air currents, its wings flapping but rarely, there is no more elegant raptor anywhere in the world than the American Swallow-tailed Kite. Formally attired in a striking black and white plumage, this is a bird of our southern swamps, at home among the cypresses, the tupelo gums, the Spanish moss, and the bromeliads. Though much reduced in range from the early nineteenth century, when it could be found as far north as Wisconsin and Minnesota, the species continues to be locally common, especially in Florida, where it reaches a peak abundance in the Big Cypress region of the southwestern portion of the state.

The swallow-tails spend only half the year in North America, usually arriving in early March and withdrawing again to South America by the end of September. During this period they have ample time to breed, most commonly fledging one or two young per nest. Throughout its range the species nests at the very tops of the tallest trees available, and consequently it is a challenge to study. Many nests are over one hundred feet from the ground, lodged in branches too slender to support a person's weight. In addition, most nests are impossible to view clearly from blinds in other trees because no nearby trees rise high enough to overlook the nests.

Aware of these problems, we were very pleased to discover a population of swallow-tails in low mangroves along the southwestern coast of Florida, not far from the boundary of Everglades National Park. Here, tree heights rarely exceeded forty-five feet, well within the reach of a good extension ladder, and nests were fully visible from our tower blinds. The major practical difficulties in studying this population proved to be moving around through the mud and tangles of mangrove roots, and surviving the assaults of hordes of biting insects.

What peculiar ecological conditions have led to the development of such diabolical swarms of flying arthropods as occur in this region is beyond our knowledge, but it is enough to note that nowhere else, including the arctic slopes of Alaska (the usual standard for insufferable insect swarms), have we ever experienced the torment that we suffered here. That the early Calusa and Tequesta Indians of Florida lived voluntarily in these mangroves invites considerable respect and admiration.

Early mornings during our studies began with a dense haze of mosquitoes and no-see-ums that seemed

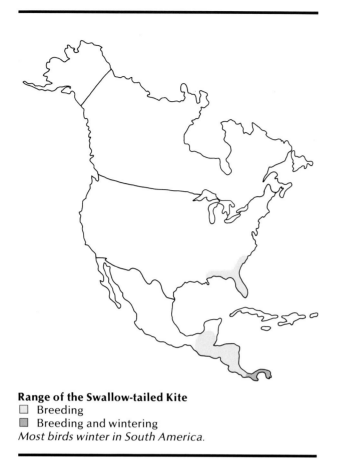

Range of the Swallow-tailed Kite
☐ Breeding
▨ Breeding and wintering
Most birds winter in South America.

These miniature fighter planes darted endlessly through the mosquito clouds that formed around the kite nests, destroying victim after victim.

Sadly, no dragonflies offered to enter our blinds. Nevertheless, with luck a breeze began to stir, and by midday, much of the insect problem for kites and observers alike had usually subsided, only to return again in the evening.

It was tempting to speculate that the tendency of the swallow-tails to place their nests at the very tops of the highest black mangroves might in part have represented an effort to escape the mosquitoes. But it could just as well have reflected the difficulty this long-winged raptor would have had in maneuvering through heavier vegetation farther down the trunks. Their nest placement, however, carried penalties of other sorts, for nests situated at the tops of trees are vulnerable to the winds and to attacks from other aerial predators. At one nest we studied closely in 1972, both young were tossed out to their destruction in the swamp below as high winds of thunderstorms buffeted the area. At another nest of 1972, we found the remains of one adult kite right under the nest, apparently a victim of another raptor—most likely a Bald Eagle or a Great Horned Owl, species common in the region.

Altogether, we had an opportunity to follow the natural history of three pairs of swallow-tails through the breeding cycle in the mangroves, two in 1969 and one in 1972. The contrasts we found between the behavior of the birds in these two years were dramatic—well illustrating the dangers of attempting to generalize about the biology of a species from a single year's data.

In 1969, the diet of the breeding pairs was heavily slanted toward tree frogs, which were widespread in the mangroves and which the kites captured on the wing by swoops into the canopy. Food was abundant in this year, and the kites had no difficulties raising their young. In the early stages of the breeding cycle, we often observed males feeding their mates at the nest, and incubation switches between adults were frequent.

The extreme drought of 1971, however, effectively wiped out the tree frog population of the mangroves, and the 1972 breeding season of the kites was one of considerable stress for lack of food. Incubation switches at the nest under close study were infrequent, as the adults spent long periods away from the nest attempting to satisfy their food needs. We only very rarely saw the male at the 1972 nest feed his mate, and we observed no tree frogs whatsoever in the diet of the pair. Instead, the kites were attempting to carry on by concentrating on green anoles (a small lizard) and nestling birds for

oblivious to repellants. To reduce the onslaughts, we even resorted at times to wearing bee hats with veils, awkward as they were. Our best defense proved to be hurrying to our blinds as fast as possible, then tightening them up sufficiently to prevent the entry of the squadrons following us. Once inside, we faced a period of resigned suffering through the bloody attacks of the inhabitants that were already there when we arrived or that came in with us.

By midmorning, the mosquitoes and no-see-ums fortunate enough to have had us at their mercy inside the blinds had finally fed to repletion (or had been squashed), and there was a brief period of recovery. But now the heat began to build up enough that we had no choice but to crack open the blinds again for some ventilation—just in time to allow in the swamp's formidable deerflies, which were becoming active. The deerflies more than made up in puncture-power what they lacked in numbers.

We took little comfort in observing that the swallow-tails had their share of misery from the insects as well. However, their problems seemed limited to the mosquitoes, and furthermore, they had help in combating these pests from the dragonflies resident in the region.

Left: A swallow-tail carries nesting material in the early nesting season. Sexes are alike in coloration and contribute about equally to nest construction and other reproductive activities. Below: A female swallow-tail arrives at the nest with a beakful of usnea moss and prepares to take over incubation from her mate.

A male swallow-tail passes an anole to his mate for feeding to the chicks.

The mangroves of southwestern Florida, an important breeding area for the Swallow-tailed Kite, are perhaps the most insufferable habitat anywhere on the continent because of incredibly dense populations of biting insects.

A male swallow-tail leaves the nest with *klee-klee-klee* calls after passing a nestling bird to the female.

A male swallow-tail lands on the back of a female for mating. Copulations are frequent and noisy in the early breeding season, and are commonly preceded by the male feeding the female.

A green tree frog rests on a mangrove root. This species was a staple food item for the swallow-tails in 1969, but was missing entirely from their diet in 1972, evidently eliminated from the mangroves by the drought of 1971.

food. Feeding rates at the 1972 nest averaged less than half the rates seen at the 1969 nests, and although the 1972 nest failed because storms tossed the young out of the nest, we seriously question if the adults could have fledged young in any case, in view of the poor food supply.

A comparison of the two years suggested a strong dependence of the kites on tree frogs for food. While they also took a variety of other food types, including anoles, snakes, and large flying insects, of these only the anoles were brought to nests with any frequency. Observers of successfully nesting swallow-tails in other regions have reported much higher use of insects than we observed, and it may be that the availability of large flying insects is comparatively low in mangrove habitat.

The tree frogs in the mangroves were all green tree frogs and similar-appearing squirrel tree frogs. The occurrence of these frogs here may depend importantly on a freshening of the brackish waters during the summer rainy season. Although they spend much of their lives in arboreal locations, these amphibians are tied to fresh water for egg laying and may only be able to breed in years of normal or high rainfall.

One of the most interesting aspects of the behavior of the young kites was the development of their abilities to recognize their own species and whether or not their parents were carrying food. Newly hatched nestlings gave cheeping cries more or less continuously during the daylight hours, and especially during feedings. At about one week of age, the cheeping cries of the young reliably followed the *eeep* calls of the female adult at the nest as the male approached with food. At this time, the young also responded with cheeping cries when Great Crested Flycatchers gave *weep* calls in the vicinity of the nest. The similarity of these calls to the *eeep* calls of the kites is apparent to the human ear as well. By two weeks of age, the young no longer responded to calls of the flycatchers. They did, however, call whenever adults came to the nest, with or without food, and whenever other large birds such as Common Grackles and Pileated Woodpeckers flew past the nest. By three weeks of age, the young no longer responded to large birds of other species flying past, but they still called when kites flew nearby with or without food. At five weeks of age, the young often did not respond vocally when adults flew past without food.

Another intriguing feature of the behavior of nestling swallow-tails in the study area, especially when compared with the behavior of nestlings of other hawks and kites, was their apparent disinclination to loft excrement over the nest edge. We repeatedly observed young backing up to the nest rim in typical accipitrid fashion. Then instead of ejecting a stream off into space, they just dribbled excrement directly down onto the nest rim. The extensive nest building by adults late in the nesting cycle, primarily using Spanish moss and usnea moss, served to cover the accumulation quite effectively, but we wonder why the birds have apparently lost the normal accipitrid pattern of lobbing waste material beyond the limits of the nest. Possibly, since telltale excrement did not tend to accumulate on the ground under the swallow-tail nests, it is an adaptation to reduce the conspicuousness of the nests to terrestrial predators, especially raccoons, which abound in the mangrove habitat. The availability of absorbent materials, such as Spanish moss and usnea, in the habitats occupied by the kites may have facilitated the evolution of such a trait.

Swallow-tailed Kites are not known to defend exclusive foraging ranges, and in fact tend to be quite gregarious throughout the year. Their nesting ranges, as determined in a recent radiotelemetry study by John Cely and James Sorrow in South Carolina, are often quite large and are probably much too large to be feasible to defend. For four breeding adults tending nests with young prior to fledging, these researchers found foraging areas ranging from 1.5 to 27 square miles in size, and for four adults tending young just out of the nest they found foraging areas ranging from 27 to 66 square miles in size. With foraging areas this extensive, there is probably no way the kites could prevent other kites from using the same areas, even if there might be some advantages in doing so.

In fact, the swallow-tails often nest quite close together in loose colonies, and it is common for such loose assemblages to include some extra nonbreeding birds. One important advantage of this sociality may lie in enhanced abilities to detect and deter potential predators. We have seen numerous examples of cooperative assault of this species on Bald Eagles and various owls, and it is impressive to observe from how far off incubating kites are able to see eagles and how rapidly they sound the alarm, soon to be joined by their mates and other kites in a mass effort to drive off the enemy.

During the years we studied Everglade Kites on Lake Okeechobee, we became aware of a spectacular concentration of Swallow-tailed Kites that forms in this region annually between July and mid-September. As studied in recent years by Brian Millsap, this appears to be a postbreeding assemblage of birds that gather to put on energy stores prior to their autumnal migration to South America. Soaring in the updrafts created by the casuarinas and melaleucas planted on the dikes surrounding the lake, these birds may be taking advantage of the large numbers of dragonflies associated with the lake. In August of 1987 in a remote cypress swamp west of the lake, Millsap located a roost of these swallow-tails that consisted of a minimum of 1,339 individuals packed into an area of only about two to three acres!

He suggested that this might represent as many as 50 percent of the swallow-tails breeding in the United States. Although the total North American population of the Swallow-tailed Kite can be estimated only crudely, future monitoring of this roost may give a practical means for assessing overall population trends of the species on this continent.

Harriers

Above: Sheltering her chick from a rain shower, a female Northern Harrier winds up quite soaked herself. Prominent facial discs functioning as sound collectors give the species keen powers of hearing. Right: The nest found in central Alaska contained only a single chick and two bad eggs when discovered, a relatively low reproductive output for a normally much more prolific species.

Northern Harrier

CIRCUS CYANEUS

AN AGILE RAPTOR of open swamps and fields, the Northern Harrier hunts steadily from flight, coursing low over the ground and catching small birds and rodents at short range with lightning-fast strikes. Very light-bodied and buoyant, this species normally flaps only intermittently, and instead remains airborne primarily by banking and sailing in a seemingly haphazard manner, exploiting the subtle uplifts provided by the winds blowing across irregular terrain.

In color pattern, Northern Harriers fall into two major categories. Adult females and immatures of both sexes possess a basically brown plumage that blends in well with their surroundings. Adult males are almost clear white underneath and pale gray above with striking black outer primary feathers. All ages and sexes exhibit a conspicuous white patch at the base of the tail formed by the upper tail coverts.

Alone among North America's diurnal raptors, Northern Harriers also have a prominent sound-focusing facial disc. This anatomical feature is shared with most owls and gives them their distinctive "owlish" appearance. Facial discs allow the birds that possess them to locate sound sources with great precision, and are extremely important in facilitating the capture of prey concealed in densely cluttered layers of vegetation. Recent studies of the acoustic abilities of Northern Harriers by William Rice have shown that this raptor can locate prey by sound alone and with an accuracy comparable to that of the most accomplished owls hunting in total darkness.

At the one blind we set up on a Northern Harrier nest, we were amazed and frustrated by the abilities of the birds to perceive the slightest noises we might make, even though the blind was positioned at a fair distance from the nest. It was always a relief when rain showers struck, providing a cover of white noise, so that we could scratch, stretch, and move about relatively normally without causing alarm in the birds.

The harrier nest we had under observation held only a single chick and two inviable eggs, although harriers commonly raise much larger broods. The nest itself was a simple platform of grasses on the ground, as is typical for the species, and was tucked in a thick carpet of waist-high brush in the floodplain of a high valley

Range of the Northern Harrier
☐ Breeding
▨ Breeding and wintering
▧ Wintering

in the mountains of central Alaska. Here the birds' close neighbors were a pair of Merlins nesting in a patch of spruce on the side of the valley. Also conspicuous in the area were numerous caribou, Dall's sheep, Long-tailed Jaegers, ptarmigan, and red foxes. The harriers eventually fledged their single youngster successfully, although we watched grizzly bears foraging within a few yards of the nest on a number of occasions and often wondered how long it might be before the nest was discovered by one of these predators.

We also found Northern Harriers in close association with Merlins at the opposite corner of the continent in southern Florida. Here, during the late winter of 1979, we set up a treetop platform for observing Everglade Kites in one area of Lake Okeechobee that by chance also hosted a nightly congregation of hundreds of thousands of roosting Tree Swallows. As might be expected, this extraordinary concentration of potential prey proved highly attractive to the bird-feeding raptors that hunted the marshes.

Each evening, as sunset approached, the swallows gathered high overhead in a cloudlike assemblage that steadily grew larger and denser while it continuously changed shape, much like a vast swarm of honeybees. Meanwhile Northern Harriers and Merlins gathered ominously below. Occasionally, portions of the swarm made abortive dives toward the marsh, but these over-anxious groups soon returned to the main swarm high overhead, and it was not until the last moments of daylight that the birds began a serious descent to roost in the sawgrass. Now in a tight, swirling, tornadolike vortex, and with a great roar of wings, the swallows poured from the sky into the marsh.

As they took up roosting locations, the swallows were vulnerable to their avian predators for a period of just a few minutes until full darkness enveloped the region. We saw as many as two Northern Harriers and three Merlins simultaneously foraging in the swallow roosting aggregation, and there could have been more because we found it difficult to see them in the dim light. And although the swallows moved their specific roost location each night to a different part of the marsh, both raptor species kept track of their movements, unerringly converging on the tornado of descending birds to reap their nightly harvest.

The steady toll of a few swallows each evening represented only a tiny percentage of the total mass of perhaps half a million individuals in the roost. Yet such predation acting over many generations of swallows most likely explains the evolution of their highly specialized roost-formation behavior. So long as the swallows remained high above the marsh, they were easily able to avoid the raptors, but once they came in to roost they had little in the way of defenses. Apparently the best they could do was to minimize the amount of daylight time they spent in the roost. In the mornings, the swallows left their roost at first light and we saw no comparable raids by the raptors.

The powerful nightly spectacle of swallows pouring into the marshes pursued by their raptorial enemies continued until March 23, when the swallows finally began their annual spring migration to more temperate regions. The Northern Harriers and Merlins did not follow them immediately, though they too disappeared from the lake within a few weeks.

Northern Harriers themselves are well known for a strong tendency to roost communally during the winter, although the functions of their roosts, like the communal roosts of other birds, have been controversial. Some biologists have favored the idea that communal roosts might function mainly in transferring information about foraging conditions. Individuals relatively unsuccessful in hunting might conceivably follow better-fed individuals out from the roosts in an effort to find better foraging regions. However, it is hard to see what advantages might lie in communal roosting for the well-fed harriers, unless they might be associated with close kin in the roosts. No evidence for close kinship of roost members has yet been assembled. Furthermore, in at least some circumstances, as we have noted with wintering birds in Arizona and New Mexico, individual harriers vigorously defend exclusive hunting grounds, so it is not entirely clear that poorly fed birds might accrue significant foraging benefits by following well-fed individuals.

In addition, other possible functions of communal harrier roosts may be of greater importance. For example, individuals clustered in groups can potentially increase their abilities to detect and escape predators. Northern Harriers disturbed at roosts by terrestrial mammals quickly communicate their alarm to other members of their roosting assemblages, and all are soon aware of the threat. Thus, the chances of a roosting harrier being taken completely by surprise may plausibly be very low for grouped individuals. On the other hand, it can be argued that the presence of numbers of harriers roosting close together may lure in predators, much as Tree Swallow roosts obviously attract harriers.

In general, however, we are much more comfortable with the possibility that harrier roosts may reduce predation threats than with the possibility that they might increase them. We also remain skeptical that the

This wintering female in the San Simon Valley of Arizona vigorously defended her feeding territory from other Northern Harriers. Easy to recognize because of a missing primary feather, she roosted nightly many miles from her feeding territory.

A tornado of hundreds of thousands of wintering Tree Swallows descends after sunset to roost in the sawgrass of Lake Okeechobee, Florida. The precise roost location was never the same in two consecutive nights, but Northern Harriers and Merlins always quickly converged to capture swallows in the aggregation during the few minutes between roost formation and complete darkness.

Northern Harriers chose this valley in the mountains of central Alaska for nesting in 1968. The active nest was tucked in a peninsula of vegetation between two gravel-bottomed braided streams, and fortunately was never discovered by the grizzly bears foraging nearby.

roosts might offer significant advantages in communicating foraging information. Nevertheless, truly comprehensive experiments to elucidate the function of these roosts have not yet been designed, let alone performed. Possibly, communal harrier roosts have indeed evolved for multiple reasons or for reasons that are as yet entirely unsuspected.

Northern Harriers are also known to nest in loose colonies, especially when prey mammals are very abundant. And sometimes in these colonial situations, they practice polygamy, with certain males simultaneously raising several broods with several mates. To what extent polygamy in this species is attributable to unbalanced sex ratios on the nesting grounds, or to the superior attractiveness and capabilities of particular males, is not easy to determine. Many studies have indeed shown an apparent preponderance of females in wild harrier populations. Some have shown that on average females produce fewer young when paired polygamously than when paired monogamously, but others indicate that females in bigamous relationships may do as well as in monogamous relationships. Males, on the other hand, have quite consistently produced more young when paired polygamously than when paired monogamously. Do females that join polygamous males really have any alternatives other than not breeding at all? This is usually very difficult to establish rigorously.

In any event, it does appear plausible that by nesting relatively close together Northern Harriers may gain some advantages in detecting and repelling potential nest predators, much as they may gain protection from predators by roosting together. Harriers nesting in colonies often make cooperative attacks on their enemies similar to the formidable cooperative attacks on predators exhibited by colonially nesting Swallow-tailed Kites, Mississippi Kites, and Everglade Kites.

Among the most spectacular aerial displays given by any raptor species are the skydancing swoops of male harriers in the early breeding season. With deep, slow wingbeats, a displaying bird rises and falls in a series of nearly vertical dives and climbs, often turning over upside down at the apex of his ascents, only to regain his orientation as he plunges earthward in the next phase of display. Skydancing displays are normally given in full view of a prospective mate, and the nearby female, often perched on the ground, but sometimes coursing below, has ample opportunity to judge the physical prowess of the male. The displays may also function in alerting other males to the territorial claims of the displaying bird. The conspicuous deep wingbeats and obvious swoops make the displaying bird readily observable from great distances and may significantly reduce his overall energy expenditures in laying claim to a full territory. Occasionally females also engage in the swooping displays, but most commonly they remain passive observers. Displays tend to be most intense when pairs or polygamous groups are nesting within sight of each other, but are also performed with great fervor by young unmated males and by males whose mates have died during the breeding season.

The overall conservation of the Northern Harrier is perhaps most critically dependent on habitat considerations. While harriers can to a considerable extent forage in disturbed habitats like those provided in many agricultural regions, they have difficulty nesting successfully in these regions unless the soil is not tilled and the hayfields are not cut through the entire breeding season. Unfortunately, as agriculture has become steadily more intensive, we have lost more and more fallow fields and marshes, with major impacts on harrier populations in many areas. For example, it is now difficult to find nesting harriers anywhere in southern California, although the species was a regular breeder in this region only a few decades ago.

Harriers are far from the only creatures that have been adversely affected by massive losses of wetlands. The basic productivity of marshland habitats makes them extremely valuable for a great diversity of wildlife species. Yet preservation of wetland habitats has been and promises to continue to be one of the most difficult of conservation tasks, in large part because the drainage of marshes has been one of the most economically attractive ways to create new lands for agricultural and urban development.

Accipiters

Above: A female Northern Goshawk lands at her nest eighty feet up in an Apache pine in southern Arizona. Goshawk nests are typically placed close to main trunks in the lower canopy zone, and the birds commonly approach them on the level or by shooting upwards from below. Right: The massive talons of an adult female goshawk are well suited for a diet of medium-sized birds and mammals. Principal prey include such species as pigeons, jays, grouse, squirrels, and rabbits.

Northern Goshawk
ACCIPITER GENTILIS

THE NORTHERN GOSHAWK is a living nightmare for squirrels, jays, grouse, rabbits, and other similar-sized mammals and birds. Weaving through the mature forests at speeds almost too fast to follow, this raptor rarely gives its intended victims much time to react. For those who allow their vigilance to lapse, the first awareness of danger often comes as goshawk talons are already piercing deeply into internal organs. The only true refuge from this formidable predator is brush too dense for it to enter. But staying in dense brush is a luxury few creatures can afford if they are also to carry on vital activities such as foraging and territory defense.

Like the other North American accipiters, the Cooper's Hawk and Sharp-shinned Hawk, the Northern Goshawk is adapted for maneuvering in woodland habitat by its relatively short wings and long tail. All three species are capable of rapid bursts of speed and quick changes in direction. They rely heavily on agility and stealth in making kills and in avoiding injury to themselves in an airspace cluttered with trunks and branches. And as we learned directly in a close study of these species in Arizona and New Mexico from 1969 through 1972, all three accipiters have a talent for surprising an adversary when the adversary's head is turned the other way. Rarely observed for more than a few moments, as they streak down a trail or ravine in headlong pursuit of prey, the accipiters are superbly crafted killing machines—the preeminent experts in guerrilla warfare among the raptors of North America.

The goshawk is a handsome dark-crowned raptor with a white eyestripe and a finely barred gray breast. The largest of the accipiters, it also has the fiercest disposition and takes the largest and most challenging prey. The ferocity of the species extends as well to a renowned willingness to defend its nests aggressively from people. Human intruders to nesting areas,

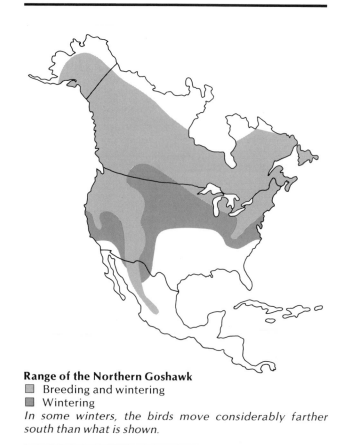

Range of the Northern Goshawk
■ Breeding and wintering
■ Wintering
In some winters, the birds move considerably farther south than what is shown.

especially those foolhardy enough to climb to nests, often find their hats removed and clothing and skin shredded by the massive talons of this species. Cackling angrily and diving repeatedly in kamikaze swoops, always from behind, the goshawks are usually successful in producing a hasty retreat in those invading their domain. In studying the species, we often carried leafy branches as we approached and checked nests. Armed with these improvised shields we were usually, but not

Left: A male goshawk lands on his nest with conspicuous white undertail coverts spread in display. A black back identifies this bird as belonging to the *apache* race of the species, the form typical of the Sierra Madres of Mexico.

Greenery collection is especially highly developed in the goshawk, but its function remains uncertain. Here a female places a Chihuahua pine sprig on her nest late in the breeding cycle.

This female Goshawk fully accepted a Cooper's Hawk chick that we fostered into her nest when her single egg failed to hatch. The chick later fledged successfully.

always, able to fend off attacks without being struck.

Goshawk nests tend to be situated in more open woodlands than those inhabited by Cooper's Hawks and Sharp-shinned Hawks. In our study area, we often found goshawks breeding in mature ponderosa pines and Douglas firs, although they also used Chihuahua pines and Apache pines. Nests were substantial platforms of sticks lined with the outer bark of various conifers, and most often the hawks placed them in the lower branches of the canopy zone. Several nests were well suited for construction of nearby blinds, and from concealment, we made intensive studies of the diet and behavior of a number of pairs.

One pair that nested two years in succession in towering Apache pines became our primary study pair. The male, an extremely beautiful black-backed individual, was an example of the goshawk race known as *Accipiter gentilis apache,* while his mate had a more familiar bluish-gray back of an *Accipiter gentilis atriçapillus.* The *atricapillus* race of the goshawk is the form found through almost all of North America, while the *apache* race is the form typical of the Sierra Madre Occidental of Mexico. However, *apache* goshawks also occur occasionally in southern Arizona and New Mexico, much as a distinctive Mexican race of the Sharpshinned Hawk, *Accipiter striatus suttoni,* can occasionally be found north of the Mexican border.

The goshawks in our study area had various diets. Our primary study pair ate birds exclusively, mainly Band-tailed Pigeons, Steller's Jays, and Mexican Jays, while other pairs took squirrels and rabbits in addition to avian prey. These differences in diet did not appear to be a strict reflection of availability of prey types for the various pairs, because it was clear that many squirrels and rabbits lived in the hunting range of our primary study pair, yet these goshawks apparently never captured them. Furthermore, when we again studied goshawks in the very same territory in 1987 (almost surely different birds after seventeen years), they were frequently taking squirrels and rabbits as prey. Perhaps the particular pair we observed in 1969–1970 avoided mammalian prey because of bad experiences, possibly injury, encountered in previous attempts to capture them. Whatever the cause, ecological theory has to allow for individual diet specializations that sometimes deviate significantly from the overall availability of prey.

In the early stages of breeding, the male of each goshawk pair we observed caught almost all prey consumed by himself, his mate, and his brood. Prey destined for his mate or brood he characteristically brought to a horizontal limb fifty to one hundred yards from the nest. Here he summoned the female with *guck* calls,

and she soon flew over to feed or to prepare the food for the young. Meanwhile the male flew to the nest and took a short turn incubating eggs or brooding small young. The male often had thoroughly bloodstained belly feathers during the intensive period of hunting in the breeding season, a testimony to his predominant role in provisioning the family.

The female only started hunting in the mid–nestling stage, when the brood began to demand more food than the male alone could supply and the young were old enough to maintain body temperatures without being brooded. Prior to this stage, a hungry female awaiting prey from her mate uttered plaintive *weer* calls, audible from hundreds of yards away. The same vocalizations were also used later as begging calls by goshawk fledglings, and were expertly imitated by Steller's Jays in the regions surrounding the nests.

The young were downy white when they first hatched, but gradually took on a streaked brown coloration as they developed juvenile feathers. Wing and tail feathers were among the first to appear through the down, and the last wisps of down did not disappear from the youngsters' heads until they had reached fledging age. By this time the youngsters had also become quite active, especially the males, and often engaged in mock "captures" of pieces of bark in the nest. Just before fledging, they began to move out onto limbs immediately adjacent to the nest structure itself, intermittently exercising their wings with rapid bursts of flapping.

In 1969, we watched the lone youngster of our primary pair take his first flight from a nest high in a tall pine rising from the bottom of a steep ravine. The youngster was actually blown off the nest in a strong gust of wind at a time when both adults were off hunting, and he came spiraling down to the ground almost directly under the nest. As his fledging appeared to be premature and clumsy, we were greatly concerned about this youngster's survival. We were especially worried about the adults' abilities to find and feed him and his own ability to avoid the many terrestrial predators in the region if he stayed on the ground.

Our fears were unfounded. The young goshawk appeared to be unruffled by his surprise fledging and immediately walked over to the small stream under the nest and began to bathe and drink. Through the rest of the afternoon, he gradually worked his way on foot up one slope of the steep-sided ravine until he was almost directly under our blind and at a considerably higher elevation than the nest. Then, in a totally confident flight he took off straight for the nest tree, losing altitude all the way, to be sure, but landing expertly on the nest itself—which he did not leave again for several days. Although this sequence of maneuvers may have been entirely accidental and not a premeditated solution to a difficult problem, we will always suspect that there was something remarkably intelligent going on in this young goshawk's consciousness.

During 1970, our primary study pair laid only a single egg. Unfortunately, this egg proved to be infertile, and when it did not hatch at the expected time, we decided to foster a young Cooper's Hawk into the nest so that we could continue to get diet information on the pair. The goshawks immediately accepted the nestling, and this youngster went on to become perhaps the best-fed nestling Cooper's Hawk in history. The adults kept it in a state of bulging repletion throughout the nesting cycle, and it ultimately fledged successfully, if a bit groggy from its relentless feasting.

The goshawk uses more greenery in nest construction than does any other North American raptor. Pine sprigs are favored building material in many areas, but in regions lacking pine, the species uses leafy branches of other trees. The top surfaces of goshawk nests often wind up looking much like shaggy green carpets.

Greenery collection is also common in many other species of the family Accipitridae, though its general functions have been long debated and remain unknown. Does the greenery help camouflage the nests from enemies, help sanitize nests by covering over waste materials, or deter nest arthropods by releasing noxious aromatic chemicals? Or is its primary function strengthening of nests (especially for species that reuse nests year after year)? As yet, no experimental tests of these hypotheses have been made, and they are not the only hypotheses that have been raised. Perhaps a number of benefits arise from the trait, and perhaps the specific benefits vary from species to species. In the Swallow-tailed Kite, which applies Spanish moss or usnea moss to the nest late in the breeding season, greenery could well have very different values than the pine sprigs used by goshawks. It is well to be wary of assuming singular overall functions for the trait.

Cooper's Hawks use lesser amounts of greenery in their nests than do Northern Goshawks, and we have never found greenery in a Sharp-shinned Hawk nest. We long puzzled over the differences among the accipiter species in this habit and sought reasonable adaptive explanations for the differences. However, we now wonder if the differences may be nothing more than a result of differences in the comparative abilities of these species to break off green living branches. In close observations of Sharp-shinned Hawks in Puerto Rico during the early 1970s, we watched birds attempting to snap off leafy branches for nesting material on a number of occasions. They were unsuccessful in doing so, apparently not out of desire, but simply because they lacked the requisite strength. A failure of a raptor to collect greenery should not be equated to a lack of value of greenery for the species.

In the late 1980s, we found our sympathies toward Northern Goshawks undergoing a subtle change when we began a program to reintroduce Thick-billed Parrots into the pine forests of Arizona for the Arizona Game and Fish Department. Thick-billed Parrots, at about fifteen inches in length and three-quarters of a pound in weight, are ideal-sized prey for goshawks, and it was only a day or two after the first releases, that we became aware of just how fully the local goshawks appreciated our efforts. The parrots, thrust into their new wilderness home from captivity, had not yet developed full flight strength, and we saw numerous tail chases by these raptors and began finding piles of parrot feathers that bore clear witness to raptor successes. In one case, we got to what was left of a radioed parrot just in time to flush a goshawk from the remains.

Nevertheless, the parrots that made it through their first few weeks in the wild were soon in much better physical condition and were a much better match for the hawks. Their losses declined markedly. Extremely fast when in good condition, Thick-billed Parrots can easily outdistance a goshawk in level flight and are very difficult for a goshawk to approach undetected so long as they stay in flocks. In addition to speed and flocking, their defenses include unceasing vigilance and a tendency to feed high up in trees where they are difficult to surprise. The first flock member to spot an approaching raptor gives an alarm call to which all immediately respond by taking to the open air as a group and circling up out of reach. The goshawk's main hope for success lies in finding birds feeding in vegetation dense enough that it can get relatively close before alarm is sounded. With luck, it can then grab a victim that has not yet attained full flight speed. Such opportunities are quite uncommon, and their rarity allows wild parrot populations to coexist in a state of balance with goshawks. Our close observations of Thick-billed Parrots under attack by goshawks gave us a keen appreciation of just how finely tuned the ageless battles between predator and prey can become.

Goshawks have made a dramatic comeback in the northeastern states in recent decades, probably largely because of the increasing area and maturity of the forests there. At the turn of the century, the landscape of New England was very different from what it is now, with most lands devoted to various forms of agriculture.

But farming in this hilly, rocky country could not compete with farming in the midwestern states and California, and large areas of New England have since returned to woodlands. The goshawk has benefited greatly from these changes in land use, although there are no guarantees that extensive forest clearing might not again return to this region.

In the Rocky Mountain states and California, as well as in much of Canada and Alaska, the goshawk is still a regular, if not abundant, species. The goshawk also occurs regularly in the forests of northern Europe and Asia, and it has recently been reestablished in the wild in Great Britain where it sometimes breeds in forests of quite short stature. The overall distribution of the goshawk is large and varied, and provides the species with considerable security from extinction. Nevertheless, some local populations, such as those in parts of Arizona, have exhibited significant recent declines, possibly resulting in part from accelerated timbering practices. The species deserves continued close monitoring because of its overall sparse population densities.

Accipiters

Cooper's Hawk
ACCIPITER COOPERII

IN THE LATE 1960s, the ornithological world awoke to the fact that a number of raptors in North America and western Europe were heading rapidly toward extinction. In eastern North America, Bald Eagles and Ospreys were in severe decline, while the Peregrine Falcon was already almost entirely wiped out. Counts of Cooper's Hawks and Sharp-shinned Hawks at migration lookouts such as Hawk Mountain, Pennsylvania, had also dropped alarmingly. However, the overall status of these woodland accipiters was relatively hard to measure because they were difficult to observe and count on their nesting grounds.

What all the affected species seemed to share was the fact that they fed primarily on birds or large fish and thus were positioned at the ends of long food chains. Raptors feeding mainly on mammals and insects did not appear to be in any difficulty. Evidence was rapidly accumulating through the pioneering studies of Derek Ratcliffe, Joe Hickey, Dan Anderson, Tom Cade, and others that the main source of difficulties lay in contamination with chlorinated hydrocarbon pesticides. In Europe, the population declines were apparently caused mainly by high mortality due to dieldrin contamination. In North America, the pesticide of primary concern was DDT (more specifically its metabolic breakdown product, DDE), which was causing drastic thinning of eggshells, high rates of egg breakage, and extremely low reproductive success. Actually, both dieldrin and DDT were used heavily on both sides of the Atlantic, and both pesticides undoubtedly contributed to the declines in both regions.

Like many other chlorinated hydrocarbons, dieldrin and DDE are extremely stable. When they are ingested as diet contaminants, they lodge preferentially in fatty tissues and are excreted only with difficulty. Because they are so readily stored, their concentrations in body tissues soon come to exceed their concentrations in ingested food. For this reason, levels of contamination tend to increase at each step of a food chain. Concentrations are relatively low in plants; are higher in herbivorous insects and mammals; still higher in carnivorous insects, birds, mammals, and fish; and reach their highest levels of all in species that feed on other carnivorous species. During the period these pesticides were

Above: A male adult Cooper's Hawk stretches his wing and tail on a transfer perch. Left: Well-wooded canyon bottoms of southern Arizona provide suitable habitat for nesting Cooper's Hawks. Unfortunately, populations of this species have declined sharply in this region in recent years.

used freely in agriculture, the raptor species residing at the ends of long food chains were ingesting especially contaminated food and not surprisingly were suffering the most severe consequences.

Although this general picture of pesticide stress has now been amply confirmed in many species, at that time no one had yet taken a careful look at the problem with North American accipiters. To further test the hypotheses that were then being vigorously debated, we decided to initiate a comparative study of pesticide contamination of Cooper's Hawks, Sharp-shinned Hawks, and Northern Goshawks. Because the accipiters were already difficult to find in the eastern states, we chose to begin studies in the Southwest, where we knew we could still locate these species in reasonably good numbers. Here we could hope to get large enough sample sizes of nesting pairs and eggs to gain clear evidence of the degree of threat these birds were under. Thus, in 1969 we began studies in Arizona and New Mexico in cooperation with Jeff Lincer at Cornell University, who joined in to run the actual chemical analyses while we performed the field work. Dick Reynolds shared field studies and egg samples of accipiters from Oregon, and Earl Shriver contributed recent egg samples of Cooper's Hawks from Pennsylvania and New York.

Cooper's Hawks were the most abundant of the accipiters in our study area in Arizona and New Mexico, and nested in a great variety of ecological zones, ranging from dry oak washes extending out into the deserts to Canadian Zone forests near the tops of the highest mountains. The other two accipiters also occupied a variety of ecological zones, but we found them to be sufficiently less common that we quickly concentrated on Cooper's Hawks as the main source of information. Our overall efforts yielded a large amount of data indicating that the accipiters of North America, with the exception of Northern Goshawks, were indeed under stress from DDE contamination. We also found many birds contaminated with dieldrin, although levels of contamination were relatively low. However, this did not rule out significant effects of this pesticide, as we were only sampling "survivors" in our study. Any birds dying from dieldrin contamination would not have been detected.

As in other DDE-stressed species, we found a considerable amount of egg breakage in southwestern Cooper's Hawks (eleven out of sixty clutches). The eggs found broken were consistently heavily contaminated and were generally the thinnest-shelled in the population. However, we also found that eggs that had been deserted without breakage were also highly contaminated and that some broken eggs were really not terribly thin, though they were relatively contaminated.

These facts suggested that pesticide contamination might cause behavioral problems in the hawks in addition to causing eggshell thinning.

From our blinds, we observed three pairs of Cooper's Hawks that had obviously disturbed reproduc-

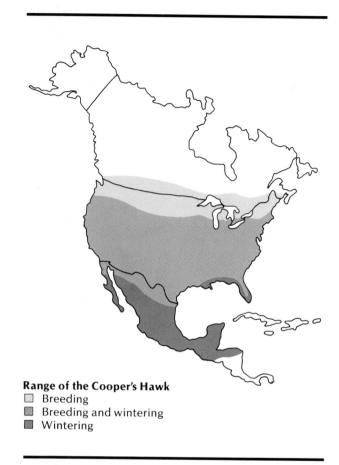

Range of the Cooper's Hawk
☐ Breeding
▨ Breeding and wintering
■ Wintering

tive behavior. The eggs from these pairs were among the most highly contaminated of all analyzed. In one case, the adult female was regularly reluctant to take food from her mate and feed it to her young. In the other two cases, pairs were extremely unenthusiastic in nest building and constructed small, frail nests.

Another of the more revealing correlations we found was that the contamination loads of individual pairs seemed to be directly related to their nesting diets, particularly the percentage of birds in their diets. The pairs at low elevations fed relatively heavily on chipmunks and lizards and had relatively low contamination in their eggs, while the pairs at the highest elevations concentrated mainly on birds and carried the highest DDE levels. Direct measurements of DDE concentrations in representative prey animals confirmed that birds, especially migrant insectivores, were the most contaminated, while resident mammals and lizards had very low levels.

However, despite the strong evidence of contamination stress in these Cooper's Hawks, the population density of the species held up well in the three years of intensive study, and it appeared that this population might still be producing enough young to absorb the stress. Cooper's Hawks in the region captured fewer birds (55 percent of their total prey) than has been recorded in diet of this species in other regions (where birds often comprise 80–90 percent of the diet), and this may have been an important factor in the continuing survival of the population.

In general, studies of accipiter species across the country have shown that Northern Goshawks tend to feed lower in food chains than Cooper's Hawks, taking many mammals and herbivorous birds. Sharp-shinned Hawks generally feed higher up the chains, with a diet devoted almost exclusively to birds, many of them insectivorous. Thus with the general biological magnification of fat-soluble contaminants, such as DDE, that occurs as the contaminants move up food chains, we might predict that Sharp-shinned Hawks would be suffering even greater problems than Cooper's Hawks, while the Northern Goshawk might be spared the brunt of the problems faced by its two smaller relatives.

Our data on contamination of these species were in general accord with these principles. Northern Goshawks showed relatively low contamination, except for one pair that we knew directly from blind studies was feeding exclusively on birds. Sharp-shinned Hawks were more contaminated than any of the Cooper's Hawks. However, we found relatively few Sharp-shinned Hawk pairs in the study area, and they were generally successful pairs, suffering no known egg breakage. Nevertheless, Sharp-shinned Hawk eggs from Oregon were more contaminated than in Arizona and New Mexico, and here Dick Reynolds documented egg breakage in two (possibly three) of five pairs he had under study. Cooper's Hawk eggs from Pennsylvania and New York were much more contaminated than the Cooper's Hawk eggs we examined in the Southwest, and eastern populations of Cooper's Hawk were known to be in catastrophic decline.

In 1972, after a considerable amount of evidence had accumulated on the insidiously harmful effects of DDT (DDE) on a great variety of species, the federal government finally instituted a ban on use of this chemical, bringing the DDT era to a close in the United States. Dieldrin use was also greatly restricted shortly thereafter. In Canada, curtailment of DDT use occurred even sooner than in the United States. Recovery of eastern accipiter populations, as could be seen in counts of the various species at Hawk Mountain, Pennsylvania, was fairly rapid in Sharp-shinned Hawks, but for

unknown reasons remained quite slow in Cooper's Hawks. However, in recent years, the counts of Cooper's Hawks at this observation point have also been climbing encouragingly, and both species appear to have now regained the abundance they enjoyed before the pesticide era.

In contrast, the Cooper's Hawk populations we had studied in the late 1960s and early 1970s in Arizona and New Mexico, which had been remarkably stable in spite of considerable DDE stress, have recently declined alarmingly. In 1987, we recensused much of our old study area in Arizona and New Mexico and found only about 50 percent of the old territories still active with breeding pairs. A more thorough census in 1988 confirmed the decline in our main study area, although we discovered that Cooper's Hawks were holding up reasonably well in other regions not many miles distant. Reproductive success of the active territories was normal in both years, and we saw no cases of egg breakage to suggest DDE stress. We do not yet know the causes of this local decline and whether it represents a long-term trend.

Our studies of Cooper's Hawks were not limited to the effects of contaminants. The many hours of blind observations gave us an opportunity to study a number of other aspects of the behavior and ecology of this species. Medium-sized and well adapted for maneuvering in woodland habitats, Cooper's Hawks are extremely versatile and opportunistic raptors, and we found them to be ideal subjects for observational and experimental investigations.

Like the other accipiters, Cooper's Hawks possess relatively short wings, long legs, and a long banded tail. In general coloration, both sexes tend toward inconspicuous browns and salmons, though adult males are distinctly bluer in their upperparts than are females. Juveniles of both sexes are heavily streaked with brown and are especially well camouflaged in their normal surroundings.

Strictly solitary in behavior, except during breeding, Cooper's Hawks are experts in ambush and surprise attack, appearing from nowhere and stopping at nothing in the pursuit of prey. They do not hesitate to enter quite brushy vegetation and sometimes even run on the ground in impetuous efforts to claim a victim. Highstrung and restless on the hunt, they fully deserve their reputation as eager avian executioners.

One aspect of the biology of this species that we found particularly interesting was the changes in eye coloration that birds exhibited as they aged. Nestlings have gray irises, but this color changes to bright yellow

Top: A male Cooper's Hawk feeds his chicks, an extremely unusual occurrence produced by the loss of his mate shortly after the hatching of eggs. Unfortunately, the male had difficulty developing skills in the procedure and commonly had his red eyes pecked by the hungry nestlings. Middle: A nesting female takes a break from incubation to drink at a nearby pool. Most Cooper's Hawk nests are near water. Bottom: Copulations typically last about eight seconds and commonly follow the transfer of prey to the female.

Last view of the world for many a small bird. Cooper's Hawks typically rely on surprise in capture attempts and are well adapted for maneuvering in highly cluttered forest habitats by their short wings and long tails.

by the time the birds are a year old. In succeeding years, the color gradually darkens through orange to red. Elderly adults of both sexes have red eyes, although it appears that color changes proceed more rapidly in males than in females, and we found it to be very uncommon for the female of a pair to have darker eyes than the male. The same eye color characteristics are also found in Sharp-shinned Hawks and Northern Goshawks.

Our interest in eye coloration was stimulated by observations of an unusual development at a Cooper's Hawk nest of 1971. Here the female adult was killed early in the nestling period, probably by another raptor, and the male took over the normally female role of ripping apart prey for the chicks. The male, who was a handsome old bird with dark red eyes, ran into immediate difficulties because he did not hold his head high enough in offering food to the chicks. The chicks pecked at his eyes as often as they pecked at the food in his bill. It appeared that red eye coloration might be a powerful releaser of the pecking response and might be a dangerous eye color for an adult to have. Our curiosity aroused, we wondered why adults ever have red eyes, why there is a progression of eye colors over the years, and why this progression takes place faster in males than in females.

To gain insight into these questions, we performed a series of simple pecking experiments with young Cooper's Hawk chicks to determine which colors elicited a pecking response and whether the shape of a red object made much difference in eliciting pecking. We constructed a model Cooper's Hawk head that could be raised and lowered on a string, simulating normal feeding motions. The model could hold different-colored eyes and different-colored and -shaped objects in the bill. For most trials we left the eye of the model yellow, and in the bill position tested yellow eyes, red eyes, plain red discs the size of eyes, and red rectangular bars—all made from colored thumbtacks. We also tested a red eye in the eye position with a yellow eye in the bill tip.

Responses of the chicks were entirely uniform. They pecked at red eyes and red objects of various sorts with equal frequency, and it did not appear to make any difference whether the red objects were in the eye position or bill position. They never pecked at a yellow eye, regardless of position.

To explain these results and the observed changes in eye coloration of adults, we developed the following hypothesis. The function of eye color changes in accipiters may be primarily to advertise age of the birds to prospective mates, with the oldest (red-eyed) birds having the greatest value as mates because of their presumed greater experience and hunting skills. Thus red-eyed birds may have an advantage in procuring mates, but they carry at the same time the disadvantage that their eyes are targets for the pecking responses of their young. On first breeding, it may be important that accipiters have yellow eyes so that they can gain experience in feeding chicks without risking eye damage. As birds become older and more proficient in interacting with nestlings, they may suffer much less risk in having red eyes.

Giving support to these ideas, we noted at several nests that young females showed considerable awkwardness in feeding their first chicks, especially in positioning their heads at the proper level relative to the chicks. Furthermore, since males normally do not feed chicks and generally interact with them much less, it is reasonable to assume that there is relatively less need for males to delay in acquiring red eye coloration.

If red eyes did not carry disadvantages, they could not very well evolve as a reliable signal of age because natural selection would very rapidly produce birds that cheat by developing red eyes as fast as possible to gain a mating advantage. The hypothesis that red eye color reliably advertises a bird as an experienced and desirable mate only makes sense if the red signal is also a handicap, especially at a young age.

The tamest wild raptor we have ever dealt with was a nesting female Cooper's Hawk of 1969. This bird and her mate had placed their nest about twenty feet up in a box-elder just ten feet from a heavily traveled road. We constructed a blind on a platform in a tree about twelve feet from the nest, but soon discovered that the blind was totally unnecessary. We took it down, and made further observations just sitting on the platform. The female was so extremely nonchalant that she often fed her young with her back to the platform, and this meant that her body obscured our view of the prey and we sometimes had difficulty identifying prey as a result. We eventually solved this problem by equipping the platform with a long stick with which we could reach over and gently lift the tail of the female to one side so we could view the prey. Her response to this adjustment of her person was never more than a momentary glance in our direction.

Her tolerance ceased, however, whenever one of us climbed the nest tree itself for periodic measurements of the young. The female would not leave the nest and stood glowering on the edge until the climber reached nest level. Then she would leap onto the top of the climber's head and foot his or her scalp aggressively with her talons, often drawing blood in the ensuing fracas.

While most other Cooper's Hawks in our study area were also very aggressive in nest defense, even to the extent of flailing at climbers who scaled their nest trees weeks after young had fledged, we did find occasional pairs that were quite wary of people. Some were impossible to study from blinds, even quite distant blinds, without causing so much disturbance of their behavior that the data obtained were worthless. In general, however, the Cooper's Hawks of this region were easy to work with, in great contrast to the Cooper's Hawks of the eastern states, which are renowned for their skittish behavior. Possibly, the relatively bold behavior of southwestern Cooper's Hawks reflects less human persecution in their history than eastern birds have suffered. Richard Knight and his coworkers have recently documented a similar correlation of strength of nest defense behavior with history of human contact for Red-tailed Hawks in various regions of North America.

Nevertheless, as our studies of Cooper's Hawks progressed, we became increasingly apprehensive that, because certain individuals were becoming accustomed to our presence, their chances for survival might be lessened. Birds that people can easily approach may be highly susceptible to molestation. We normally banded all young Cooper's Hawks we located in the study area, but only a small fraction of the young were exposed to us on more than the day of banding. However, the returns we received from recoveries of our banded individuals were limited almost exclusively to birds that had had an opportunity to become very familiar with us, either through repeated days of observation from nearby blinds and platforms or through repeated handling for weighing and measuring through the nestling period. Further, essentially all these recovered birds were victims of various forms of human predation. The recovery rate of tamed or partially tamed nestlings was much greater than that of untamed nestlings, a fact strongly suggesting that we were not doing the birds a favor by allowing them to see us at close range on a repeated basis. The effects of our species on raptors can sometimes be quite subtle and surprising.

Accipiters

Sharp-shinned Hawk
ACCIPITER STRIATUS

DENSE STANDS OF immature Douglas fir in the West and hemlocks in the East provide favored nesting habitat for the most secretive of North America's raptors, the Sharp-shinned Hawk. A single-minded predator of small birds, this is not a species that survives by intimidation, but one that relies on stealth and camouflage, both in gaining close approach to its victims and in avoiding capture by larger raptors. No larger than a jay and feathered mainly in browns and grays, the sharp-shin is named for a sharp keel on the leading edge of its legs.

In its habitual surroundings of forests and forest edges, the sharp-shin is an animated spook, an avain wind-up toy with five gears for full-speed ahead and no neutral nor idle. It rarely perches in conspicuous locations and rarely flies above the canopy, except during migration. So even though it is a commoner species than is often recognized, it is a difficult species to find and a difficult species to study closely.

In essence, the sharp-shin is a miniature edition of the Cooper's Hawk. However, large female sharp-shins are sufficiently close to small male Cooper's Hawks in bulk to lead to frequent mistakes in identification, even among experienced raptor biologists. The two species are colored very similarly, occupy similar habitats, and fly with similar alternations of flapping and sailing. Under many conditions it is very difficult to judge size of a hawk, and the subtle differences in shape between the species are often difficult to discern. Sharp-shinned Hawks tend to have tails that are more squared off at the end than the rounded tails of Cooper's Hawks, and the head of an individual flying overhead tends to project farther in front of the wings in Cooper's Hawk than in the Sharp-shinned Hawk. But these are quite small and variable differences, easy to mistake.

The most reliable way to differentiate these species is through vocalizations. Alas, they do not commonly vocalize except near nests. The repetitive *kew kew kew kew kew* alarm calls of the sharp-shin are much more mellow than the strident *kek kek kek kek kek kek* alarm calls of Cooper's Hawk, and once these calls are heard they are easy to remember.

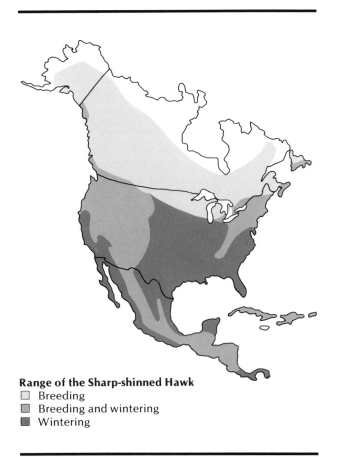

Range of the Sharp-shinned Hawk
☐ Breeding
◩ Breeding and wintering
◼ Wintering

More than any other North American raptor, the Sharp-shinned Hawk exhibits a strong difference in size between sexes. Male sharp-shins average about three

and one-half ounces in weight, while females weigh almost twice as much at about six and one-third ounces. Thus in this species, as in almost all raptors, it is the females that are superior in size, a pattern contrary to the usual pattern in birds and one usually referred to as "reversed sexual size dimorphism." Causes of this dimorphism have been one of the most contentious topics in the study of raptors, and the number of different hypotheses advanced to explain the phenomenon continues to increase steadily. Whatever the primary causes may be, the principal correlation that has been noted is that the extent of size difference between sexes seems to be strongly related to the extent that the species takes birds as prey. The size differences between males and females are quite modest in species that take mainly mammals, insects, or other invertebrates.

The best-known hypotheses to explain the size dimorphism center on potential advantages in reducing food competition between sexes and on potential advantages in promotion of clear-cut dominance relationships and harmonious pair bonds. Certainly the size differences between sexes often do result in differences in diet of the sexes, but debates continue as to whether these differences are the primary cause of the dimorphism or only a secondary effect.

Our data for both sharp-shins and Cooper's Hawks in Arizona and New Mexico confirm that males and females of these species do take significantly different prey during the breeding season. In our observations, sharp-shin females often captured prey the size of grosbeaks and robins, while males mainly took birds the size of juncos and smaller. In Cooper's Hawks, females quite frequently captured jays and pigeons, while males more commonly took chipmunks and robin-sized birds. It is hard to believe that these differences in diet were neutral in their impacts on foraging success of pairs, and we find it difficult to accept that the sexual size differences might be retained if they led to appreciable disadvantages in foraging. Our sympathies are strongest for hypotheses that view the sexual size differences as an adaptation to increase food supplies available to pairs during the breeding season, especially for species where food supplies tend to be scarce in the late breeding season when both adults are hunting—a situation that apparently occurs with some frequency for bird-feeding raptors, judging from our observations in the Southwest.

During our studies of the three North American accipiters—Sharp-shinned Hawk, Cooper's Hawk, and Northern Goshawk—we were also very curious to determine if there was significant competition among the species. How the accipiters space their nesting territories provides one kind of evidence on this question. Species that are not in strong competition often tolerate one another in close proximity, while species that compete strongly often avoid each other or actively exclude each other from their territories. While we saw very few direct interactions between the accipiters, we did find a very interesting pattern of nest spacing that strongly suggested a degree of competition between species—something that was also suggested by similarities in the prey species they depended on.

The general spacing between adjacent nests of Cooper's Hawks was about a mile, but dropped to a half mile in areas of apparently excellent habitat. Similarly, the closest nesting of adjacent pairs of Sharp-shinned Hawks was approximately a half mile. Further, we never found Sharp-shinned Hawks nesting closer than about a half mile from Cooper's Hawks. At the same time, the spacing of Cooper's Hawk nests relative to Northern Goshawk nests generally ran about a mile.

The interesting fact was that on four occasions we found Sharp-shinned Hawks nesting immediately adjacent to Northern Goshawks. As goshawks and sharp-shins overlapped to only a very limited extent in the sizes of prey they were taking, this result appears to be quite consistent with the possible importance of food competition in controlling nesting distributions.

However, another factor aside from competition may be important in influencing the nest spacing of these species. The larger species represent significant threats of predation to the smaller ones. Cooper's Hawks may space themselves at considerable distances from the larger Northern Goshawks to reduce the chances of attack by this species on their young. The same could be said about the spacing of sharp-shins, the smallest of the three species, relative to Cooper's Hawks. On the other hand, it would not appear to explain the very close nestings we observed of sharp-shins (the smallest) and Northern Goshawks (the largest). However, it is important to note that Sharp-shinned Hawks in this region were extremely inconspicuous in behavior and typically nested in the densest possible tangles of vegetation. So dense, in fact, that we commonly heard them banging their wings against branches and limbs as they flew to their nests. They may have achieved considerable protection against nearby nesting goshawks by choosing nesting locations that the relatively large goshawks would have great difficulty reaching. As direct evidence of this, we once watched a female goshawk attempting to capture fledgling sharp-shins at a nest in a dense white fir. The goshawk came crashing through the branches right in front of us, as we sat concealed in a blind thirty feet from the nest, but she never made it to the nest itself, and the young sharp-shins scattered to safety.

Possibly both competition and direct predation threats were important determinants of the observed nesting distributions. In a sense, the sharp-shins nesting close to Northern Goshawks may have been indebted to the goshawks for creating spaces in the nearly continuous array of Cooper's Hawk territories where the sharp-shins could find enough food for nesting. About the only places we were able to find nesting sharp-shins in this region were either next to active goshawk nests or in old Cooper's Hawk territories that were inactive. At the same time, the sharp-shins nesting close to goshawks had to find a solution to the direct threats represented by the goshawks to their own safety. The fact that all four sharp-shin pairs that nested close to Goshawks were successful in raising young suggested that their choice of nest sites in dense, cluttered vegetation represented an adequate solution.

The Sharp-shinned Hawk is the last of the accipiters to initiate breeding activity, generally beginning nest building in late April or early May in the southwestern states. As in the other accipiters, both sexes participate in nest construction, using their feet and bills to break off dead twigs from standing trees in the vicinity of the nest, then carrying them to the nest in direct flights under the canopy. Nest-building activities are concentrated in the early to middle morning hours and are interspersed with bouts of mating activity, preening, and foraging. Nests usually have linings of chips of the outer bark of trees, and are usually placed on horizontal branches against the main trunks of conifers. They are generally quite difficult to locate. The best clue to their existence is often a scattering of feathers of prey birds which can be found on the ground in the nest vicinity. New nests are built each year, but they are occasionally placed on top of old nests. Building on top of old nests is much more common in Cooper's Hawks and Northern Goshawks.

During the early stages of breeding, essentially all hunting is done by the male of a pair. On his return with prey, the male announces his arrival at a perch near the nest with repetitive high-pitched *kew kew kew kew kew kew* calls, which are essentially the same as the alarm calls of the species. The female soon flies in to take the prey with repeated *eee* calls, which also continue while she is feeding. As egg laying approaches the female becomes more and more lethargic, often just perching for long periods, fluffed up and quiescent, apparently saving her reserves and avoiding the poten-

Dense Canadian Zone fir forest in southern Arizona hosted
a pair of Sharp-shinned Hawks in 1972.

This female sharp-shin at a nest in the Huachuca Mountains of southern Arizona belongs to the Mexican race *suttoni*. Solid rufous thighs set this race apart from *velox*, the race found through most of North America, and in fact, this photograph, taken in 1971, constitutes the only proof yet obtained of *suttoni* occurring north of the Mexican border.

In Arizona, a typical sharp-shin clutch includes four eggs. Unlike the eggs of Cooper's Hawks and Northern Goshawks, sharp-shin eggs are usually heavily spotted, presumably to reduce their conspicuousness. On Puerto Rico, however, a population of sharp-shins free from most threats of predation has evolved nearly unspotted egg coloration.

A male Puerto Rican Sharp-shinned Hawk is perhaps the most handsome of all the North American accipiters. Puerto Rican sharp-shins are much more extroverted in behavior than their continental counterparts.

A female sharp-shin tends her partially hatched brood in a Douglas fir. Male adults do all the hunting at this stage while females care for eggs and young and carry on nest defense activities. Unlike male Northern Goshawks and Cooper's Hawks, male Sharp-shinned Hawks do not incubate while their mates feed on prey.

tial damage to her unlaid eggs that might result from undue activity.

Eggs are most commonly laid on alternate days, and clutch size in the Southwest is most commonly four or five eggs. Unlike the plain bluish-white eggs of Northern Goshawks and Cooper's Hawks, sharp-shin eggs are highly camouflaged with brown blotches and specklings, giving them a very attractive appearance. Incubation lasts about thirty-four or thirty-five days and generally begins with the laying of the next to last egg.

Females do all the incubation of eggs and cover them almost constantly except when working on prey brought in by males. As a female feeds, a male sometimes flies to the nest and occasionally even spreads out his breast feathers as if to settle on the eggs, but we have never seen a male actually follow through and cover the eggs. At best, the males might do so only ineffectively because of their relatively small size. In this respect, the Sharp-shinned Hawk differs markedly from the Northern Goshawk and Cooper's Hawk in which males do generally cover eggs while their mates feed on prey. During the nest-building and incubation periods, males usually feed their mates three or four times per day.

For about the first half of the nestling period, females continue to attend their nests, brooding the nestlings when they are not feeding them. But thereafter, females also begin to hunt and supply food for the brood. Throughout the nestling period, prey are ripped apart for the young by the female, and if the male returns with prey at a time when the female is off hunting, the prey is just dropped in the nest cup and left for the female to handle when she returns. By the late nestling stage, pairs commonly bring as many as ten to twelve prey to the nest daily. Begging calls of the young are very similar to the *eee* calls of female adults soliciting food from their mates.

The nestling period lasts about four weeks, but males develop more quickly than females and generally fledge several days earlier. Fledging generally occurs in middle to late July and is a gradual process, with youngsters first moving out to branches near the nest and quickly returning when adults arrive at the nest with food. At this stage, youngsters begin ripping apart prey for themselves, though most feedings still take place at the nest supervised by the adult female. In time, the fledglings begin to fly out to meet returning parents and take prey from them at locations away from the nest vicinity. Young usually remain dependent on adults until middle to late August and are slow to develop their own capacities to hunt.

In Puerto Rico, there are no native terrestrial mammals, and the only resident accipiter is the Sharp-shinned Hawk. As the sharp-shins of this island are not exposed to the threats that are represented by larger accipiters or by large tree-climbing mammals, we were very anxious to compare their behavior to the behavior of sharp-shins on the mainland. Before moving to Puerto Rico in 1972, we made several predictions about what differences we might find in the sharp-shins there. First, we speculated that they would be much more extroverted in their general demeanor. For example, we predicted we might observe the conspicuous white undertail covert display that is commonly seen in Cooper's Hawks and Northern Goshawks around nests, but which we never saw in mainland sharp-shins. Also we guessed that the conspicuous aerial advertisement displays we had seen in the large accipiters high over their nesting areas might be prominent in sharp-shins on Puerto Rico, though we had not yet seen them in sharp-shins of Arizona and New Mexico. Finally, we predicted that we might find that the highly cryptic spotted egg coloration of Sharp-shinned Hawks on the mainland might tend in Puerto Rico toward the plain white egg coloration typical of Cooper's Hawks and Northern Goshawks.

All of these predictions were fulfilled. The sharp-shins on Puerto Rico have very different personalities from their mainland cousins, and were, as expected, much more extroverted in behavior, with conspicuous tail covert displays and frequent swooping aerial displays. Furthermore, their eggs, while not completely white in the clutches we observed, were much paler and less camouflaged than on the mainland, with only very indistinct blotches and spots. Although Sharp-shinned Hawks are predators themselves, many facets of their biology can be viewed as responses to predation threats represented by other species.

The Sharp-shinned Hawk is one of the more common raptors of North America, and it also occurs south through the West Indies and Central and South America to northern Argentina. A total of ten geographic races are recognized through this extensive range. *Accipiter striatus velox* is the common form of the species through most of North America, but just south of the Mexican border, *velox* is replaced by *suttoni,* a very intensely colored race with dark upperparts and solid rufous thighs. It has long been debated whether this race might also occur north of the border. In 1971 we were able to resolve this question when we found and photographed a female *suttoni* nesting successfully in the Huachuca Mountains of southern Arizona.

Buteos and Allies

Above: On Puerto Rico, Red-tailed Hawks are the most common diurnal raptor of the dense rainforests where they feed on a great variety of vertebrate and invertebrate prey. Hanging in the winds over the treetops, they make most kills in the upper canopy and are the principal enemy of the endangered Puerto Rican Parrot. Right: Dark-phased red-tails, like this migrant in eastern Oregon, are more common in the western states.

Buteos and Allies

Red-tailed Hawk
BUTEO JAMAICENSIS

PERHAPS THE MOST familiar raptor of North America is the Red-tailed Hawk. Distributed from Alaska and northern Canada south to Mexico and Florida, as well as throughout much of the West Indies, this species occupies a great diversity of habitats and feeds on a wide range of foods. Moreover, in physical appearance the red-tail exhibits such a variety of patterns from place to place that it was originally described as several different species. Only more recently have detailed studies revealed the prevalence of numerous intergrades linking together the various geographic forms of this hawk.

In its many guises, the red-tail ranges from clear white to completely black underneath, though the most frequent ventral color pattern is a distinct cummerbund of dark spots contrasting with a light throat and upper breast. Upperparts vary from brown to black. Even the tail color is highly inconsistent, ranging from solid red to banded brown and gray, with an almost infinite diversity of spotting and streaking patterns.

The great variability of the red-tail extends also to behavior and ecology. Medium-large in size and powerfully proportioned, with a relatively short tail and sturdy broad wings, this raptor is basically a soaring predator of small mammals. However, the red-tail exhibits enough versatility in habits that it is very difficult to characterize the species' habitat tolerances or feeding preferences. Its nesting habits are equally diverse and equally difficult to summarize.

We made intensive studies of red-tails during the years we spent in the Puerto Rican Parrot conservation program. Much to our surprise, the red-tails proved to be the major mortality threat faced by this highly endangered parrot in its last refuge, the lush rainforests of the Luquillo Mountains near the eastern end of the

Range of the Red-tailed Hawk
- ☐ Breeding
- ■ Breeding and wintering

island. For this reason, we felt it was advisable to study these raptors in some detail.

Red-tails were more densely concentrated in the Luquillo Mountains than has ever been documented anywhere else in the range of the species. On northeastern slopes at high elevations, we found one region where there were four territories, complete with nests, packed into just 0.92 square miles of terrain, for an

A "Harlan's Hawk" lands at its nest in the Yukon Territory of Canada in 1968. Once considered a separate species characterized by longitudinal streaks and spotting on the tail, this form is now considered only a color variant of the red-tail.

Yearling red-tails characteristically have banded tails lacking red coloration, but are otherwise so diverse in coloration that they are frequently hard to identify.

A first-year Red-tailed Hawk pauses during fall migration in eastern Oregon. The dark cummerbund is a common, but not invariable, characteristic of light-phased red-tails.

astonishing average of 4.3 pairs per square mile! The high densities here were apparently a result of good food supplies in combination with superb foraging conditions. The extremely steady updrafts of wind caused by the northeasterly trades interacting with the mountain topography allowed the red-tails to hang effortlessly over the canopy as they hunted, efficiently exploiting the food resources in their territories.

The high red-tail density in the upper Luquillo Mountains was especially remarkable because closed-canopy forest does not initially appear at all similar to the open and mixed habitats that red-tails generally occupy on the continent. Nevertheless, our observations revealed that Luquillo's red-tails were well adapted to local conditions, treating the surface of the forest canopy very much as if it were an open field, and making many of their kills at canopy level.

Red-tail territories did not overlap and occupied essentially all lands within our principal study area on the northeast side of the mountains. Although unpaired individuals were frequently seen moving through the area, they were challenged vigorously by the territory owners and driven to boundary regions between pairs. Only by flying at great altitudes above the territories were intruders able to escape harassment.

Territories were exceedingly stable over the several-year period of our investigations, suggesting that the red-tail population was at saturation. Yet although all pairs under study built nests, considerably less than half were successful in fledging young in any year. Possibly this relatively low productivity was a direct result of the close packing of territories and the large amounts of time that pairs were obliged to spend in territorial defense.

Red-tail nests were difficult to study in the Luquillo Mountains. Even though we could spot the nests high up in tall trees from our distant above-canopy lookouts, getting to them on the ground and actually finding them again from the ground was troublesome because of the density of rain forest vegetation. In fact, nests were often completely invisible from the ground below, and it sometimes took several days of climbing nearby canopy trees to actually pin down a nest location.

One nest in a vine-shrouded cecropia in 1975 was well suited for close observations from a nearby blind, and here we documented the adults feeding their single chick prey ranging from lizards, tree frogs, and centipedes to crabs, pigeons, and the introduced rats and mongooses. The most interesting prey were the giant centipedes, which usually arrived at the nest alive, though obviously in stunned condition. The chick had

great difficulty dismembering and swallowing these tough-skinned arthropods, and frequently failed to do so. As they revived, some of the centipedes finally just crawled off the nest and down the trunk of the nest tree.

Feedings were frequent during the days we studied this nest, except for one day when the usually dependable trade winds were neutralized by a weather system moving into the area. On this day, the adults did not bring a single prey to the nest. No doubt the windless weather made aerial foraging impractical, while the birds' success in hunting from perches may have been relatively low.

The great diversity of prey species brought by the red-tails to the nest under close study indicated remarkable foraging flexibility. However, it was at nests of the Puerto Rican Parrot that we learned just how far the predatory capacities of the red-tails extended. At one parrot nest of 1975, a red-tail actually crawled down inside the four-foot-long hollow stub attempting to get at the parrot nestlings shortly after the adult parrots had flown off on a foraging trip. Only quick action on the part of John Taapken, who was watching the nest from a nearby blind, prevented the red-tail from killing the parrot youngsters. John ran to the nest tree, and by shouting and banging on the trunk managed to flush the hawk before it reached the bottom. We also learned of two earlier instances in which observers had seen or obtained evidence of red-tails entering holes to take nestling parrots, so the attack of 1975 was not unique.

Nestlings are not the only-aged parrots vulnerable to these hawks. Several observers have seen red-tails take free-flying parrots. Although we never witnessed a successful attack, we saw several near misses and in one instance obtained strong circumstantial evidence – plucked remains – of a successful attack on a breeding female near her nest. The extensive variety of hunting approaches used by these hawks makes it difficult for the parrots to achieve any real security against them.

About the only potential prey we did not see the Luquillo red-tails capture was snakes. However, this was most likely due to the scarcity of snakes in this region. In other areas, red-tails are renowned as frequent snake-predators. For example, at one old red-tail nest in a cliff pothole in California, a site later used for nesting by a pair of California Condors, we found the tail rattles of four different Pacific rattlesnakes in the litter. The red-tail's fondness for snakes may exceed that of any other North American raptor.

In northwestern Canada and Alaska, at the opposite corner of the species' range from Puerto Rico, the red-tail occurs as a form that for many years was given full species status as "Harlan's Hawk." As originally described, Harlan's Hawk (*Buteo harlani*) was supposedly separable from the red-tail by a tail coloration that is normally gray in adults and shows spotting and longitudinal dark streaks instead of the transverse dark bars that are usual for western red-tails. The difficulty in conceiving of Harlan's Hawk as a true species has always been the difficulty in finding two Harlan's Hawk individuals that look alike in tail coloration. Just about every conceivable intermediate condition between red and gray tails with varying amounts of longitudinal and transverse barring and spots can be found in large samples of museum skins collected in the western states, Canada, and Alaska. Some individuals have red tails or partially red tails combined with longitudinal streaks, while others have transverse bars on tails that are mostly gray, and many individuals have both transverse bars and longitudinal streaks on the very same feathers. With this kind of mish-mash in tail color characteristics, the general consensus is that it seems doubtful that Harlan's Hawk, whatever it may be, is a separable, reproductively isolated species, and that until strong evidence for its distinctiveness is found, the form should best be considered a common color variant of the red-tail that breeds in the northwest corner of the continent.

In 1968 we had an opportunity to watch several pairs of relatively pure "Harlan's Hawks" at their nests in the Yukon Territory of Canada and in the Alaska Range of Alaska. We saw and heard nothing in the behavior of these birds to suggest that they were anything but red-tails. The long, harsh *keearr* alarm vocalizations, the kinds of nest construction, diet, hunting behavior, in fact everything we could determine, seemed totally typical of *Buteo jamaicensis*.

Among other well-marked color variants of the red-tail are melanistic, or black, individuals. Black red-tails are most common in the western states. One particularly fine adult of this coloration nests in a cliff only a couple miles from our current home in southeastern Arizona. Red-tails also seem, more than other North American species of raptors, to have a tendency toward albinism, producing white and partially white individuals. In late 1979, we came across such a bird perched on a snag in an open field in central Florida east of Lake Okeechobee. This was one of the most striking raptors we have ever seen—completely white except for a brilliant red tail.

The great morphological and behavioral plasticity of the red-tail places this species in an especially favorable position for long-term survival, no matter what ecological disasters may lie ahead. By virtue of its relatively low position in food chains, the red-tail was spared the devastating population declines suffered by many other falconiforms in the DDT era, and for the same reason it may well survive future chemical catastrophes. Further, its broad food preferences, its adaptability to human-modified habitats, and its general lack of interference with human interests, together with its tolerance of climatic extremes ranging from harsh deserts to humid rainforests, probably equip it, as much as any raptor could possibly be equipped, to withstand the challenges of a changing planet.

Buteos and Allies

Broad-winged Hawk
BUTEO PLATYPTERUS

THE BROAD-WINGED HAWK is probably the most abundant diurnal raptor of the eastern woodlands of North America, where it feeds mainly on a great variety of small vertebrates, ranging from salamanders and frogs to chipmunks and nestling birds. Its plaintive calls drifting through the mature oaks and maples sound much like those of another resident of the same habitats, the Wood Pewee, and together, these two species seem to embody the peaceful spirit of upland deciduous forests.

The broad-wing is a relatively small buteo and is marked mainly with brown streaks and bars that help conceal it in its usual wooded surroundings. Rarely found far from cover, this raptor is much more often heard than seen, but sometimes can be observed rising above the canopy with a snake or mouse in its talons. Less tied to water than the Red-shouldered Hawk, the broad-wing nevertheless often settles near bogs and swampy depressions and usually places its twiggy nest well below the treetops in the first main crotch of a moderately large tree.

The first buteo nest we ever watched in detail from a blind belonged to a pair of broad-wings. These birds had chosen a site high in an oak atop a wild-strawberry-covered hill near Dryden, New York. Our efforts to become familiar with the nesting activities of the hawks and the fruiting activities of the strawberries provided very pleasant diversion from the intense grind of graduate studies at nearby Cornell University.

Yet we came to know the Broad-winged Hawk most intimately in a completely different setting—the virgin wilderness of the Luquillo Mountains in eastern Puerto Rico, where we also studied the Red-tailed Hawk. Here a tiny population of a distinctive subspecies of the broad-wing lives in company with tropical hummingbirds, tanagers, parrots, and todies. Nesting in bromeliad-laden hardwoods and coping with nearly two hundred inches of rain per year, this population faces a very different world from that of its migratory relatives in the eastern United States. Still, the Puerto Rican birds are quite clearly Broad-winged Hawks, with vocalizations and behavior quite similar to mainland populations of the species.

In early 1976, we had the good fortune to locate the first three nests ever discovered of the Puerto Rican Broad-winged Hawk. Herb Raffaele located additional nests in the same year for the only other population of broad-wings known for the island, that of Rio Abajo in the northwestern limestone hills region. One of the Luquillo nests was well situated for blind observations, and we made an intensive study of the diet of the birds at this nest, as we were anxious to determine if the species represented any significant threats to the endangered Puerto Rican Parrot.

Like the diet of the broad-wing on the mainland, that of the Puerto Rican subspecies proved to be mainly small vertebrates, especially frogs and lizards, though we also saw occasional rats and frequent centipedes, and sometimes birds, some even as large as nestling pigeons. Overall, this diet was very similar to that of the red-tails of Luquillo Forest, though the broad-wing is a much smaller bird (less than half as heavy) and apparently cannot match the capacities of its larger cousin in taking some of the larger prey available. Fewer rats figured in broad-wing diet than in red-tail diet, and while we found evidence of red-tails even occasionally taking mongooses, we found no evidence of broad-wings doing so.

Nevertheless, with both species taking pretty much the same foods in Luquillo Forest, it is of interest that they have apparently been able to coexist in harmony, especially in view of the high density of red-tails in the forest and the exceedingly aggressive territoriality shown by red-tails to one another. The broad-wings were not excluded from red-tail territories, suggesting strongly that the two species had indeed reached some sort of ecological accommodation.

The truce between the red-tails and broad-wings seemed mainly to result from differences in their hunting behavior. The red-tails, at least on the windward slopes of the mountains, hunted mainly from the air, and mostly exploited the animal life of the upper branches of the forest canopy. In contrast, we never saw the broad-wings hunting from flight, and virtually all their foraging activities were concentrated well beneath the forest crown, where they characteristically watched for prey from relatively low perches. Thus, in the regions

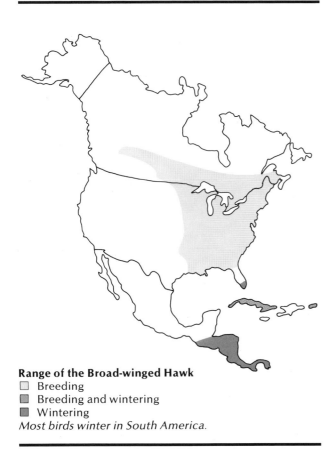

Range of the Broad-winged Hawk
☐ Breeding
▨ Breeding and wintering
▨ Wintering
Most birds winter in South America.

where the broad-wings coexisted with the red-tails, they were in fact using quite different habitats. Apparently, they were not actually hunting and eating the same specific populations of prey and were not in strong competition, despite their similarity in diet.

Giving apparent support to this interpretation is the fact that broad-wings in Luquillo Forest normally occur only on the windward slopes, while red-tails occur on all sides of the mountains. On the leeward slopes the red-tails have few updrafts to utilize for aerial hunting, and in fact their hunting behavior switches heavily toward hunting from perches at all levels in the forest. If the broad-wings were present in the same leeward areas, the two species probably would compete strongly for food. Very likely the broad-wings do not occupy leeward slopes because of this potential competition and their inabilities to dominate red-tails.

The total population of Broad-winged Hawks in the Luquillo Mountains probably does not exceed fifty individuals, and the same is probably true for the Rio Abajo population. Yet these populations have apparently been stable for at least the last century, and judging from early reports of Jean Gundlach and Alexander Wetmore, the species may not have been any more widespread at the turn of the century than it is now. Long-term stability of such small populations raises intriguing genetic questions, as these birds are very likely highly inbred and deficient in genetic variability, yet they seem vigorous and productive.

Although we never saw them hunt from the air, the Puerto Rican broad-wings frequently soared into the skies and sometimes engaged in dramatic aerial displays that distracted us from our parrot observations. In these displays one bird locked talons with another, and the two descended rapidly toward the forest canopy, whirling around like a windmill running wild, and separating only moments before they collided with the treetops. Whether we were watching courtship or fights in these encounters was not clear. But in other species where such displays have been seen, particularly certain eagles and kites, they have commonly involved male-female pairs, suggesting courtship activity. Regardless of function, these whirling displays are among the most striking avian spectacles known, and they were especially impressive in the misty setting provided by the steep-sloped rainforests of the Luquillo Mountains.

In the eastern United States, broad-wings provide another of the most impressive avian spectacles to be seen in North America – massed fall migration to the tropical regions of Central and South America. Viewed from strategic lookouts along the Appalachian Mountains, the fall flights of broad-wings bring ever-increasing numbers of hawk-watchers together from all over the world. One of the most rewarding of these observation points, and certainly the most famous, is Hawk Mountain, located along the Kittatiny Ridge of eastern Pennsylvania. In good flight years, broad-wings drift and soar

The first nest ever found of the Puerto Rican Broad-winged Hawk was placed on a base of airplants and vines. It held two chicks close to fledging in May of 1976.

A female Broad-winged Hawk stands aside her nestlings high in an oak atop a forested hillside in upstate New York, a habitat shared with Ovenbirds, Scarlet Tanagers, Black-throated Blue Warblers, and Veeries.

From the North Lookout of Hawk Mountain in Pennsylvania, it is sometimes possible to see thousands of migrating Broad-winged Hawks in a single fall day, as well as lesser numbers of most other diurnal raptors of the eastern states. Once an assembly point for gunners, this site was acquired by Rosalie Edge in the mid-1930s and was transformed into the most renowned of North America's sanctuaries for the birds of prey. Breeding raptors of the sanctuary area include Turkey Vultures, Northern Goshawks, Cooper's Hawks, Sharp-shinned Hawks, Red-tailed Hawks, and Broad-winged Hawks, but the primary attraction of the sanctuary is the steady stream of migrating raptors passing the lookouts in the fall.

Wintering Broad-winged Hawks in the Florida Keys are mostly immatures that may well have missed their proper migration bearings and found themselves trapped by the seas in the southernmost land areas of the peninsula.

Broad-winged Hawks are usually the most abundant of the raptors migrating past Hawk Mountain of eastern Pennsylvania in the fall. Here the broad-wing migration starts in late August, peaks in September, and dwindles to nothing in October. Farther south, in Panama, the migration pulse of broad-wings peaks in October.

past the slopes of Hawk Mountain in many thousands from late August to early October. From this location, it is also possible to see at close range essentially all other species of diurnal raptors that occur in the eastern states and Canada. Flights are especially dramatic during the periods of fresh northwest winds that follow cold fronts. While there are other raptor observation points in North America that surpass Hawk Mountain in their tallies of migrating raptors, none exceeds this site in scenic beauty and general biological interest. The numbers of raptor observers migrating to Hawk Mountain each fall have grown to exceed the numbers of migrating hawks by a considerable margin.

The broad-wings and other raptors of Hawk Mountain have unique significance in the history of raptor conservation, for it was here in the mid-1930s that Rosalie Edge and Maurice and Irma Broun began a lonely but ultimately successful battle to stop the senseless slaughter of migrating hawks that was at that time a socially acceptable pastime. Until these efforts, droves of gunners gathered each fall to fire endlessly at the raptors passing by the mountain lookouts. The carcasses of dead and dying hawks accumulated by the hundreds in the forests below.

The halting of the raptor massacres at Hawk Mountain was at first viewed as a strange misunderstanding of local custom perpetrated by outsiders unfamiliar with the serious threats posed by raptors to human society. But in time, similar efforts have spread throughout the country, creating a whole new environment of interest in and respect for birds of prey, with incalculably positive implications for wildlife conservation in general. What was once a minority viewpoint toward raptors has become a growing consensus that seems destined to endure. The lonely defenders of Hawk Mountain have left a unique and priceless legacy.

Buteos and Allies

Red-shouldered Hawk
BUTEO LINEATUS

WHILE BROAD-WINGED HAWKS are birds of the upland deciduous and mixed deciduous-coniferous forests of the eastern states, Red-shouldered Hawks are found primarily in the moist river bottoms and wooded swamps of this region. Here they feed heavily on aquatic animals such as frogs and crayfishes, though they also take many small mammals and insects, and occasional birds. In many respects, the red-shoulders resemble the Common Black Hawks of the Southwest in their habitat preferences and diet. Very likely they are unable to occupy the same range as the black hawks because the two species would be in strong competition if they did. Nevertheless, a geographically disjunct population of red-shoulders does occur farther west than the black hawk range – in coastal California – again associated primarily with riparian woodland.

Red-shoulders, broad-wings, and black hawks are all almost exclusively still-hunters, watching intently for prey from low perches within the forest canopy, then descending to capture it in short pounces. In this respect, they are similar to yet another buteo of the riparian zone of the southwestern states, the Gray Hawk. But the Gray Hawk takes few aquatic creatures as prey and specializes mainly on lizards, thus avoiding severe direct competition with the black hawks occurring in the same region. Together, these four species are the

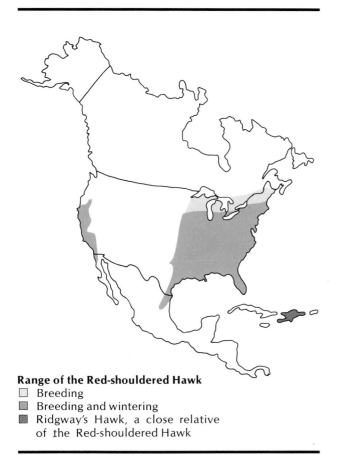

Range of the Red-shouldered Hawk
☐ Breeding
▧ Breeding and wintering
▨ Ridgway's Hawk, a close relative
of the Red-shouldered Hawk

woodland buteonine raptors of North America and form a ecological group distinct from the open-country buteonines of the continent, which include such species as the Swainson's Hawk, Ferruginous Hawk, Short-tailed Hawk, White-tailed Hawk, and Rough-legged Hawk.

In coloration, adult Red-shouldered Hawks possess a rich orange-chestnut barred breast and a similarly hued shoulder patch. The tail is black with white bands, while the upper sides of the wings are basically black with numerous white spots. From below, the bases of the primary feathers of a soaring bird appear light in color, creating a white "window" patch toward the ends of the wings. The head color is generally brown, but in birds from Florida the brown is so pale as to appear almost white from a distance.

In habitat preferences and diet, Red-shouldered Hawks are diurnal or daytime counterparts of the Barred Owl of the eastern states, just as Red-tailed Hawks, with their more open-country habits, are diurnal counterparts of the Great-horned Owl. The vocalizations of the Red-shouldered Hawk serve to link this species closely with Ridgway's Hawk on the island of Hispaniola in the Caribbean, and it seems likely that these two species share a close common ancestry. The many morphological and behavioral similarities of red-shoulders and Ridgway's Hawks have been well documented in intensive natural history investigations by Jim and Beth Wiley. Other close relatives of the red-shoulder are the Gray Hawk and the Roadside Hawk of Central and South America. Interestingly, we have been struck by a strong similarity in the vocalizations of the Red-shouldered Hawk and the Common Buzzard of Europe. Nevertheless, studies of Brian Millsap suggest that on morphological grounds the Common Buzzard belongs to a quite different group of buteos and that its closest relative in the New World may be the Red-tailed Hawk.

Ridgway's Hawk in effect appears to be a population of Red-shouldered Hawks that has evolved to fill the normal niche of the Broad-winged Hawk on Hispaniola – that of a mainly upland forest buteo – and it is of special interest that Hispaniola is the only major island of the West Indies, except for Jamaica, that lacks a resident population of Broad-winged Hawks. Very likely, there is simply not enough ecological space on Hispaniola to allow coexistence of two woodland buteo species. Perhaps the Red-shouldered Hawk got to the island first, became well adapted to local conditions there as Ridgway's Hawk, and has been able to exclude colonization by Broad-winged Hawks ever since. Meanwhile, Broad-winged Hawks may have been the first to reach other islands in the region, serving as a barrier to further spread of Ridgway's Hawk.

Red-shouldered Hawks reach their peak abundance in the Spanish-moss-draped cypress swamps and river bottoms of the southeastern states, especially in Florida, and it is here that we have had most contact with the species. Its *kleeah* proclamations resounding through the swamps in early spring are among the most pleasing sounds in nature – sounds that seem to announce the end of winter and the beginning of the breeding season for many species. The wet woodlands of this part of the country are filled with pairs of red-shoulders. In bottomlands like those that border Fisheating Creek in Florida, pairs replace one another with almost metronomic regularity along the watercourses.

Often exceedingly tame, Florida's red-shoulders are a common sight perched along hammock edges and drainage ditches, patiently scanning the ground for potential prey. Anglers of the region learn to guard their catches and bait buckets well when this species appears in the vicinity. Nesting everywhere from dense cypress swamps to hammocks in relatively open marshes and even in saltwater areas dominated by mangroves, the red-shoulder has adapted to virtually all aquatic regions

A Florida red-shoulder in flight reveals distinctive "wing windows" at the bases of his primary feathers.

A female red-shoulder in upstate New York arrives with a short-tailed shrew for her brood. Red-shoulders have disappeared almost completely from this region and many other regions of the northeastern states in recent decades, though the causes of disappearance are not certain.

A Florida Red-shouldered Hawk surveys his domain in Everglades National Park. Florida's red-shoulders are far less wary than their northern relatives and frequently hunt relatively open habitats.

The Patuxent River of Maryland is the home of a thriving and stable population of Red-shouldered Hawks. The forests of this floodplain, although not virgin, include some of the most impressive old-growth timber in the eastern states.

of the state. The major factor that appears to limit its distribution in these regions is presence of adequate numbers of hunting perches. Red-shoulders are rarely seen in truly open Everglades habitat where snags are few and far between.

In years past, Red-shouldered Hawks were also abundant in the moist woodlands of the northeastern states, though they are now common in this region only in a few localities that are still in relatively undisturbed condition. One of these is the Patuxent River bottoms of Maryland, especially the stretch of this river running through the Patuxent Wildlife Research Center. For many decades, researchers at the center have been tracking the health of the local red-shoulder population, and it has remained exceedingly stable, although housing developments throughout this general region have now made the Patuxent population virtually an island population.

In 1976 and 1977, we lived in a pre–Civil War slave cabin just off the east end of Patuxent. Here we had an opportunity to hike the towering old-growth woodlands of the Patuxent River on many occasions and to observe the local red-shoulders on a daily basis. One pair nested near the edge of the clearing where we lived, and we set up a blind to watch another pair at its nest along the main part of the river farther to the north. Far more wary than the red-shoulders of Florida, the Maryland birds were nonetheless very similar in diet and general behavior, though we rarely saw them hunting along forest edge habitats like those commonly used by the Florida birds.

Another robust, but relatively isolated, red-shoulder population still thrives in Pocomoke Swamp of the eastern shore of Maryland. As the most northerly well-developed cypress swamp in the states, Pocomoke is also home for one of the most northerly populations of Swainson's Warblers, a species often considered to be symbolic of the cane thickets of our southern states. This species, and associated Prothonotary Warblers, Barred Owls, Pileated Woodpeckers, Red-bellied Woodpeckers, and Parula Warblers, are core members of a distinctive southern swamp community somehow existing as an outpost just south of the Delaware border.

The Red-shouldered Hawks of southern California, once known as Red-bellied Hawks, seem to have adjusted much better to encroaching civilization than the red-shoulders of the northeastern states and have become a familiar bird of suburbia and the freeways, often nesting in groves of eucalyptus and other exotic trees. It is hard to imagine a much more thoroughly disturbed region in the states than the riparian zones of southern California, and it is surprising that the species has been able to accommodate itself as well as it has to the habitat changes taking place there.

How the species has been able to survive development pressures in California while it has failed to do so in many regions of the eastern states would be well worth careful study. The ability of a number of raptors to adapt to urban conditions is now a subject of great interest among biologists and may well be of great importance in future conservation of these species. Examples of species making such adaptations include the European Sparrowhawks recently invading urban areas of Scotland and the Merlins recently occupying urban areas of Saskatchewan. Many of the Peregrine Falcons released in reestablishment efforts in the eastern United States have also adopted urban environments.

In many respects, the Red-shouldered Hawk is an ideal species for biological research. In many regions it is relatively tolerant of close observation, and it often occupies territories that are sufficiently small that much of what happens in the activities of a pair can be seen from a single well-chosen vantage point if the topography is right. Despite these advantages, wildlife biologists have undertaken relatively few intensive studies of this species.

Perhaps the most thorough red-shoulder studies yet made have been those of Jim Wiley, who has concentrated on observations from blinds and lookouts in both Florida and California. Jim's researches have revealed many interesting facets to the behavior and ecology of this species, including the fact that the size of prey brought to nests bears a strong relationship to where it is caught. In his observations, the adults almost never brought small prey such as insects to nests unless they were caught in the near vicinity, while larger prey were brought in both from relatively close and relatively great distances. This feature of nest provisioning seems to make excellent intuitive sense, as the costs of transporting small items from great distances could well exceed the benefits gained. It seems likely that other raptors may make similar decisions in provisioning their young, but determining whether this is so poses formidable practical difficulties with many species. The red-shoulder is one of the few for which such data can be collected with accuracy and rigor in at least some habitats.

Buteos and Allies

Gray Hawk
BUTEO NITIDUS

ALONG THE SOUTHERN borders of Arizona, New Mexico, and Texas, birds typical of Mexico and other Central American countries intermingle with more temperate species in a region of especially high avian diversity. Nowhere else in North America is the variety of raptors so great. At one time of the year or another, thirty of the thirty-four diurnal birds of prey that have bred regularly in North America occur in this region.

Among the tropical species that attain their northern limits here is an intriguing woodland buteo that was once known by the colorful name of Mexican Goshawk, but in recent years has been more usually referred to as the Gray Hawk. A very handsome, medium-sized raptor with a solid gray head and back and a finely barred gray breast, this species is one of several that are found almost exclusively in the linear bands of cottonwoods that follow the major streams of the region. Studies by Rich Glinski indicate that only about fifty-five pairs of Gray Hawks occur north of the Mexican border, almost all of them in Arizona's San Pedro and Santa Cruz drainage basins, including Sonoita Creek. Although the number of pairs in the United States has been growing slowly in recent years, the population remains very small and the species remains in a highly vulnerable status in North America.

Of major concern is the health of the riparian cottonwood groves in which not only Gray Hawks, but also Common Black Hawks, and to a lesser extent Zone-tailed Hawks, usually nest. Cottonwood saplings are unable to survive in areas that are heavily grazed, and few cottonwood areas free of cattle remain in the Southwest. In many riparian zones, the only cottonwoods left are old giants that are slowly dying out, with no younger individuals coming along to replace them. That the main problem is cattle can be quickly appreciated by the healthy regrowth of cottonwoods that occurs in the

few areas where cattle have been excluded. Clearly, without the removal of grazing pressures, at least periodically, the long-term survival prospects for this tree are poor.

Preservation of cottonwood communities in the Southwest has much wider significance than just the conservation of Gray Hawks and Common Black Hawks. These are among the richest habitats in overall avian

Range of the Gray Hawk
☐ Breeding
▨ Breeding and wintering

An adult Gray Hawk circles near its nest along the San Pedro River. A specialist on lizards, this species is rarely found far from well-developed riparian forests.

Arizona's San Pedro River has many stretches that flow year-round. Lined with cottonwoods and floodplain mesquite forests, these stretches provide habitat for a number of southern raptors, especially Gray Hawks and Zone-tailed Hawks. Unfortunately, many regions along the river are now being invaded by exotic salt cedar.

A female Gray Hawk guards her nest along the Santa Cruz River.

Seldom seen except in the vicinity of their nests, Gray Hawks generally keep below canopy and are almost accipiterlike in their general behavior, making rapid, agile flights through the cluttered vegetation. The old name applied to this species – Mexican Goshawk – has considerable merit.

diversity known anywhere on the continent. Yet according to the Nature Conservancy, cottonwood-willow riparian forests are now the rarest forest type in North America.

Rich Glinski's studies have also indicated another habitat requirement for the Gray Hawk. The birds apparently need access to substantial hunting areas that are relatively heavily wooded but open at ground level, like the habitat structure provided by mature mesquite-hackberry bosques. The Gray Hawk depends critically on lizards for food, and it apparently needs such habitat to be able to hunt effectively. In many regions, the large mesquites adjoining the riparian zone have been heavily cut for firewood, as this is one of the best woods known for heating and cooking. In other areas, mature mesquite (and cottonwood) forests have been lost because of declining water tables produced by ceaseless pumping of ground water supplies for agriculture. The original mature mesquite woodlands that used to occur in places such as along the Santa Cruz River near Tucson have almost completely disappeared. While low brushy mesquite has been spreading rapidly in the Southwest at the expense of good grassland, there are now extremely few areas where the mesquites are mature enough to offer good hunting grounds for the hawks.

That both cottonwood nesting areas and mesquite-hackberry hunting grounds are critical for Gray Hawks seems the most likely explanation for the absence of this raptor from Aravaipa Canyon, a well-watered tributary of the San Pedro River. This canyon possesses an excellent riparian zone of cottonwoods and sycamores, but it is too deeply incised in the surrounding terrain to allow the development of an extensive parallel floodplain forest. So even though Gray Hawks thrive farther downstream where the Aravaipa joins the San Pedro, they do not appear to find adequate conditions for survival in Aravaipa Canyon itself. At the same time, Aravaipa Canyon remains a superb home for Black Hawks and Zone-tailed Hawks, whose foraging requirements are rather different.

In addition to being stressed by destruction of mature cottonwood and mesquite communities, the Gray Hawks of North America are also threatened by another habitat modification that we have already mentioned in our discussion of Mississippi Kites—widespread invasion of the bottomlands of many river systems by an exotic tree known as salt cedar or tamarisk. This species is a native of the Old World, and has been widely introduced into the Southwest to control erosion along streams. Once established, it often completely overwhelms the native riparian vegetation and creates a dense monoculture of very brushy dark woodland that is little used by most birds. Difficult to eradicate, it is having massive effects on native wildlife resources. Approximately half the avian species found in the southwestern states are completely dependent upon natural or relatively natural riparian vegetation, so the stakes in stalling or reversing the encroachment of salt cedar are enormous.

While the cottonwoods of the southwestern states have overwhelmingly positive values for avian communities, this tree does pose a number of hazards for those interested in studying member species of these communities. In particular, we have had our share of difficulties in dealing with cottonwoods in several efforts to put up blinds for observing Gray Hawks. Cottonwoods have very brittle branches, so it is essential when climbing this species to stick to main trunks to avoid a sudden catastrophic return to ground level. We have always been uneasy with the risks in ascending cottonwoods and have had a number of near calamities as limbs that appeared safe snapped off without warning. Main trunks also pose problems, including very thick bark to which it is sometimes difficult to attach blind supports securely. But our first Gray Hawk blind in a cottonwood foundered on still another cause—ants. This blind was one we assembled with Rich Glinski to help launch him in his intensive Gray Hawk studies. It was a sturdy enough structure, but an overwhelming force of these arthropods soon claimed it, forcing a strategic withdrawal with no hope of successful counterattack.

Another effort to set up a blind at a Gray Hawk nest in a cottonwood led eventually to a split beam under the platform as we tried overly hard to achieve a sturdy support framework. While the blind held together well enough to allow use, it was surely the most precarious structure we have ever put together. We finally cut short observations as the split in the support beam progressively widened and the shape of the platform evolved in ominous directions.

Nevertheless, so long as we still trusted the structure, we had an excellent viewpoint from which to watch the resident pair of Gray Hawks that were nesting on another trunk of the same tree. The adults, obviously uninterested in our substandard blind, confidently fed their two young a diet of lizards and small mammals. Though we did not see any avian prey, extensive blind observations of other nesting pairs by Rich Glinski have revealed that these hawks also take birds with some frequency. His overall data indicate a diet consisting of about 80 percent lizards and snakes, 10 percent mammals, and 10 percent birds. A major dependence on spiny lizards and whiptail lizards has been unmistakable.

Since aquatic prey are quite uncommon in the diet of Gray Hawks in Arizona, it is curious that these birds are so tightly tied to habitats with permanent flowing streams. We have never found them in completely dry canyons, whether vegetated with cottonwoods or not. Gray Hawks do come to streams to drink, and it is possible that they have difficulties obtaining enough moisture for survival just from the tissues of their prey. However, other raptors of this region, like Zone-tailed Hawks and Red-tailed Hawks, often nest in completely dry canyons, so it is unclear why Gray Hawks might not do likewise. Possibly the tie to permanent streams is not so much physiological as ecological, and may result from the favorable vegetation structure and vigorous prey populations in ecosystems with water tables close to the surface.

A migratory species, the Gray Hawk arrives in Arizona in middle to late March and begins nesting activities immediately. Females normally lay eggs in early May and incubate for about thirty-three days. The usual brood of two or three young stays in the nest for five to six weeks before fledging and then is dependent on the adults for another month or two after fledging. The birds head south again to northern Mexico by early October.

Like Common Black Hawks, Gray Hawks are not often seen soaring overhead except during courtship, and they carry on most activities within cover. Thus it is a challenge to see either of these species actually hunting. You almost always hear Gray Hawks before seeing them, and their loud descending alarm calls leave no doubt as to their displeasure with intruders in the vicinity of the nest. Other vocalizations include a very musical note of rising and falling inflection that sounds more like the call of a peacock than that of a typical buteo. This call carries very clearly through the galleries of cottonwoods, and it is one of the first sounds heard in the hours before dawn as resident Gray Hawk pairs announce their territorial holdings to one another.

In flight, Gray Hawks are relatively swift and accipiterlike, but they also often perch for long periods scanning their surroundings. The old name, Mexican Goshawk, is actually quite appropriate in a behavioral sense, though the species is not closely allied with the true goshawks in ancestry.

Many features of coloration and body proportions, for example shape of the legs and feet, suggest a close relationship of the Gray Hawk to the Red-shouldered Hawk. The black and white banding of the tail is closely similar in the two species, and both exhibit similar wing shape and parallel pattern of wing banding that is visible when the birds are soaring overhead. The similarities of these two species set them apart from typical buteos in a number of ways, and some ornithologists have urged their separation, along with the Roadside Hawk and Ridgway's Hawk, into a distinct genus, *Asturina*.

The major task for conservation of the Gray Hawk is clearly one of habitat protection. Encouragingly, the Bureau of Land Management (BLM) has recently set aside as a giant preserve, a significant part of the species' range in the United States. This preserve includes thirty-three miles of cottonwood bottomlands along the San Pedro River, one of the last permanent streams in Arizona. The San Pedro drainage hosts approximately half of the Gray Hawk pairs that nest north of the Mexican border, and about half of these pairs are found within the boundaries of the preserve. In importance, the preserve is comparable to another BLM reserve, the Snake River Birds of Prey Area in Idaho, which encompasses eighty-one miles of riparian habitat and serves as a major refuge for Prairie Falcons, Golden Eagles, and Ferruginous Hawks. Establishment of the San Pedro Riparian National Conservation Area can be largely credited to the efforts of Dean Bibles, and was accomplished primarily by a complicated series of land swaps between the BLM and various private land owners. This conservation area, together with the Patagonia–Sonoita Creek Reserve established earlier by the Nature Conservancy, represents a major step toward guaranteeing a North American future not only for the Gray Hawk, but also for many other southern species dependent on riparian cottonwood communities.

Buteos and Allies

Short-tailed Hawk
BUTEO BRACHYURUS

LIMITED TO FLORIDA within the United States, the Short-tailed Hawk is a bird of the tall pines, hardwood hammocks, and cypress swamps, mainly in the southern and central parts of the state. Although the species occurs in two color phases, light and dark, neither is a very conspicuous pattern, and until you become familiar with the short-tail's mode of hunting and with its vocalizations, you are unlikely to be aware of its existence.

Florida's short-tails most commonly hunt by making use of the updrafts that form along the boundaries between tall isolated groves of cypresses or pines and the surrounding low prairies and marshes. These cliffs of vegetation deflect any moving air upward into standing waves that can support almost effortless soaring by large birds. As the morning breezes begin to stir, the short-tails rise from the trees to take positions over such vegetational features and commonly reach altitudes of several hundred feet from the ground. Other large birds move into the air columns about the same time, and the short-tails soon become hard to pick out among the many specks of soaring vultures, anhingas, storks, kites, and other raptors. This hunting habit, coupled with the species' overall low density, makes this hawk very difficult for human observers to detect, and very likely equally difficult for its prey to detect. Perhaps the best way to pick out the species from other soaring birds is to look for tiny specks that do not move. The short-tail rarely circles when hunting, and instead just hangs in the air facing into the wind for long periods.

Despite its relatively inconspicuous nature, the short-tail is one of the most attractive raptors found within the borders of the United States, and we long hoped for a chance to observe it closely. We were especially anxious to study a nesting cycle of short-

Range of the Short-tailed Hawk
☐ Breeding
▇ Breeding and wintering

tails, because the diet of this species primarily is small birds, and we wanted to determine if the species faces the same seasonal stresses in food supplies we had found in the bird-feeding accipiters.

An opportunity to hunt for nests of the Short-tailed Hawk finally materialized in 1978 and 1979 when we were studying Everglade Kites on Lake Okeechobee. In both years, we made intensive searches of the swamps

A female dark-phased Short-tailed Hawk rests on her nest edge in south-central Florida. The nest, placed atop bromeliads and orchids in one of the tallest cypresses in the region, gave the adults unobstructed access from above. Prey brought to the nest were exclusively small birds, but the single chick did not survive to fledging.

A wintering dark-phased short-tail hunts over the prairies near Flamingo in Everglades National Park. Hanging high in the wind, short-tails rarely circle and generally capture prey in long stoops out of the sky.

This cypress nest tree of a pair of dark-phased Short-tailed Hawks was approached only by wading through hip-deep sloughs clogged with muck and aquatic vegetation. The nest itself, close to a hundred feet from the ground, had a commanding view of the entire swamp.

and hammocks northwest of this lake, especially along Fisheating Creek, where many previous sightings of short-tails had been made. Eventually, we found an active pair, but this was only after dozens of fruitless searches that led us to wonder if the species had suffered a significant decline in the region.

Our searches in 1978 yielded only a lone territorial bird of the light phase that built several nests along Fisheating Creek but never acquired a mate. Clear white underneath and dark above, with an attractive chestnut patch on both sides of the neck, this bird was noticeably smaller than the Red-tailed Hawks and Red-shouldered Hawks occupying the same region, and it spent long periods calling and circling over its nest grove in an apparent attempt to attract a partner for breeding.

Expanded efforts in 1979 finally turned up a pair of dark-phase short-tails in a remote cypress swamp farther north. These birds had solid black bodies and were active over the central reaches of the swamp. Viewing the swamp from prairies outside, we strongly suspected a nesting was in progress from seeing the male bird streak into the swamp carrying prey.

Unfortunately, it was already late spring and the cypresses were rapidly leafing out, making it difficult to spot a nest structure from the ground, especially considering the abundance of nestlike bromeliads on the cypress branches. Finding a nest was unlikely unless we might actually see one of the adults fly to it, and that was impossible from the outside of the swamp. We had to get closer, and this meant slogging though opaque waist-deep waters and stubbing our shins on innumerable cypress knees and submerged logs, always wondering what we might step on next. Fortunately, after covering the swamp quite thoroughly on foot, we finally saw the male adult overhead carrying a twig, and he flew straight to one of the airplants in a nearby cypress, making a twisting, flapping landing. At last we had an active nest. The nest was only partly built and incubation had not yet started, so it appeared we had a chance to follow a full breeding cycle of the species.

The nest was placed atop a mass of bromeliads and flowering orchids nearly a hundred feet from the ground in one of the tallest cypresses in the region. As this was the latest nest ever recorded of the species in Florida (incubation began on about May 26), it may have been a renesting effort after a failure earlier in the year. An unoccupied nest in a nearby cypress, apparently also of short-tails, suggested that the swamp had been occupied by short-tails in the recent past, although there was no way to determine conclusively if this second nest dated from the same year.

The height of the active nest and the density of nearby vegetation made good observations from the ground impossible. We soon decided that a tree blind was a necessity if we were going to be able to get any detailed information on the feeding ecology of the pair. Unfortunately, the only suitable cypress for a blind had a major fork in the main trunk about eighty feet from the ground, which meant that we would have to construct the blind near the top of a trunk that was slanting up into the sky at an alarming 45 degree angle. The diameter of the trunk at the place where the blind would have to be placed was none too great, and we had some misgivings about the safety of what we were doing. Fortunately, the trunk proved to be strong, and we wound up with a blind perched at the highest point in the swamp with a spectacular view not only of the Short-tailed Hawk nest some thirty feet distant, but also of the entire region.

Swallow-tailed Kites, nesting several hundred yards away, cruised past the blind with regularity, and far below were Wild Turkeys, Wood Storks, Barred Owls, deer, bobcats, and raccoons. Overhead, we could watch the aerial activities of the short-tails, as well as the ominous buildup of thunderheads that drenched the swamp with rain each afternoon. There are few wild habitats to match the beauty of a mature cypress swamp, and it was often difficult to concentrate on activities at the short-tail nest with so many seductive distractions on all sides.

Shortly after we began observations of the pair from the treetop blind, we saw the adult female hard pressed to defend her nest from a formidable enemy. As she sat incubating, a large yellow rat snake appeared, working its way upward through the bromeliad base of the nest. Once she became aware of the snake, the female spread her wings fully and held them extended in an impressive display that greatly increased her apparent size and ferocity. Simultaneously footing aggressively at the snake, she managed to drive it into a quick retreat back down the trunk of the cypress.

The short-tails hatched their single chick on June 29, and the male adult began bringing prey to the nest to pass to the female for feeding to the youngster. The pair fed exclusively on other birds, mainly from the surrounding prairie regions, and in fact we had our first good look at a Bachman's Sparrow as a prey item brought to this nest. Sadly, the single chick in the nest lost vigor about a week after hatching and soon disappeared, so we were unable to complete a study of a full nesting cycle. Causes of the chick's difficulties were unknown, although it became reluctant to take food toward the end and may well have perished as a result. As we were not climbing the nest tree itself during this period, we did not have a chance to inspect the chick closely before it disappeared. Nevertheless, it is worth noting that the same dermestid beetle larvae that were becoming a problem by attacking Everglade Kite nestlings in 1978 and 1979 were also found in this short-tail nest when Jeff Lincer climbed and inspected it a short time later.

Our efforts to find and study Short-tailed Hawks took us into some of the most pristine wildlife areas of Florida. They also gave us one of the most extraordinary wildlife experiences to be hoped for in this age—a moment in which we believed we had seen an Ivory-billed Woodpecker. This will-o-the-wisp species had last been seen nearly a decade earlier in a region of Florida not far distant. By the late 1970s, many considered the species to be extinct in the states, and reported sightings were generally viewed with considerable skepticism. None of the recent sightings had been clear enough or long enough or substantiated well enough with photographs to be fully believable. Our sighting was not troubled by these problems but nevertheless reinforced the caution with which contemporary ivory-bill sightings should be regarded.

We were hiking a hammock northeast of Archbold Biological Station looking for short-tails when a large bird flew up from a log at our feet and landed clinging to the vertical trunk of a pine about fifty feet distant. Immediately apparent were large and conspicuous white triangles on the back of the bird formed by the white secondary feathers of the folded wings—a diagnostic field mark of the ivory-bill that distinguishes this species from the otherwise quite similar Pileated Woodpecker (a species with a uniformly black back). Had the bird flown on at this point, we would have had no doubt whatsoever that we had seen a living ivory-bill.

But the bird did not fly immediately, and instead it shifted from one side of the trunk to the other for perhaps another thirty seconds, allowing ample opportunity for a careful inspection of its plumage with binoculars. Unfortunately, a detailed look revealed that in fact the white triangles on the bird's back were not pure white but were somewhat cream-colored, and in fact the white area on the left wing was marred by two black secondary feathers intermixed with the white ones. Furthermore, the bird did not have the pure white bill of an ivory-bill, but the typical black bill of a Pileated Woodpecker, and the details of the bird's head-color pattern matched a Pileated Woodpecker in all respects. Clearly, this was not really an Ivory-billed Woodpecker, but was most likely a freak Pileated Woodpecker (or

less likely a hybrid of the two species) bearing most of the wing coloration of an ivory-bill.

With the sighting of this bird, thoughts of Short-tailed Hawks had vanished for a time, and in truth even if a screaming short-tail had circled low over our heads, we might not have noticed it. We hiked on back toward home wondering just how many of the "ivory-bill" sightings of recent decades might trace to similar sources.

The Short-tailed Hawk itself is a species that is frequently misidentified because of its similarities to other species. In particular, wintering Broad-winged Hawks in southern Florida are often nearly clear white underneath and are very similar in size and shape to short-tails. Often such broad-wings winter in the Florida Keys, and many records of short-tails from this area undoubtedly trace to this species. In general, the hawks of the genus *Buteo* are especially hard to differentiate as many are so variable in plumage. A knowledge of behavior is as important as good eyesight in making reliable identifications.

The short-tail's almost exclusive diet of birds is unusual for a buteo, and like other raptors feeding heavily on birds, the species exhibits a considerable size difference between the sexes. Short-tails capture prey in long stoops, sometimes in the canopy of hammocks, but perhaps as often in the open fields surrounding wooded areas. One of the most accessible places to watch this species hunting, especially in winter, is over the prairies of Everglades National Park near Flamingo. Short-tails are also often seen foraging over Anhinga Trail in the park. Another place where there is a good chance of seeing the species at any time of year is in Corkscrew Swamp Sanctuary in Collier County. The short-tail is not a species you expect to see every day in the field in southern Florida, unlike the abundant Red-shouldered Hawks and Red-tailed Hawks, but there are places where it can be found with some reliability.

Nevertheless, the difficulties in finding this species have made it hard to monitor the health of the Florida population. The species has almost surely suffered significant losses due to the continuing development of many regions of the state. The fact that we found no short-tails in many of the wild areas west of Lake Okeechobee where the species was known formerly also raises concerns that short-tails have been having some difficulties in undisturbed regions. Here surely is a species deserving more attention from conservationists.

Buteos and Allies

Swainson's Hawk

BUTEO SWAINSONI

ONLY ONE WOODLAND buteo, the Broad-winged Hawk, and one open-country buteo, the Swainson's Hawk, migrate all the way from North America to South America in winter. All other North American species in this genus, with the possible exception of the Zone-tailed Hawk, go no farther than Central America, and some barely reach the Mexican border. To be strictly accurate, small populations of both Broad-winged

Range of the Swainson's Hawk
- ☐ Breeding
- ■ Wintering

Most birds winter in South America.

Hawks and Swainson's Hawks also winter in Florida and a number of resident broad-wing populations occur in the West Indies. Nevertheless, the great majority of individuals of both these species are truly intercontinental travelers.

These migrations take the hawks down through Central America and across the Panamanian isthmus, where they collect in huge assemblages of tens of thousands of birds in the fall. Swainson's Hawks finish their southward journeys in the pampas of Argentina, settling in habitats similar to the open grassland and brushland habitats they occupy in North America during the summer. The final destination of most migrating broad-wings is the forests of northern South America, though some get no farther than southern Central America.

The entire southward migration for Swainson's Hawks takes about a month and a half to two months, and biologists have long speculated as to whether this species takes any food at all during this long journey. No one has witnessed prey capture attempts in the migratory swarms in Costa Rica and Panama, and at sites in this region where flocks of Swainson's Hawks have roosted overnight, no one has found traces of pellets or fecal material. Recent calculations of Neal Smith, David Goldstein, and George Bartholomew on the energy requirements of migration suggest that Swainson's Hawks could put on enough fat to enable them to survive the entire migration, providing the birds do not use any significant amounts of flapping flight en route. This restriction accords well with field observations that document soaring and gliding as the main modes of travel during the journey.

Regardless of whether or not they feed on migration, the fact that nearly the entire populations of Swainson's Hawks and Broad-winged Hawks funnel through

Panama during migration allows a potential for censusing these populations. In efforts during the mid-1980s, Neal Smith was able to document, by actual counts of birds on photographic negatives, that the total populations of each of these species must consist of nearly a million birds, clearly ranking them among the most abundant raptors of North America.

Of the other North American raptors, only a few make comparable seasonal migrations, most notably Swallow-tailed Kites and Mississippi Kites, and some populations of Turkey Vultures, Peregrine Falcons, and Ospreys. The general absence of raptor species making a full migration to South America may relate to a number of things. Possibly one important factor is that most raptors find it difficult to fly across long stretches of water. Eastern raptors, in particular, face a formidable barrier to southward progress in the Gulf of Mexico, unless they swing far to the west in their routes of travel. Soaring conditions are generally poor over water, and most raptors have to rely on powered flapping flight to cross such barriers, an energetically expensive way to progress for large birds. Thus it may have been difficult for many raptor species to establish migration routes taking them into South America. Only five species of raptors, the Osprey, the Swallow-tailed Kite, the Northern Harrier, the Peregrine Falcon, and the Merlin, are known to move regularly into the West Indies or across the Gulf of Mexico in migration, and these are all species that relative to their body size have especially long, thin, powerful wings suiting them for such arduous journeys.

Some evidence indicates that the wintering populations of Broad-winged Hawks and Swainson's Hawks found in southern Florida may primarily represent individuals that missed their bearings in their first fall migration and got trapped in southern portions of the peninsula by the oceans to the east, south, and west. Most individuals of these species wintering in Florida have been juveniles, not yet fully experienced in migration. There have been actual sightings of migrating flocks of broad-wings circling over Key West, heading tentatively out to sea, then returning once again to the safety of land. Some flocks have been seen to fight onward to the south, but the finding of weak and starving individuals on the Dry Tortugas not much farther along suggests that individuals that continue south over the Gulf of Mexico may be doomed.

Though its wings are not so long and thin as to place it among the species comfortable with long overwater migrations, the Swainson's Hawk has relatively long pointed wings for a buteo, which allow reliable identification of the species from a considerable distance. To what extent the relatively long wings are a reflection of the long migrations practiced by this species is unknown, but at least a rough correlation between wing length and length of migration exists in many avian groups. For example, the nonmigratory Sharp-shinned Hawks of Puerto Rico have much shorter wings than migratory populations of sharp-shins on the mainland, although they are very similar in weight to mainland sharp-shins.

In other aspects of appearance, Swainson's Hawks, like many other buteos, exhibit a great variety of color patterns from completely black to primarily white underneath. In typical light phase, the species has a white throat and belly separated by a dark brownish band across the upper breast. Intermediate-phase birds have a reduced white throat and a white belly heavily marked with rufous-brown barring. Completely dark individuals are rare.

On its breeding grounds in the western states and western Canada, Swainson's Hawk is known mainly as a predator of small mammals and insects, but like many other large raptors taking both invertebrate and vertebrate prey, this species normally brings only vertebrates to nests as food for developing nestlings. In part, this reliance on vertebrate prey during breeding may stem from the fact that vertebrate skeletons offer a rich source of calcium for bone development of nestlings. But probably more important, it may stem from the high transport costs of satisfying the energy and protein needs of developing nestlings with relatively small prey such as insects.

In any event, the diet we have seen at several nests of Swainson's Hawks in the southwestern states has been exclusively small mammals, lizards, and birds. These are the sorts of prey the species evidently needs for successful breeding, despite the fact that stomach analyses of Swainson's Hawks over the years have shown a very high proportion of insects in the diet.

One nest we watched in western New Mexico in 1971 was in the top of a sturdy soaptree yucca that reached about twenty feet into the sky. The pair attending the nest included a light-phase male and an intermediate-phase female, and the nest contained two downy white nestlings. Swainson's Hawks were very common in this region, nesting in everything from mesquites to cottonwoods. Perhaps because of the heavily overgrazed, brushy condition of the land, the hawks found an abundance of ground squirrels and small birds to feed on, and we even once saw them bring in a

In flight around its nest, an adult Swainson's Hawk exhibits the distinctive two-toned wing coloration and pointed wing tips that allow identification of this species from long distances.

As in most raptors, the female Swainson's Hawk generally remains in attendance at the nest, while the male does most of the foraging for the brood. Adults at this site were often together at the nest when the male brought in food, and young were fed a diet made up entirely of small vertebrates.

A male Swainson's Hawk lands with a banner-tailed kangaroo rat in midafternoon. How he may have captured this strictly nocturnal mammal is unknown.

Swainson's Hawks often nest in soaptree yuccas in western New Mexico. The tallest trees in the region, these yuccas provide excellent nest sites for Red-tailed Hawks as well. Old nests of both species are often used by nesting Great-horned Owls.

banner-tailed kangaroo rat to the nest. How they managed to capture this strictly nocturnal species during the middle of the day we may never know, but it did not appear to have been a highway victim scavenged by the birds, as it was not crushed in any way. At another nearby nest in 1987, we again found a whole, uncrushed banner-tail, so the Swainson's Hawks evidently have learned effective ways of catching this species.

Recent studies by John Kirkley and James Gessamen have explored the crucial relationship between water needs of nestling Swainson's Hawks and their diet characteristics. Like young of most other raptor species, young Swainson's Hawks have no opportunities to drink water until after fledging, and must meet all their water needs during development from the moisture present in prey they receive from their parents. Further, because Swainson's Hawk nests are often placed in extremely hot environments, the nestlings are often faced with a special need for water to allow them to regulate body temperatures by evaporative cooling. Certain prey contain enough water in their tissues to supply such needs; others do not. In particular, young ground squirrels are a much more favorable food for nestlings than fatty adult ground squirrels with respect to water content, and it appears that, were nesting Swainson's Hawks to feed exclusively on adult ground squirrels, their nestlings would not obtain enough water to survive. Presumably diet of the species is normally varied enough to avoid such difficulties.

In late summer and early fall, the Swainson's Hawks of the Southwest often gather in large flocks in agricultural lands, where they take large numbers of grasshoppers before heading farther south on their annual trek to South America. In the late 1960s, we also saw large flocks of the wintering population of Swainson's Hawks in Florida using agricultural lands. Here the birds had learned to follow tractors, as farmers plowed their fields in preparation for planting. This process exposed many small rodents to view—some of which were crippled as the blades of the plows cut through the soil. Processions of Swainson's Hawks commonly drifted along behind, diving intermittently to

the ground to grab these unfortunate creatures. Sometimes the hawks collided in midair when more than one bird attempted to capture the same rodent simultaneously. The huge crops taken on by the hawks graphically illustrated the ease and efficiency of foraging in this way, and the major challenge faced by these birds appeared to be locating active tractors.

Another intriguing foraging method we have watched Swainson's Hawks employ in Arizona is fire following. When the grasslands are aflame, Swainson's Hawks stream in from miles around to take advantage of the prey species suddenly deprived of cover and safety. Such behavior is also well known for many other raptor species of open country, such as White-tailed Hawks and Aplomado Falcons.

Swainson's Hawks have also adjusted well in other ways to agricultural practices. A number of researchers have noted that a large fraction of the nest sites used by the species in certain regions have been trees planted as hedgerows and around farm structures, and evidently the species has increased as a result of these plantings. However, the suitability of agricultural lands for foraging by Swainson's Hawks depends greatly on the specific characteristics of agricultural practices. As a general rule, pasturelands and hayfields provide good foraging habitat. Wheat fields and alfalfa fields do not, apparently because they provide too much cover for prey. Thus Swainson's Hawks have not proved to be tolerant of agricultural practices in all areas. For example, the species has completely disappeared from the highly agriculturalized southern San Joaquin Valley of California in recent decades.

As a very handsomely marked, open-country species, the Swainson's Hawk is a welcome sight in our western states, and it is still abundant in many regions, especially where grazing is still the major land use. Like other species that winter beyond our borders, however, its long-term conservation can be only partially controlled by local practices. Nevertheless, in the relatively short term, the general tolerance of this species for disturbed, partially agriculturalized regions favors its survival.

Buteos and Allies

Rough-legged Hawk
BUTEO LAGOPUS

POLEWARD FROM THE frigid Brooks Range across the North Slope of Alaska flow a number of snow-fed rivers bearing intriguing names, many of them Inupiaq in origin. The Sagavanirktok, the Kuparuk, the Itkillik, and the Colville are among the largest, and as they descend from the mountains, they meander first through rolling tundra-covered foothills, then through a broad plain of tundra and lakes, finally reaching the Arctic Ocean after journeys of several hundred miles.

The lands these rivers pass through are all underlain by permafrost. Forlorn and desolate in mood, they are lands of sphagnum moss, dwarf willows, tiny birches, and miniature rhododendrons; lands of perpetual daylight in the summer months and perpetual darkness in winter. The Arctic Circle lies hundreds of miles to the south.

Although the overall relief of the region is modest, the rivers of the North Slope have cut bluffs and cliffs here and there along their courses. Mostly these are entirely insignificant patches of rock and talus. They are, nevertheless, large enough escarpments to support thriving populations of cliff-nesting raptors. Peregrine Falcons, Gyrfalcons, and Rough-legged Hawks are the primary residents. Common Ravens are also live here, though in less abundance, and like the rough-legs, they provide an important service to the Peregrine Falcons and Gyrfalcons by constructing stick nests that these species can subsequently occupy. Golden Eagles, common on the cliffs of the Brooks Range, occur only on some of the higher escarpments along the southern fringe of the region.

In the terrain between the rivers, a fairly limited community of prey species fuels the economy of the cliff-nesters. Small mammals, primarily lemmings and various species of voles, form the main food of the Rough-legged Hawks, while the resident ptarmigan and

ground squirrels sustain the Gyrfalcons. The Peregrine Falcons take mainly small birds, while the ravens, as is their custom elsewhere, feed opportunistically on a variety of plant and animal species, many of them as carrion. Certain of these food species, particularly the small mammals, exhibit dramatic cycles of abundance and scarcity, and the Rough-legged Hawks especially, because they are almost entirely dependent on such

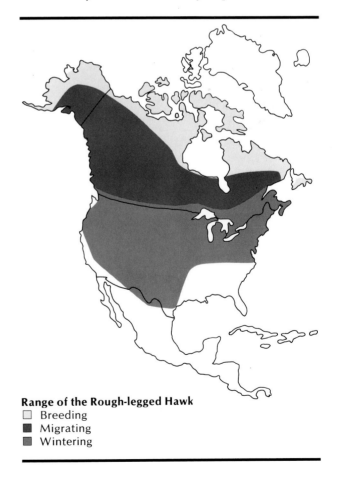

Range of the Rough-legged Hawk
- ☐ Breeding
- ■ Migrating
- ■ Wintering

117

An Alaskan rough-leg nest of 1987 was placed on a gentle slope in a region of excellent prey availability. Both adults at this nest were of the light phase. Prey brought here were primarily small mammals captured in the near vicinity, and the young were well fed and healthy.

Two of the nestlings engage in a tug of war over food.

As one nestling lofts excrement over the nest edge, the other two watch attentively, and nest sanitation is maintained.

The female rough-leg, a light-phased bird, was the parent in attendance at the nest found near the Sagavanirktok River. The chick, apparently suffering from a lack of food, called almost constantly and aggressively commandeered each prey brought to the nest, not waiting to be fed by his parents.

The bluffs along the Sagavanirktok River of Alaska are modest in size, but they are the only escarpments for many miles and host a surprising abundance of nesting raptors. In 1987, however, small mammal populations were at a low point in the region, and most Rough-legged Hawk territories were vacant.

In flight, light-phased rough-legs commonly exhibit white tail bases, black bellies, and black patches along the leading edge of their wings, but the species is highly variable in coloration, like many open-country raptors.

prey, have to contend with severe fluctuations in food availability.

Confined almost completely to treeless tundra on their breeding grounds, Rough-legged Hawks and Gyrfalcons compete for honors as the most thoroughly arctic nesters of America's diurnal raptors. The breeding distributions of the two species overlap broadly, and although the Gyrfalcons of some regions extend closer to the pole than the rough-legs, Gyrfalcons also regularly breed farther south in the mountains of interior Alaska and Canada. Building nests of dwarf willow and birch branches on exposed ledges and slopes, the rough-legs make the best of what few woody materials are available in their surroundings and cope as best they can with the dense clouds of mosquitoes that are nurtured in the soggy pools and streams dotting the surface of the landscape.

Normally, rough-legs are the most common of all the arctic raptors, but in July of 1987, when we had an opportunity to visit Alaska's North Slope, small mammals were at a low point in their cycle of abundance, and we found more pairs of Gyrfalcons than of rough-legs. Numerous old rough-leg territories along the river bluffs were host only to empty nests, and the few pairs that were attempting to breed were having only moderate success.

One nest we watched from a blind held but a single youngster, and a very scrawny one at that. His parents, apparently unable to find adequate numbers of small mammals, were bringing in mostly small birds, and the youngster appeared to be in a state of acute hunger.

In view of the apparent food stress at this nest, we were curious as to whether the parent birds might be attempting to increase prey captures by extending their hunting activities through the late evening and early morning hours. Certainly there was enough light around the clock to make this possible. But though we watched for signs of such an adjustment in a twenty-four-hour vigil, activities ceased at about nine at night and the pair did not resume hunting until an hour of the morning that would be appropriate for raptors in the lower states. A twenty-four-hour watch of an active Golden Eagle nest nearby revealed a very similar schedule of activities. The raptors of the midnight sun appear to need their rest as much as their observers.

The adults of the rough-leg pair included a light-phased female and a most strikingly beautiful black-phased male. Both exhibited the broad black subterminal band to the tail typical of the species, but beyond this they were quite different in appearance. The female, heavily streaked with dark brown and with a black belly and black patches near the bases of her primary feathers, remained in close attendance at the nest. The all-dark male, arriving only at irregular intervals, was a dead-ringer for a Zone-tailed Hawk, differing mainly in the amount of white banding at the base of the tail. A close similarity of rough-legs to zone-tails was also apparent in alarm vocalizations—in both species a high, thin descending scream that breaks up into a sort of yodeling when the birds beat their wings in flight. Whether these two species commonly have a chance to hear each other in nature, however, is questionable. By the time the southernmost wintering rough-legs reach the summer range of the zone-tail in Arizona and New Mexico, the zone-tails have normally long departed for a wintering range farther south.

The nest of the rough-leg pair rested on an inconsequential rib of gravel and rock projecting from a low bluff overlooking the Sagavanirktok River. On the flood plain directly below we watched the activities of a family of seven arctic wolves, not more than a couple hundred yards away. We wondered how the rough-leg nest could possibly survive predation by these canines, as it was an easy stroll to reach the nest from the top of the bluff, and just as easy a stroll from the bottom of the bluff to the top. Five of the wolves were just pups, tumbling and wrestling with each other on the green tundra carpet, and like the rough-legs they came in two color phases, white and black. In the late evening and early morning hours, the pack held extended choruses of mournful calling with other wolves perhaps another mile upriver. Possibly, the distant howlers were additional members of the same pack, but we never caught sight of them. The nearby remains of a slain caribou gave testimony to the wolves' predatory capacities, and we could only wish the rough-legs the best of luck in the weeks that lay ahead.

Perhaps the rough-legs' choice of such a vulnerable nest site was dictated by the fact that a pair of Gyrfalcons was occupying what may have been their customary nest on a more substantial and protected cliff a quarter mile away. For the most part, the rough-leg and Gyrfalcon pairs appeared to be avoiding one another, though we did see occasional aggressive aerial encounters.

Avoidance of nesting Gyrfalcons may also have been the reason why another rough-leg pair, about seventy miles distant, nested completely apart from any cliff whatsoever. This nest, with three young close to fledging in mid-July, was placed on nothing more than a gentle slope in the tundra, and here again Gyrfalcons were nesting in the nearest cliff a quarter mile away. Old rough-leg nests on the cliff strongly suggested that it might have been the rough-legs' usual home.

This second pair of rough-legs was occupying a region with much better small mammal populations than those available to the first pair and was doing much better in provisioning its brood. We saw only small mammals brought to this nest and found virtually nothing but mammal fur as prey remains at the site. In directly observing the adults' activities, we found that they had little trouble locating prey, hunting much in the manner of White-tailed Hawks. Circling and hanging in the breeze high over the tundra, they occasionally hovered for a few seconds, then moved on to new locations to scan the ground—and finally descended in long direct stoops to capture their victims.

While the first pair of rough-legs was somehow succeeding in the very midst of a wolf pack, the second pair was situated only a short distance from an active den of five red foxes. That they too were unmolested in spite of this tangible threat and in spite of the total vulnerability of their nest site to terrestrial predators was again noteworthy, as was the fact that both rough-leg nests were surviving what appeared to be substantial threats of aerial predation by nearby nesting Gyrfalcons. Perhaps the persistence of both nests was due to the close attendance they received from the adult females and the abilities of the females to spot approaching predators and intercept and harass them at long distances from the nests.

Like most other raptors reaching the far north, the Rough-legged Hawk has a circumpolar distribution. Peregrines, Gyrfalcons, Merlins, Golden Eagles, Ospreys, Northern Goshawks, and Northern Harriers, among the diurnal raptors; and Snowy Owls, Boreal Owls, Hawk Owls, Great Gray Owls, and Short-eared Owls, among the nocturnal species, all occur both in the New World and in the Old World. Very few raptor species limited to more southerly latitudes can make this claim. Very likely, this effect is largely traceable to the fact that especially in past ages only minor barriers to dispersal have existed between northwestern Alaska and Siberia.

The name, Rough-legged Hawk, is derived from the feathering of the legs found in this species, an unusual characteristic for a buteo, but a characteristic found also in the Ferruginous Hawk and Golden Eagle among the New World falconiforms and in most owl species and in ptarmigan and grouse, where even the toes are often feathered. Presumably the feathering of legs and toes functions mainly in heat conservation for these extremities, and this is why the characteristic seems to be associated primarily with birds of cold climates and nocturnal habits. The correlation of feathering of legs or toes with cold climates is not perfect, however, as none of the falcons, including the Gyrfalcon, possess such feathering, and some species with leg-feathering, for example a number of eagle species in the genus *Aquila,* live only in quite low latitudes.

In winter, the rough-legs of the New World migrate as far south as northern Mexico. Those we have had an opportunity to observe in southern Arizona have appeared to be very limited in their habitat preferences, occupying only certain specific grassland regions year after year and avoiding brush-covered terrain completely. At least superficially, grassland is the closest habitat match to tundra that Arizona has to offer.

For the most part, the Rough-legged Hawk, like the Gyrfalcon, has suffered very little from the advances of civilization, primarily because it nests so far north of developed regions. However, on its wintering grounds, the rough-leg is vulnerable to human pressures, such as shooting, habitat destruction, and collisions with powerlines and automobiles. To date, such pressures have certainly been taking their toll, though there have been no indications of long-term declines of the species at migration overlooks like Hawk Mountain in Pennsylvania. Presumably, the chronic wintering losses are more than made up for by productivity on the nesting grounds.

Ferruginous Hawk
BUTEO REGALIS

THE FERRUGINOUS HAWK is a very solidly built, "chesty" raptor inhabiting the Great Plains and intermontane grasslands of the western states and southern Canada. But although it is the largest of the North American buteos, it is one of the least familiar members of this genus for most naturalists. Formerly known as the Ferruginous Rough-legged Hawk, because of its feathered legs, it is a much more heavy-bodied bird than the true Rough-legged Hawk, and much more powerful. The rusty color of the bird's leg, back, and shoulder feathers is the source of the term, "ferruginous."

The Ferruginous Hawk feeds nearly exclusively on medium-sized mammals such as gophers, ground squirrels, and rabbits. It is so thoroughly adapted to open country that it commonly rests right on the ground and hunts from the ground, even in areas that offer apparently suitable perches in the form of posts, snags, and phone poles. Because of these terrestrial tendencies, the species is often overlooked and its abundance underestimated.

Ferruginous Hawks, like most open-country buteos, occur in various light and dark color phases. In typical light phase, the species is nearly clear white when viewed in flight from below, with a conspicuous rufous V formed by the legs against the lower abdomen and tail. The topsides of the wings are basically gray with rufous patches. In the much rarer dark phase, the body is solidly black with a rufous wash, and the wings are two-toned black and white when viewed from below. The tail in both dark and light phases is basically a dirty white underneath, and this is often a very useful field-mark for distinguishing this species from most other large raptors at a distance.

Other North American buteos exhibiting a tendency toward color phases are Swainson's Hawks, Red-tailed Hawks, Rough-legged Hawks, White-tailed Hawks, and

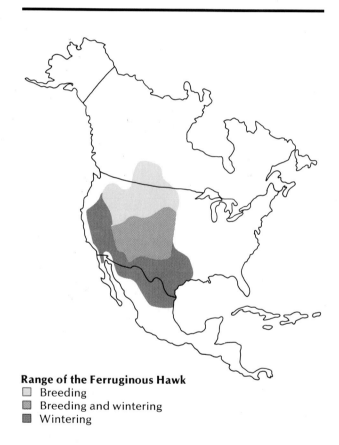

Range of the Ferruginous Hawk
- Breeding
- Breeding and wintering
- Wintering

Short-tailed Hawks. At least on this continent, the trait seems somehow related to habitat, as the woodland raptors, with only very rare exceptions, do not exhibit such polymorphism. Giving added support to this conclusion is the fact that dark color phases of the Red-tailed Hawk are much more common in the open country of the western states than in the more forested regions of the eastern states and West Indies. Only the Broad-winged Hawk, among the woodland species, shows any tendency toward color phases, but here again the tendency toward dark individuals is limited to the most western population, which nests in Alberta.

Just why there is such a strong tendency toward color phases in the open-country species is one of the more interesting unresolved questions in the biology of raptors. Conceivably it may have something to do with individual recognition at a distance for species that are primarily dependent on visual, rather than vocal, identification cues. Alternatively, as Dennis Paulson has suggested, it could in some way relate to interactions with prey species, perhaps increasing the difficulties that prey might have in recognizing their predators. Recent studies of the Red-tailed Hawk in Arkansas by Charles Preston suggest that different color-phase birds actually tend to position themselves differently in perching, perhaps to make themselves maximally inconspicuous to prey. Whatever its primary function, it is interesting to note that in most species exhibiting this polymorphism, including the Ferruginous Hawk, light-phase individuals greatly outnumber dark-phase individuals. This fact may ultimately prove to be important in elucidating the significance of the variability. Only the Short-tailed Hawk, among the polymorphic North American raptors, is characterized by a preponderance of dark-phased individuals.

In keeping with its strong open-country habitat preferences, the Ferruginous Hawk is one of the few raptors that commonly nests on the ground, although where cliffs or trees are available within its range, the species readily uses them, presumably because they give superior protection from terrestrial predators. An active nest we examined in southern Idaho in 1981 was placed in the top of a low juniper adjacent to a region of sagebrush and grassland stretching unbroken to the horizon. The nest itself was a bulky structure, consisting mainly of massive dead branches of juniper. These were far larger than the branches generally used in nest construction by other similar-sized buteos and accipiters, and suggested an uncommon degree of strength in the species. Other observers have similarly reported unusually large materials incorporated into Ferruginous Hawk nests. In the latter part of the nineteenth century, during the period of rampant slaughter of buffalo on the Great Plains, Ferruginous Hawks were sometimes found attending nests constructed largely of ribs taken from skeletons of these giant mammals. Observations of Ferruginous Hawks carrying relatively large prey, such as adult rabbits, further suggest a substantial physical prowess in this species. Yet in spite of these clear

manifestations of power, the talons of the Ferruginous Hawk are actually quite small for a raptor of this size.

Ferruginous Hawks often hunt right from the ground, perching on hillsides where they have a view of their surroundings and can take off in short shallow glides to surprise victims leaving cover. At other times they hunt from low perches. In still other circumstances, such as we have observed in wintering birds in Arizona, they perch on the ground amidst burrows of mammals such as gophers, waiting for unwary prey to become vulnerable at close range. Under such conditions the hawks sometimes make successful captures by thrusting their talons into the piles of loose earth the mammals are pushing up from below. In addition, Ferruginous Hawks sometimes hover over open fields, much like American Kestrels, Rough-legged Hawks, and Black-shouldered Kites, and they sometimes hunt from soaring flight.

In studying Ferruginous Hawks using various hunting methods in Idaho, James Wakely found that males of this species were successful in 16.6 percent of their capture attempts overall. However, success was consistently greater than 20 percent for birds hunting from right on the ground among mammal burrows and for birds hunting from high soaring or hovering flight. Birds hunting from low flight were less successful, and those hunting from low perches did worst of all, with only about 10 percent of their attempts resulting in kills. Yet in spite of the relatively low success rate in hunting from low perches, this was the most commonly used hunting method, probably mainly because it requires only low energy expenditures and yields a relatively high rate of return on investment.

Irrespective of hunting method, the Ferruginous Hawks in Wakely's studies did not concentrate their foraging efforts on areas where prey density was greatest, but in areas where prey vulnerability was highest because of a dearth of cover. In earlier times, most ecologists assumed that habitat quality for raptors could be specified simply by counting prey numbers or measuring prey biomass per unit area. Studies such as Wakely's, however, have by now clearly demonstrated that for many species, prey abundance is not equivalent to prey availability. And while the data obtained from prey censusing efforts are a start toward understanding why birds of prey concentrate their foraging efforts in certain areas, the best way to measure habitat quality for these species is surely to study their rates of prey captures relative to their foraging expenditures in various habitats. Prey numbers are often only a small component in the equation, and such factors as

A Ferruginous Hawk nest, placed on the top of a juniper, was located on the edge of a vast region of open prairie in southern Idaho.

Light-phase Ferruginous Hawks are easily identifiable by their rusty-colored legs contrasting with white underparts. Their legs, like the legs of Rough-legged Hawks and Golden Eagles, are completely feathered. All other diurnal raptors in North America have naked legs.

A dark-phase Ferruginous Hawk strokes through the skies of northern New Mexico. A powerful predator of small and medium-sized mammals, this species is almost always found in open country where it commonly perches directly on the ground.

Massive juniper branches, far larger than the branches used by other buteos in nest construction, formed the fabric of an Idaho Ferruginous Hawk nest. A century ago, nests of this species on the Great Plains were sometimes built of buffalo ribs.

availability of hunting perches for the raptors, density of concealing vegetation, and activity levels of the prey are commonly far more important. As a general rule, most individuals of most prey species are simply not highly vulnerable to capture most of the time.

Around their nests, Ferruginous Hawks have a reputation for being exceedingly sensitive to human activities, and they are one of the falconiform species most likely to desert nests, at least early-stage nests, after disturbance. Correspondingly, studies of Richard Olendorff, John Stoddart Jr., Clayton White, and Tom Thurow have documented that nesting success in these hawks depends heavily on the degree of remoteness of nesting sites from developed areas. Such sensitivity argues for great caution in conducting reproductive studies with this species, and overall conservation of the species apparently must include effective safeguards to minimize human activities on the breeding grounds. The Ferruginous Hawk has the most restricted overall range of any of the buteos found in North America, and its total population has recently been estimated to not exceed four thousand pairs. The species merits special concern, as it could quickly drop to a truly threatened status in the event of future environmental stresses.

In the winter of 1987, we encountered a most unusual Ferruginous Hawk with Arnie Moorhouse in the Sulfur Springs Valley of Arizona. The bird was perched on the ground, and we were attracted because it was only able to flutter and stagger ineffectively as we approached. We immediately made a successful effort to capture the bird to examine it for signs of injury.

In the hand, the bird seemed in good weight, and indeed it had a full crop. We found no broken bones or signs of recent injury. But what soon caught our attention was the appearance of the bird's right eye. At first glance we were aware that the eye seemed somehow strange, though we were not quite sure why. Close examination, however, revealed that the eye had what appeared to be two pupils, which lent the bird a decidedly unnerving appearance. Had the bird been shot? Was one of the pupils actually an entry point for a lead pellet? If so, the eye had healed over remarkably well. There was no disfiguration to its shape, and the cornea appeared unblemished. Further, there were no ragged edges to either of the irises surrounding the pupils. It all looked relatively natural, yet at the same time horribly supernatural. Until seeing this bird, we were quite unaware of how confidently we all rely on the cosmic rule of one pupil per eye – and how viscerally disturbing any deviation from this rule might be.

Whether the bird's inability to fly was in some way related to its unusual eye was unclear, but in any event we were surprised by the bird's overall good physical condition. Somehow it was surviving in spite of its handicaps, though how it was managing to feed itself remains a mystery.

Buteos and Allies

White-tailed Hawk

BUTEO ALBICAUDATUS

THE SOUTHEASTERLY SEA winds blow humid, warm, strong, and steady, and bring mostly cloudy skies to the south coast of Texas. These forces provide a unique combination of direct and indirect environmental conditions that are important to the ecology of one of the most geographically limited of North America's raptors, the White-tailed Hawk. North of the Mexican border, this relatively large buteo is rarely found anywhere else

but in the Lone Star State, although it also occurs south through Central America into South America, where it is replaced in certain regions by two other very similar buteos, the Red-backed Buzzard and Gurney's Buzzard. These three hawks may in fact all be geographic forms of a single species, though each is presently accorded full species status, perhaps rightly so.

In Texas, the white-tail is most frequently seen in the flat transition habitats between the coastal beaches and the dense thorn-scrub vegetation farther inland. In this zone of open grasslands and marshes with scattered low shrubs, prickly pear, and Spanish daggers, the hawk finds very favorable hunting conditions for its primary prey of rabbits and other small mammals, and it often achieves quite dense local populations.

A prime example of good white-tail habitat exists in the coastal pasturelands lying just inland from Port Mansfield south through the Laguna Atascosa National Wildlife Refuge. Here, in the springs of 1987 and 1988, we had an opportunity to observe the activities of half a dozen pairs and become familiar with many aspects of their behavior. The birds had spaced their nests at distances of approximately a mile, and the low relief and open nature of the habitat allowed us to observe the entire foraging ranges of specific pairs from single vantage points.

Range of the White-tailed Hawk
◼ Breeding and wintering

White-tailed hawks are aerial hunters who prosper in the coastal gales. Hanging high in the sky, they face directly into the wind, with their long wings beating rarely, but nevertheless in constant motion extending in and out from the body, while their tails simultaneously flex up and down. By these adjustments, the birds maintain nearly stationary positions in the face of continual small variations in the steadiness of the winds.

In flight, the White-tailed Hawk bears a strong resemblance to the light phase of the Short-tailed Hawk, both in coloration and in behavior. Both species have light-colored tails with a dark subterminal band, light underparts, and dark cheeks. And both hunt mainly by hanging high in the wind, patiently inspecting the ground below.

The top surfaces of White-tailed Hawk nests are commonly lined with grasses—often whole grass plants including roots—an unusual sort of lining for a raptor, but a relatively soft one, like the moss lining of nests of Swallow-tailed Kites.

A female White-tailed Hawk gently descends to her nest in the brisk southeasterly winds. Blowing almost constantly, these winds provide steady uplift for nearly effortless hang-hunting by the hawks.

The windswept coastal prairies of southern Texas, with prickly pear, Spanish daggers, and scattered mesquites and huisache, form the principal North American habitat of the White-tailed Hawk, a raptor preying mainly on small terrestrial mammals and birds.

Poised perhaps two hundred feet from the ground, a foraging white-tail is not conspicuous to human observers, but it has a commanding view of the terrain and any potential prey leaving cover. Characteristically the hawk remains in one position for a fairly extended, leisurely inspection of the ground below, then drifts to another position, moving from one end of its territory to the other and back again in stages. When prey is sighted, the hawk begins an approach, often a long uninterrupted stoop to the ground. Sometimes, however, the bird makes a phased descent, pulling up short at intermediate heights, sometimes hovering for a second or two as if pondering the possibilities of success. Then finally, it either continues on down in a capture attempt, or thinking the better of the situation, shifts over to soar back up to greater altitudes and resume general scanning.

In many respects this hunting behavior strongly resembles that of the Short-tailed Hawk. Both species forage from such high altitudes that they are likely to be overlooked, and both hang in the wind as they patiently inspect the terrain for potential victims. It is also important to note that the details of shape and coloration for the light-phase forms of both species are strikingly similar. Both species have a short tail relative to their wingspread, and in both the tail is basically white with a dark band near the end. Further, both have dark gray or brown upperparts and largely white underparts with dark cheeks and a chestnut patch in the shoulder or neck region. Major differences between the species lie in overall size and in the fact that they concentrate on quite different prey—birds in the case of the short-tail, and mammals in the case of the larger white-tail. While the underlying causes of the great visual similarity of these two species are presently obscure, they represent an intriguing subject for future research.

Alarm cries of the White-tailed Hawk are a curious *raa kadick kadick kadick kadick* when disturbed at the nest, but the birds are not at all bold in defending nests and mainly circle so high overhead at such considerable distances that you hardly notice their scolding. Possibly because of the battering winds in the region, the white-tails generally place their substantial coarse nests in compact shrubs relatively close to the ground, eschewing sites in taller and less stable vegetation. Nests are often in bushes or Spanish daggers on small rises or dunes, where the birds have an unobstructed view of their surroundings and can detect the approach of potential predators from a great distance.

One nest we watched from a distance for a number of days was placed about eight feet from the ground in a mesquite tangled with vines. This nest was deeply concave and grass-lined. It held but a single egg, which we suspected may have been inviable, because most pairs in the region already had chicks at fledging age. This pair attended their egg only fitfully, and it appeared that they might well have been in the process of desertion, after having incubated long past the expected hatching date.

However, detailed studies of nesting pairs by Craig Farquhar have revealed that normal incubation of this species is surprisingly inconsistent. Pairs frequently leave their eggs unattended for several hours at a time, yet with no apparent detrimental effects on hatching success. This style of incubation represents a strong departure from the usual falconiform pattern. It is possible that what we interpreted as desertion behavior was in fact only typical incubation behavior.

At another nest only about four feet from the ground, we watched adults alternately feeding one fledged chick right on the ground and a chick still in the nest. Two other nests slightly higher from the ground also held two chicks apiece. Two chicks per nest appeared to be the norm, and they were very dark in color, quite unlike their parents in general appearance.

Aside from resident Bay-winged Hawks, Crested Caracaras, Black-shouldered Kites, Black Vultures, and Turkey Vultures, we found few other raptors in the region occupied by the white-tails. Migrating flocks of Broad-winged Hawks, Swainson's Hawks, and Mississippi Kites passed through in the early breeding season, but were largely gone by the time the white-tails had young in their nests. The virtual absence of Red-tailed Hawks was especially interesting in view of the widespread distribution and abundance of this species in North America. However, whether the rarity of red-tails here is a result of this species being an inferior competitor to the white-tails, as has been suggested by Tom Howell for Nicaragua, or the result of other more subtle factors, is not immediately obvious.

Red-tails are certainly capable of thriving in some habitats with strong winds, as we had earlier studied a dense population of this species hang-hunting over the very windy upper elevations of the Luquillo Mountains of eastern Puerto Rico. Likewise, it is questionable that the absence of tall trees for nesting in coastal Texas might be a serious impediment for red-tails, as this species readily nests in quite low yuccas in the grassland regions of New Mexico. A detailed comparative study of the red-tails and white-tails of southern Texas examining what factors limit distributions and reproductive success and how the two species interact could be of considerable interest in understanding why these species occupy the habitats they do.

Recent intensive studies of the white-tails by Mark Kopeny have revealed that the species has been experiencing a significant recent increase in abundance and range in Texas. Its overall ecology appears to be quite compatible with the cattle grazing practiced on most of the coastal prairies and scrublands. So long as these lands are not plowed under for crops or allowed to grow up to dense brush, the White-tailed Hawk should be able to endure as a most interesting resident of North America.

Buteos and Allies

Zone-tailed Hawk
BUTEO ALBONOTATUS

IT WAS A cool spring morning in the San Simon Valley of eastern Arizona in 1970. As we stopped by the side of the road, the usual Turkey Vultures were circling leisurely overhead in a tireless quest for carrion, while Cactus Wrens, Mourning Doves, and Gambel's Quail called from stations in the mesquite thickets. A peaceful scene; nothing out of the ordinary; nothing to suggest violence or stress. Then suddenly, one Turkey Vulture of a group of three partially folded its wings and powered into a stoop toward the ground in a remarkably unvulturelike maneuver. The stoop, as it turned out, was directed at a Mourning Dove, which just barely avoided capture by dodging to one side as the vulture came barreling in at a shallow angle out of the sun.

Was this really a Turkey Vulture? It certainly looked like one as it circled back up into the sky and hastened to rejoin its flock-mates, who had moved a half mile down the valley. The long wings tipped up at an angle from horizontal and the two-toned pattern of the wings all seemed normal for the species. However, a closer look through binoculars revealed that what seemed like a vulture's naked head was really just a bright yellow cere merging with a conspicuous naked patch of skin in front of the bird's eyes. The bird's head was otherwise fully feathered. And what we had taken to be excrement-covered white feet lying flush against its tail was actually a white band of the tail itself. What had appeared to be a Turkey Vulture gone crazy was really a Zone-tailed Hawk doing what it knows best – using its Turkey Vulture-like appearance to get close to unsuspecting prey.

That the Zone-tailed Hawk might be a true mimic of the Turkey Vulture was first pointed out by Edwin Willis in 1963 and has been vigorously debated ever since. Willis noted the close similarity in size, coloration, and flight characteristics of the two species and the fact that zone-tails do not occur outside the range of the Turkey Vulture. He also called attention to the curious black coloration of juvenile zone-tails, representing an abrupt departure from the usual streaked appearance of other young buteos, but which might be expected in a species dependent on its visual resemblance to the dark Turkey Vulture. Only at close range can white speckles be seen on the body feathers of juvenile zone-tails. From any distance they appear solid black. Willis's hypothesis was an excellent one, and one we have come to believe is very likely correct after watching this species on numerous occasions in southern Arizona and New Mexico.

The close association of zone-tails with Turkey Vultures extends much further than Willis suspected,

At her nest in southern Arizona a female zone-tail stands guard over her chick, awaiting the return of her mate with food. Most prey at this nest were open-country birds such as meadowlarks.

In Arizona, Zone-tailed Hawks often nest in tall streamside sycamores and cottonwoods, though they also commonly breed in pines at high elevations.

A female Zone-tailed Hawk stands guard near her nest. Long talons of this species are consistent with the fact that it often takes birds as prey.

In flight, the Zone-tailed Hawk bears a very close resemblance to the Turkey Vulture, especially in its uptilted two-toned wings and overall black coloration. Whether the zone-tail uses this resemblance to approach prey that normally consider the Turkey Vulture innocuous has been a controversy for decades.

Range of the Zone-tailed Hawk
☐ Breeding
▨ Breeding and wintering

for we have found that zone-tails in southern Arizona and New Mexico almost invariably nest very close to Turkey Vulture roosts, and the species has a strong tendency to fly with groups of Turkey Vultures as it hunts. While it is not difficult to tell the two species apart when they are at very close range, at the usual distances above the terrain that they forage, the similarities are uncanny. On more than one occasion we have been photographing zone-tails in groups of Turkey Vultures, only to find that once the photos were processed, many were of Turkey Vultures alone. We suppose that our difficulties in telling the two species apart represent the difficulties faced by other visually oriented species. It also seems reasonable to suppose that for those kinds of prey that can learn over time the futility of responding in panic to soaring Turkey Vultures, the close resemblance of the two species must allow zone-tails an important advantage in making close approaches without causing alarm.

Small birds are the sorts of prey that might be most capable of learning that Turkey Vultures are not a threat, and as we learned in observations of foraging zone-tails and in close study of pairs of zone-tails at their nests, small birds, such as meadowlarks and doves, form an important part of the zone-tail's diet. It would be remarkable if a slow-flying raptor like the zone-tail would be able to capture such prey without some special adaptations.

The relatively long toes and claws of the zone-tail also strongly suggest a dietary emphasis on birds. These characteristics are not usually found in buteo hawks, but are conspicuous in bird-specialists such as Peregrine Falcons and certain accipiters, presumably aiding these species in grasping prey covered by loose feathers. Zone-tails also take considerable numbers of lizards and mammals (in some areas they seem to concentrate quite heavily on lizards), and these are also prey that might be capable of learning Turkey Vultures are no danger.

Zone-tails do not always hunt together with Turkey Vultures, and when they are flying alone they appear to have greater difficulty deceiving potential prey. Over a period of several days in 1976, we watched the reactions of Mourning Doves feeding in an open field in southern Arizona as Turkey Vultures and zone-tails came in over the region. So long as the vultures and zone-tails came in as a group, we saw relatively little response in the doves, but if a zone-tail came in alone, they took off in a startled panic. Remarkably, they also often took off in alarm if Turkey Vultures came in singly. The doves seemed to have difficulties telling the two species apart, and appeared to be making their decisions as to whether to flee or not at least in part on the basis of how many Turkey Vulture-like birds were foraging together.

We saw these same responses repeatedly, so we have little doubt that we were observing a real difference in the responses of the doves to single and grouped birds. These observations suggested a strong advantage for zone-tails that ally themselves with Turkey Vultures in foraging. The extent of this advantage was apparently reflected in the success rates in capture attempts we recorded over the years. Of a total of forty-five attempts at prey when zone-tails were foraging alone, only 6.7 percent were successful. In contrast, of ten attempts made in the presence of Turkey Vultures, 30 percent were successful, a statistically significant difference. If future observations confirm this difference, it will constitute powerful evidence for the mimicry hypothesis.

In actual prey capture attempts, a zone-tail almost always delayed its stoop until after it had spotted prey and flown on some distance in typical leisurely Turkey Vulture fashion, although its eyes obviously remained glued to the prey. Once it had soared on out of view of the prey, it doubled back in a shallow stoop, taking full advantage of cover to get as close as possible to the prospective victim without being seen. As it neared the prey, the zone-tail finally darted out from cover at the last instant, catching its victim by surprise. Thus, the zone-tail apparently uses its resemblance to the Turkey Vulture mainly to locate prey without alarming it, and not actually in approaching prey in capture attempts.

Zone-tail hunts are tremendously exciting to witness. The main impediment to making observations lies in finding zone-tails in the first place. We have found it worthwhile to scan every group of Turkey Vultures encountered in the zone-tail's range; more than occasionally one individual in the group may in fact turn out to be one of these "invisible" black buteos.

The kind of mimicry apparently shown by the zone-tail is known as "aggressive mimicry," and for this type of mimicry, as well as for some other types, the whole system can break down if the mimic becomes too numerous with respect to numbers of the model species. Zone-tailed hawks, while not exceedingly rare, are very thinly spread in our southwestern states, and it is uncommon to find two pairs nesting closer than about five to six miles from one another. This highly dispersed distribution gives further support to the mimicry hypothesis. Overall, in a Texas-to-Arizona survey of this species we conducted in 1976 with Rich Glinski, we documented a total of only about a hundred known nesting locations north of the Mexican border. Although additional pairs undoubtedly exist in the states and although zone-tails also occur south through Central America into South America, they are not known to occur in dense concentrations anywhere.

The most surprising setting in which we have encountered Zone-tailed Hawks was the floodplain rain forest along the Manu River in southeastern Peru. Here in the spring of 1989, we found a zone-tail regularly hunting over a swale of dead palms that was home for a small nesting colony of Blue and Gold Macaws. Also cruising regularly over the area were Greater Yellow-headed Vultures, which are very similar at a distance to the Turkey Vulture and may serve as an alternative model species for the zone-tails of this region. Twice in one morning we watched the zone-tail dive into a vine-covered tree close by the macaw nests. Once it came up with a struggling lizard in its talons. We were not able to determine if the second attempt was also successful. Nevertheless, it is noteworthy that the bird returned to make a second capture attempt in the very same tree it had earlier hunted successfully. It was clearly the same bird, judging from several flight feather peculiarities.

In Arizona, zone-tails characteristically nest high in tall trees, sometimes in cottonwoods along desert streams, sometimes in pines in more mountainous regions. In contrast, some Texas zone-tails nest on cliff ledges. Clutch size of the species is usually only two eggs, but the eggs are quite large. One of the first people to recognize this fact was a renowned egg collector of the 1870s, Major Charles Bendire, who learned of its importance under unusual circumstances. It is worth repeating his account of this discovery, in his *Life Histories of North American Birds*, as a cautionary tale.

On May 3, I paid a second visit to this locality [Rillito Creek near Tucson] and found one of the birds [zone-tails] on the nest, where it remained until I rode up to the tree and rapped on it with the butt of my shotgun. This caused it to fly off about 50 yards farther up, on the opposite site of the dry creek bed, where it alighted in a smaller tree. As the bird appeared so very tame I concluded to examine the nest before attempting to secure the parent, and it was well I did so. Climbing to the nest I found another egg, and at the same instant saw from my elevated position something else which could not have been observed from the ground, namely, several Apache Indians crouched down on the side of a little cañon which opened into the creek bed about 80 yards farther up. They were evidently watching me, their heads being raised just to a level with the top of the cañon.

In those days Apache Indians were not the most desirable neighbors, especially when one was up a tree and unarmed; I therefore descended as leisurely as possible knowing that if I showed any especial haste in getting down they would suspect me of having seen them; the egg I had placed in my mouth as the quickest and safest way that I could think of to dispose of it – and rather an uncomfortably large mouthful it was, too – nevertheless I reached the ground safely, and with my horse and shotgun, lost no time in getting to high and open ground. . . . I found it no easy matter to remove the egg from my mouth without injury, but I finally succeeded, though my jaws ached for some time afterward.

Those who ignore the lessons of history are sometimes condemned to relive them. Having forgotten all about Major Bendire's travails, one of us, Noel, indeed had the misfortune to replicate them, on a more modest scale and with a different species – coincidentally not far from where the Major made his famous getaway. The setting was a particularly high Cooper's Hawk nest of 1970 that we were checking periodically to follow its progress. On the occasion in question, Noel could see from the ground that the nest contained well-developed nestlings, but on making the climb he found, unexpectedly, that the nest also contained an especially large, but inviable, egg. Since we were then routinely analyzing accipiter eggs for pesticide residues, it was important to collect this egg.

Unfortunately, there was no obvious way to get the egg safely to the ground. Noel had made the climb without any sort of pack and needed both hands free for the descent. Needless to say, the possibility of climbing all the way down and then all the way back up with a proper container was ruled out as too much trouble. Consequently, without any premonitions of disaster and without even any stimulus from nearby Apaches, he slid the egg casually into his mouth.

The descent of the tree was uneventful, except for our unsuspecting victim's growing appreciation that a whole addled Cooper's Hawk egg can have a very peculiar and unpleasant flavor. However, when it came time to remove the egg at the base of the tree, he found, like Major Bendire, that this was a most unbelievably difficult task. Jaws open only just so far, and the egg proved to be almost impossible to grasp and advance past the front teeth. The realization of this fact, coupled with a realization that the essence of stale Cooper's Hawk was rapidly soaking off the shell and heading straight for nausea centers of the brain, led to dark thoughts about oxygen deprivation, catastrophic convulsions, and cardiac arrest.

Did Major Bendire experience the same desperate thoughts? His published account is silent on this question. Since the egg he collected was fresh, rather than addled, he presumably missed out on some nausea values with his egg. But any advantage here might well have been overwhelmed by the urgency of his predicament with respect to the Apaches. In any event, the jammed Cooper's Hawk egg, like Major Bendire's zone-tail egg, only came free after a seemingly interminable period of painful jaw contortions.

In the long run, conservation of the Zone-tailed Hawk presents some interesting complications, as this species' survival may depend on the good health of its apparent model species, the Turkey Vulture. Turkey Vulture populations have been a subject of some concern in the southwestern states. Although the vultures still seem reasonably common, counts conducted by Amadeo Rea in recent years suggest progressive declines as a long-term trend. Should Turkey Vulture populations of this region ever drop below some hypothetical threshold, possibly the zone-tails would be unable to sustain themselves because of declines in hunting efficiency. Conservation of the zone-tail may make sense only if considered in tandem with conservation of the Turkey Vulture, and the factors limiting Turkey Vulture populations in the Southwest have not as yet received any detailed study.

Buteos and Allies
Common Black Hawk
BUTEOGALLUS ANTHRACINUS

WHEN FLYING, A Zone-tailed Hawk bears a strong resemblance to a Turkey Vulture; at rest the zone-tail is a twin of another species, the Common Black Hawk. Black hawks and zone-tails are very close to the same size, and both are completely dark in color, except for white bands on the tail. Moreover, both species can often be found nesting in the very same river bottoms in the southwestern states. The great similarity in appearance and range of these two hawks led to considerable confusion in early records of their occurrence, even among experienced naturalists. Confusions between the two continue to bedevil bird-watchers and to immerse many written accounts of the species in clouds of uncertainty.

Yet the two species can be readily distinguished by vocalizations, are shaped quite differently in flight, and feed on quite different prey. It does not seem likely that they are true mimics of each other. Soaring overhead, the black hawk displays much broader wings than the zone-tail, and its tail is quite short, projecting only a short distance beyond the trailing edge of the wings, quite unlike the long tail of the zone-tail. Another characteristic helping to distinguish these two species in flight is the presence of a small white patch at the base of the outer primary feathers in the black hawk and absence of this patch in the zone-tail. Once these differences are learned, it is relatively simple to separate the two species under most conditions.

Only during migration are you likely to see a Common Black Hawk at any distance from a permanent stream, so during much of the year any large black raptor with a white band on the tail flying over dry desert regions will almost surely turn out to be a zone-tail. The black hawk is closely tied to aquatic ecosystems both for feeding and nesting, and while zone-tails sometimes nest near black hawks, they feed in a great variety of ecological zones, many of them far from water. Were it not for the fact that tall trees are concentrated near streams in the desert regions, the zone-tails probably would not show any significant tendency to nest in the same areas as black hawks.

Unlike the zone-tails, black hawks are perch hunters, carefully scanning the riparian forest floor and streambeds from positions relatively low in trees or from prominent rocks in the watercourses. From such vantage points they are able to locate the fish, frogs, snakes, lizards, and aquatic insects that form their usual diet. Black hawks characteristically catch their prey in short descending pounces from perches, and although they eat a mix of terrestrial and aquatic prey, aquatic creatures make up the bulk of the species' diet throughout its North American range. Farther south, in Central and South America, the Common Black Hawk also concentrates on aquatic fare. There it often occurs in mangrove swamps, where it is an enthusiastic predator of crabs and is known regionally as the Crab Hawk.

North of the Mexican border, the Common Black Hawk breeds exclusively along well-wooded permanent watercourses. Such habitat is quite limited in the southwestern states, and in 1976 and 1977, we conducted an extensive survey with Rich Glinski of the black hawk population of the states, hiking many of the permanent streams of Arizona and New Mexico to find nesting pairs and to evaluate detailed habitat preferences of the species. This was a thoroughly enjoyable project, taking us through some of the wildest country of the Southwest, and yielded an overall estimate of about two hundred pairs. These were largely concentrated in Arizona and to a lesser extent, New Mexico, although a very few pairs also occur in Texas and occasionally in southern Utah.

The center of distribution is along the streams draining the Mogollon Rim country into the Salt, Gila, and Verde rivers of central Arizona. This is a wild roadless region of Indian reservations and forested mountain streams that still remains largely inaccessible to all but the most dedicated hikers. Here, in the best riparian habitats, we found some stretches where black hawk pairs were spaced at intervals as close as a mile to a mile and a half from one another.

The streams of this region are notable for placid stretches lined with cottonwoods, sycamores, walnuts, and alders alternating with vertical red-rock gorges too narrow to allow the development of any riparian vegeta-

Range of the Common Black Hawk
☐ Breeding
▨ Breeding and wintering

At a nest in a sycamore along a tributary of the Gila River, the parent black hawks brought in a great variety of foods for their single chick. Included were water snakes, frogs, and fish so large the birds could hardly carry them. In Central America, the species also takes large numbers of crabs.

In flight, the Common Black Hawk is broader-winged and shorter-tailed than the Zone-tailed Hawk, though the color patterns of the two species are very similar.

High-quality habitat for Common Black Hawks is found along the permanent streams draining the Mogollon Plateau of central Arizona. Here the hawks nest primarily in cotton-woods and sycamores and feed intensively on fish and other aquatic life.

The vocalizations of the Common Black Hawk differ markedly from those of the Zone-tailed Hawk and allow certain identification of the birds around nests. Whereas zone-tails give thin descending whistles in alarm, black hawks give a series of sputtering short notes that are quite reminiscent of the calls of Bald Eagles.

tion. In many stretches, the only way to follow the canyon bottoms is to wade and swim down the watercourses themselves, hoping that forward progress will not be blocked by nonnegotiable waterfalls or chutes. The polished rock surfaces slickened by a surface layer of algae often urge you along faster than seems safe, and it is sometimes impossible to see far enough ahead to anticipate difficult stretches before being thrust into them. Too narrow and too broken up with boulders and debris to allow boating or rafting, many of these streams present an unending succession of unpredictable challenges and should not be attempted alone and without waterproof containers for food and other gear. Flash floods from the summer thunderstorms can close off escape routes along the canyon bottoms within minutes and leave a hiker stranded for many hours.

Despite the difficulties, the black hawk's domain is an entrancingly beautiful one of stream-chiseled rock formations and grotesque flood-battered tree trunks piled high with debris on their upstream sides. The deep clear pools provide welcome refreshment from the midday heat and a source of aquatic insects to sustain many of the resident birds of the region. American Dippers concentrate on the larvae and nymphs of these insects, and submerge themselves completely beneath the water surface to hunt their victims. Emerging adult insects are vulnerable to Black Phoebes sallying from boulder to boulder along the water's edge. Those insects reaching higher elevations above the water must take their chances with swifts and swallows coursing ceaselessly overhead. Canyon Wrens also take their toll, and proclaim their ownership of the precipitous rocky walls with loud cascading calls that ring and echo down the chasms.

The black hawks are most commonly found along the more peaceful stretches, but generally keep just ahead and out of sight around the bend. Only at nests do they make a stand and challenge an intruder with angry cries, flying from tree to tree, landing on rocky outcrops of the canyon walls, or circling overhead. The alarm calls of the hawks are very reminiscent of the alarm cries of Bald Eagles: a series of sputtering, staccato notes very different from the long drawn-out tremulous screams of nesting Zone-tailed Hawks.

In 1976 and 1977, we watched a number of pairs of black hawks from blinds and found them to be reasonably tolerant of such observations. Our primary study pair was nesting in a tall sycamore along a tributary of the Gila River. The nest, which was reachable by a sixty-foot caving ladder, held only one chick, and he was being very well fed on a diet of frogs, fish, and snakes, some of which were so large that the birds were barely able to carry them to the nest. The adults kept the nest well decorated with greenery, and it was a substantial platform of twigs in a sturdy crotch of the sycamore. Such nests are often strong enough to last for many years and to be reused many times by the hawks. Probably more than half the nests we have found over the years have been built on limb junctions where large dead branches have fallen into live crotches, providing especially well-braced support for the structures.

Common Black Hawks nesting in North America generally arrive in March and depart again in October. Egg laying normally starts in April, and the clutch usually consists of only one or two eggs. Young most commonly hatch in late May and fledge in July, but they remain dependent on their parents for food through August and into September. As they develop, juvenile black hawks, unlike juvenile zone-tails, acquire a streaked brown plumage similar to the juvenile plumage of most all buteonine raptors. After fledging, they tend to remain within the territories of their parents until their first fall migration. Black hawks normally migrate solitarily, though we have sometimes seen a number pass by during a single October day along mountain ridgelines of southern Arizona.

For many years, Jay Schnell has made a thorough study of the Common Black Hawks of Aravaipa Creek in eastern Arizona. Here the hawks occupy a very narrow canyon bottom incised in a region of towering cliffs and are especially dependent on aquatic prey as there is very little area of bottomlands adjoining the stream flowing through the canyon. In close observations at nests, Jay has found that more than 70 percent of their diet is fish and frogs, mostly caught within quite short distances of the nests.

The black hawk pairs of Aravaipa have formed an exceedingly stable array over the years, and this canyon constitutes one of the most reliable, and certainly one of the most spectacular, locations for finding the species in North America. Here black hawk pairs are interspersed with pairs of Zone-tailed Hawks and Cooper's Hawks along the riparian zone. Higher slopes and cliffs of the canyon host Peregrine Falcons, Prairie Falcons, and Golden Eagles. Fortunately, the security of this thriving community of diurnal raptors is well assured by inclusion of a large portion of the canyon in a preserve of the Nature Conservancy and a wilderness area of the Bureau of Land Management.

Although the United States population of Common Black Hawks appears to be self-sustaining at present, the species exhibits a relatively low reproductive rate and is not the sort of raptor that could absorb much in the way of increased threats of mortality or habitat destruction. Unfortunately, as we have discussed earlier, many cottonwood riparian areas of the Southwest are suffering from overgrazing and invasion by exotic salt cedar. In addition, the introduction of exotic watercress into the perennial streams may be reducing foraging opportunities for the black hawks in some regions—dense mats of this surface plant may significantly obscure the visibility of prey to the hawks, just as dense mats of floating water hyacinth are a problem for Everglade Kites in some areas of Florida. Furthermore, the riparian zones of Arizona and New Mexico are in high demand as recreation areas and for housing developments. In accessible riparian areas, Common Black Hawks have not been faring well in the face of human disturbance and harassment. One nesting female of a pair we had been monitoring along a relatively heavily used creek in east-central Arizona in 1977 was shot right on the nest, a fate that others have undoubtedly met as well.

The conservation of the Common Black Hawk depends on maintaining important regions of riparian habitat, like that found in the Aravaipa Canyon preserve, free from excessive development and disturbance. Less than half of the known black hawk nesting territories are on public lands, and the long-term future of many of the private lands on which the bird lives is uncertain. Unfortunately, black hawks do not occur commonly in the recently created San Pedro Riparian Preserve of the Bureau of Land Management. The primary protection for the species at present comes from the remoteness of many regions where it does occur.

Buteos and Allies

Bay-winged Hawk
PARABUTEO UNICINCTUS

ONE OF THE most intriguing birds of the Sonoran Desert of southern Arizona is the Bay-winged Hawk, also known as Harris' Hawk. These hawks often place their nests in the arms of giant saguaro cacti, and they often use the tops of the saguaros as hunting perches. Yet Bay-winged Hawks are not limited to saguaro-dominated deserts. They also do well in various thorn-scrub brushlands and have been expanding their range in such habitats in recent years. In the last two decades, populations have become established in mesquite-dominated regions of the San Simon and Sulfur Springs valleys of eastern Arizona, for example, and the species has long been a resident of mesquite thickets in many other regions. The Bay-winged Hawk, as a whole, has a North American range that extends from the Colorado River basin in the west to central Texas in the east, and it also occurs as a common raptor in brushy country south through Central America and into South America.

In appearance, the bay-wing is a medium-sized raptor, whose chief distinguishing features are an overall dark brown coloration, set off by handsome chestnut patches on the legs and shoulders. The underwing coverts are also a rich chestnut color and give the bird a very attractive pattern in flight. From a distance, another of the most obvious features of coloration is a conspicuously white base to the tail, visible either from above or below. Immatures are fairly similar to adults in appearance but possess a streaked brown and white breast instead of a solidly dark-brown breast.

The biology of the bay-wings is highly unusual. Unlike any other North American hawks, they commonly breed in groups, with more than two adult birds attending many nests. They also hunt in groups and commonly breed several times a year. Moreover, they occupy some of the most rigorous habitats with respect to temperature extremes of any North American raptor.

Intensive research on these peculiarities was started by Bill Mader in the early 1970s and has been continued in more recent years by Jim Dawson, Jim Bednarz, and others. Bill Mader's pioneering studies in Arizona revealed that many nests of Bay-winged Hawks were attended by trios of adults, in every case studied, a female with two adult males. And in at least several cases, he was able to determine that both males copulated frequently, and apparently successfully, with the female, so it seemed very possible that true polyandry was involved, with both males contributing genetically to the broods. Whether or not both males actually fertilized eggs, all members of the trios he studied helped feed

Range of the Bay-winged Hawk
▨ Breeding and wintering

the broods and defend the nests, and overall, Bill found that trios appeared to be much more productive of young than pairs. Follow-up studies by Wayne Whaley in the same region also indicated that groups of bay-wings hatched and fledged more young than did pairs.

More recent studies of a large color-banded population in Arizona by Jim Dawson have revealed a bewildering diversity of reproductive patterns in the species. In Dawson's study area, which overlapped Mader's and Whaley's study areas, Bay-winged Hawks also commonly bred in groups, but Dawson's groups most commonly consisted of more than three birds, often including peripheral individuals who rarely came close to nests, but nevertheless passed food to the "core" bay-wings attending the nests. The existence of these peripheral individuals was only determined by careful long-term observations from blinds. The composition of groups attending nests was highly variable, ranging from pairs, to polygynous assemblages of one male with several females, to a more common association of one female with several males. One nest we were shown by Dawson in 1989 was tended by two males and two females. Each male copulated with both females, and both females closely attended the brood.

Most commonly, Dawson's breeding groups appeared to be family groups in which fledglings, especially males, retained an association with their parents for several years. Nevertheless, some group members were immigrants from other families, and helpers were by no means restricted to young males. While more than one male typically attempted copulations with the single egg-laying female generally found in each group, only one male was seen to copulate successfully with this female in most groups. So while polyandry and polygyny definitely occur in some groups, as demonstrated conclusively by genetic analyses of offspring, the usual pattern appears to be monogamous pairs assisted by one or more nonbreeding helpers, mostly previous offspring.

Monogamous pairs assisted by helpers have also been the usual pattern reported for Bay-winged Hawks in New Mexico by Jim Bednarz. But farther east, in Texas, several recent studies of Bay-winged Hawks have indicated that group breeding is rare. Thus, the reproductive strategies employed by the species vary considerably both within areas and on a geographic basis. The causes of this variability have not yet been determined with certainty.

Bay-winged Hawks are surprisingly docile raptors, rarely showing strong aggression to one another within groups, although Jim Dawson has found that groups

Above: In Arizona, Tucson's Bay-winged Hawks often use the limbs of giant saguaros as hunting perches. From such viewpoints they can efficiently detect the rabbits and quail that form a large fraction of their diet. Right: A fledgling Bay-winged Hawk ends his first tentative flight atop the fruit-laden arm of a saguaro. Fledglings, especially males, often retain an association with their parents for several years and assist in caring for later broods.

do maintain well-defined exclusive territories, which are defended from other groups by aggressive interactions when intrusions occur. For the most part, territorial violations are rare, with the various groups avoiding trespass of each other's territorial boundaries. When violations occur, however, the intruders are quickly driven from the territories by harassing flights of the territory owners. Earlier reports that the species was nonterritorial seem to trace mainly to the observers' failure to recognize that apparent intruders who have been tolerated by nesting birds were actually members, often peripheral members, of the groups attending the nests, and were not really intruders from other groups.

Within groups, the extent of tolerance between individuals is extraordinary. In fact, the birds commonly land and perch peacefully on top of one another on saguaros under circumstances that apparently have nothing to do with mating behavior or aggression. Such behavior, known as "backstanding," sometimes involves as many as two birds stacked up in series on top of a third for periods up to several minutes.

At least in part, this great mutual tolerance is very likely related to frequent cooperative hunting within groups. As first studied by Bill Mader and later investigated by Jim Dawson and Jim Bednarz, group hunting is highly developed in the species and groups enjoy much greater success in foraging than do individuals. In part, the increase in success with group size occurs because team hunting makes it feasible for the hawks to kill prey that are normally safe from capture, especially prey that have taken cover in dense vegetation. With some individuals working actively to flush prey from cover while others stand by ready to capture it in the open, the prey have few chances for escape. In one such capture we witnessed with Jim Dawson in 1989, a group of five bay-wings piled in successively on a cottontail rabbit, diving right into the brush and quickly dispatching the unlucky animal.

The prey taken are frequently large enough to provide food for several individuals, so that all can share in the rewards of group hunts. The birds find themselves highly interdependent in foraging as a result. The advantages of cooperative foraging may also underlie the strong tendency for the species to breed in groups. When only two individuals cooperate in breeding, group hunting is difficult during much of the breeding cycle—the incubation and early nestling periods.

Bay-winged Hawks are primarily dependent on mammals for food, but Bill Mader's studies indicate that they also take birds with considerable frequency. His research well illustrates the importance of proper methodology for diet studies of raptors. Bill compared his blind observations of the kinds and amounts of prey adults brought to nests with the feather, fur, and bone remains found in the same nests during the same periods of time. By direct observations, over 35 percent of the diet was birds, but by examination of prey remains, the proportion of birds was only 17.5 percent, a difference presumably resulting from a relative impermanence of bird remains in nests. A similar difference in determining bay-wing diet by direct observations and by prey remains has been confirmed by Jim Dawson. Thus, the use of prey remains to determine diet of this species can lead to major errors, and should be avoided unless it can be confirmed independently that prey remains give relatively unbiased estimates for the particular bay-wing population in question.

The same problem occurs in other species. Jim Wiley, for example, has found major biases in using prey remains to establish the nesting diet of Red-shouldered Hawks, and we have found unacceptably large biases in using such data to determine the nesting diet of Cooper's Hawks. Yet many studies of the food habits of falconiform species continue to be based only on prey remains at nests, with no attempts made to determine just how realistic the data are. Comprehensive observations of raptors from blinds are often the only way to gain reliable information on many aspects of their biology.

The Bay-winged Hawk's relatively strong dependence on birds for food is reflected in its possession of two morphological features that seem to cut across essentially all groups of raptors. Like other bird-feeding hawks, bay-wings have relatively long toes and claws and exhibit a strong size difference between sexes. The long toes and claws apparently aid in gripping elusive prey covered by hard-to-grasp feathers. Just how the size difference between sexes relates to bird-feeding has been much more controversial, as we have already discussed in the chapter on the Sharp-shinned Hawk. The Bay-winged Hawk, despite its extremely unusual breeding and foraging habits, exhibits the expected amount of size dimorphism for its diet, a fact that may prove crucial in the ultimate evaluation of various hypotheses concerning size dimorphism, especially those that relate dimorphism to various social interactions, such as pair-bonding.

The tendency of Bay-winged Hawks to breed more than once a year has now been confirmed in great detail, both by Bill Mader, Jim Dawson, and Wayne Whaley in Arizona and by Jim Bednarz in New Mexico, and places this species among a very limited group of raptors. The only other North American falconiforms known to regularly produce more than one brood a year are Everglade Kites, Black-shouldered Kites, some populations of American Kestrels, and apparently some Crested Caracaras. All are species that occur in the southern reaches of North America and are largely year-round residents in their breeding ranges. The nesting cycles of most raptors are sufficiently long that seasonal constraints largely rule out multiple-brooding, especially if the species are migratory.

In the Everglade Kite, extremely long breeding seasons coupled with highly unpredictable food supplies have apparently been important factors leading to the development of regular mate desertion as a component of multiple-brooding. Bay-winged Hawks have a breeding season nearly as long as that of the Everglade Kite (ten months of the year in some areas), yet mate desertion is at most a very rare occurrence in this species. Instead, the composition of breeding groups has been quite stable in successive breeding attempts. Under good conditions, groups have begun new breeding attempts long before fledglings from previous breeding attempts have become independent–thus overlapping their investments in nesting attempts through time. Such overlap may be one of the important advantages of group breeding, because with additional individuals to care for fledglings, there is less potential conflict of interest in caring for more than one breeding attempt simultaneously.

Why have Everglade Kites developed a mate-desertion strategy coupled with ephemeral use of nesting territories? And, in contrast, why have Bay-winged Hawks, at least in some areas, adopted a strategy of overlapping broods with stable pair-bonds, helpers at nests, and stable territories? The differences may have been produced largely by the regularity with which the two species approach the limits of their respective food supplies. Everglade Kites, with their boom-or-bust population trends, may be chronically "under-populated" under good food conditions, and there may generally be ample space for individuals to find good new feeding areas and form new pair relationships. Bay-winged Hawks, with their much more stable populations, may commonly approach saturation of their favored habitats. There may be few openings available for new pairs to exploit, thus making mate desertion and ephemeral pair-bonds unprofitable strategies, especially if they might lead to reductions in the sizes and hunting success of foraging groups.

In August of 1974, we had a chance to join Bill Mader for several days to observe Bay-winged Hawk nests in his study area. One nest was twenty feet up in a saguaro cactus, and here we were able to see the single youngster take his first flight and make his first uncertain landing on the thorny top of a fruit-laden saguaro limb. Stepping gingerly on the thorns, he had his first taste of a chronic problem that all bay-wings have to cope with in this region–impalement. By the time they reach independence, bay-wings must learn how to pull cactus thorns out of the bottoms of their feet or suffer severe consequences. Most become adept in this process, using their bills to pluck out the offending needles from one foot while standing on the other, never seeming to conclude that perching on cactus might not be worth the pain and trouble involved.

The other nest we observed with Bill Mader was about ten feet up in a palo verde and held only downy chicks. The bay-wings at this nest were remarkable in that they were also still caring for a hopelessly crippled fledgling from a previous nesting attempt, a bird that could not fly or forage effectively on its own. While the efforts of the adults to rear this fledgling were doomed to failure and were a wasted investment in a genetic sense, the adults very likely had no way to determine whether the fledgling was beyond recovery. What emotions these hawks may have felt in continuing their solicitous care can only be conjectured, but it is impossible not to consider parallels with human treatment of the infirm and terminally ill.

By standing in the nest cup and providing shade in which the youngsters could huddle, the adults at the palo verde nest sheltered their brood as best they could from the hot midday sun. Midsummer temperatures in the deserts near Tucson often reach 110 to 115 degrees Fahrenheit, a severe stress for all wildlife in the area. That the Bay-winged Hawk can breed successfully in such a rigorous environment is yet one more component of the remarkable adaptability of this most unusual species.

Sadly, the saguaro habitats of southern Arizona are being rapidly lost to housing developments. Suburbia has now nearly submerged the study area of Bill Mader that we visited in 1974, and when we again visited the area in 1989 with Jim Dawson, we were amazed by the extent of the changes. The entire region between Tucson and Phoenix is on its way to becoming a giant sprawling city, and this can only have major impacts on the bay-wings living there. While we were encouraged to see that the species can still do relatively well in partially developed areas, often nesting in backyard orna-

Known as "gang hawks" for their tendency to hunt in groups, Bay-winged Hawks in flight reveal conspicuous white tail bases that are hidden in perched birds.

Above: The female of the palo verde nest in Arizona's Sonoran Desert was highly solicitous of her young, shading them from the broiling midday sun and feeding them the prey supplied by the two male adults.

146

Nestling Bay-winged Hawks in the Sonoran Desert regions of Arizona face some of the most rigorous temperature extremes endured by any diurnal raptor species. Possibly because daytime temperatures often reach 110 to 115 degrees Fahrenheit, pairs of this species tend to nest only where they have access to reliable water supplies.

The low Sonoran Desert flatlands near Tucson, Arizona, support dense populations of Bay-winged Hawks. The giant saguaro cacti and palo verdes provide shelter and food for many prey species, as well as nest sites and hunting perches for the hawks.

In perching on cactus, such as this prickly pear, Bay-winged Hawks often wind up with thorns imbedded in their feet. Most individuals become expert in removing these thorns with their bills.

mental trees, it still hangs on only in areas that contain at least fair amounts of native habitat. If thoughtful zoning laws could be developed that would preserve substantial patches of native vegetation, possibly the Bay-winged Hawk could continue to survive in this region. It does not exhibit any strong behavioral intolerance of people here, and residents generally leave it unmolested.

Before we condemn development pressures too strongly, however, it is also well to consider a potentially important correlation noted by Jim Dawson in his studies. Bay-winged Hawks in the Tucson area seem to show a strong distributional correlation with availability of water. Much of the available water in this region comes in the form of artificially constructed cattle ponds, and Jim has frequently observed the hawks gathering at such ponds to drink. Where such ponds have not been created, the hawks seem to be much more sparse than where ponds exist, and the abundance of bay-wings in the region may actually be closely dependent on partial development of lands for cattle-grazing purposes.

Finally, it is important to consider that in the long term, the Bay-winged Hawks of this region may be affected by changes in the distribution of one of their primary hunting-perch trees, the saguaro cactus itself. As has been well documented for the Tucson region in the past century, saguaros have been slowly disappearing from low elevation flatland regions while they have been simultaneously increasing on steep mountain slopes, apparently because of warming climatic trends. Bay-winged Hawks are essentially limited to the flatland regions, and if trends continue, the saguaros may march right out of the bay-wing's range into the mountains. Together with other vegetation changes, the decline in saguaro populations might greatly decrease the quality of future habitats available for the bay-wings in the region, quite apart from the changes caused by urbanization.

Ospreys

Above: Darkness descends on an Osprey nest in a black mangrove snag of Everglades National Park. When such snags are available in proximity to good food supplies, they are favored nest sites for the species, but in areas lacking such sites the species sometimes even nests on the ground. Left: Even in migration far from water, Ospreys often carry fish, as though they are reluctant to risk such journeys without a guaranteed food supply.

Osprey
PANDION HALIAETUS

NO RAPTOR EXHIBITS greater skills in capturing fish than the Osprey. Certain other species, such as the Bald Eagle and the Common Black Hawk, also take fish with fair frequency. But none pursues this prey with anything like the Osprey's single-minded focus, and none captures fish with the same heroic crashing dives from high in the sky.

Aiding the Osprey in its foraging are a number of anatomical peculiarities. Dense, oily feathers provide protection against immersion. Curiously crooked wings may adapt the species for jolting collisions with the water surface and subsequent lift-offs into the air. Unusually long legs with very short stiff feathers allow a low-resistance penetration of the bird's talons through the water to the depths occupied by prey. Highly curved talons and feet soled with spiny spicules help it grip slippery prey. The species is clearly a specialist locked anatomically to its food supply, much as the Everglade Kite is structurally matched to a diet of snails with its long, nearly straight talons and bizarrely shaped bill. To be sure, Ospreys have occasionally been documented taking nonpiscine prey such as birds and mammals, but such events are highly exceptional.

The Osprey is also unusual in being the only diurnal raptor besides the Black-shouldered Kite and the Peregrine Falcon to have a nearly worldwide distribution. Never found far from water, except during migration, this species is entirely dependent on healthy aquatic ecosystems, and where fish are especially abundant, it is sometimes found nesting in substantial colonies. Such colonies were once known for Gardiner's Island and Plum Island in Long Island Sound, Lake Istokpoga in Florida, and until recently, the upper keys of Florida Bay. Donald J. Nicholson, for example, found seventy-five occupied Osprey nests on relatively modest-sized Lake Istokpoga in 1910, and we saw as

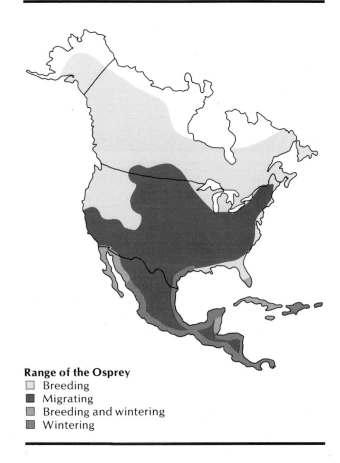

Range of the Osprey
☐ Breeding
■ Migrating
▨ Breeding and wintering
▨ Wintering

many as a couple dozen Osprey nests simultaneously active on a single small island in the northern keys of Florida Bay during the late 1960s.

Sometimes elevated nest substrata are unavailable in regions of favorable food supplies. Under such conditions, and if sites safe from terrestrial predators exist, Ospreys occasionally build nests right on the ground. We have seen ground nests in the Florida Keys, and ground nesting was a common trait for the Osprey colony of some three hundred pairs on Gardiner's Island many years ago. Normally, however, Ospreys are well known for their choices of highly conspicuous nesting sites at the tops of towering trees and dead snags, or on power poles, duck blinds, channel markers, communications towers, and even billboards. One renowned pair in southern Florida built their nest atop the boom of a temporarily idle construction crane. The owner, to his everlasting credit, retired the crane from active duty, allowing the Ospreys to follow through with their nesting efforts.

Although Ospreys do not hesitate to make deep dives that carry them completely under the water in their attempts to capture fish, they most typically take fish available close to the surface, such as mullet and pike. Nevertheless, they occasionally tackle prey too large to lift from the water. Not always able to extricate their talons from such prey, they may occasionally drown as a result. Early reports of large fish being recovered with Osprey skeletons still attached apparently trace to such blunders.

Ospreys may also make fatal mistakes in attempting to take fish capable of counterattack. On one occasion, as we were boating in northern Florida Bay in 1971, we happened upon an Osprey floating at the surface that may have made just such an error. This bird was totally exhausted and waterlogged and made no effort to flee our approach. When we hauled it into our skiff, we found that it had a deep abdominal wound which had allowed sea water to enter its body cavity, apparently weighing the bird down to such an extent that it was impossible for it to become airborne. After allowing the sea water to drain from its body cavity, we wrapped the bird in spare clothing to prevent it from struggling and to allow it to regain its normal body temperature. Later we gave the bird to John Ogden, who was then studying the Ospreys of the region. The bird recovered quite quickly, and John was able to release it successfully near where we had found it. Although we can only speculate about what had happened to this Osprey, our best guess is that it may have grabbed a large sea catfish by the tail, only to have the dangerous pectoral spines of its struggling victim slash into its abdomen.

Like Everglade Kites, Ospreys are very active in foraging, using flapping flight and hovering for the most part as they search for food from heights of about fifty to one hundred feet above the water surface. For a relatively large bird such as the Osprey, such flight is energetically demanding, but there are few opportunities for the species to hunt from perches, and the thermals or topographic updrafts adequate for continuous soaring are characteristically missing over bodies of water.

Colin Pennycuick has calculated that sustained flapping flight is energetically impossible for birds that exceed about twenty pounds in weight, and indeed the larger vultures, such as the California Condor, do not employ flapping flight for more than brief bursts. The Osprey falls well below this aerodynamic limit, at a body weight of three to four pounds and a wingspread of five to six feet, although it is far larger than many raptors that hunt primarily from soaring flight. Only when migrating over terrestrial regions is the Osprey able to consistently conserve energy by soaring in thermals and topographic updrafts. But even in migration, Ospreys commonly carry fish, as if they are greatly concerned about keeping their energy reserves in good shape.

Male Ospreys also sometimes carry prey for extended periods during display flights over their nesting areas, flapping and hovering vigorously, with their bodies inclined at a steep, almost vertical angle, and at the same time calling repeatedly with loud *chereeeeks*. These flights are highly conspicuous and may serve primarily to convince females of the physical stamina of their mates. Females generally remain perched at their nests during these displays, just as they remain very attentive at their nests during most of the nesting cycle. Almost all hunting through to the end of the nestling period is done by males.

Adult Ospreys are basically black above and white underneath. They have white heads, except for a black crown and a broad horizontal black line from the bill through the eye to the back of the neck. Nestling Ospreys, in contrast to nestlings of most other raptors, are highly cryptic, or camouflaged, in their first down—their mottled pattern makes them almost impossible to see in their nests from above. Such coloration suggests significant threats of predation from other avian species, as does the cryptic coloration of Osprey eggs and the very close attendance of female Ospreys at their nests. In North America, the threats may come primarily from Bald Eagles and various crows and ravens, and the conspicuous nature of Osprey nests makes them obvious targets for such species.

Osprey nests have also been favored targets for predation by people, especially by egg collectors, although this has been much more of a problem in Europe than in North America. Egg collecting as a hobby has now fortunately died out almost completely in the New World. Harassment by egg collectors, however, was an

When landing at the nest, Ospreys descend into the wind, feet outstretched to cushion the impact.

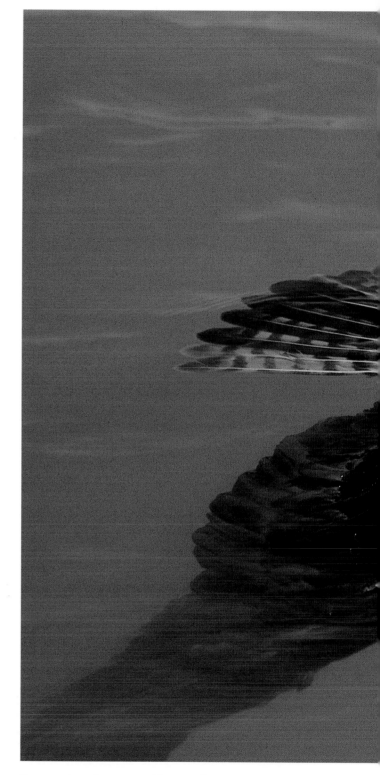

On occasion, Ospreys tackle prey that are risky to handle. This may have been the fate of this waterlogged bird found floating in Florida Bay with a giant gash in its abdomen.

In feeding on fish, Ospreys typically start with the head and work backwards. Their adaptations for such prey include feet that are soled with spicules to aid in gripping slippery individuals.

Through most of the breeding cycle, male Ospreys capture all prey for their families. This nest in the Florida Keys, only about five feet off the ground, was built largely of masses of turtle grass.

important factor in the loss of the Osprey population of Britain around the turn of the last century, and has been a major obstacle to the natural reestablishment of the species in Scotland, despite massive efforts to guard vulnerable nests. Nevertheless, the Ospreys which returned on their own to Scotland in the 1950s, apparently repopulating the country from Scandinavia, are still continuing to increase, and may yet come close to approaching their original abundance.

Both European and North American populations of Ospreys exhibit a curious migration pattern unknown for other raptors. Yearlings from north temperate regions migrate south in typical falconiform fashion, wintering in African and tropical American locations, respectively. But then instead of returning to their summer homes the following spring, the young Ospreys almost always remain on the wintering grounds through another whole year. They finally move northward in their third calendar year to enter the breeding populations near the nest sites where they hatched. Assuming adequate year-round food supplies in the wintering areas, and assuming that birds might still be too inexperienced in foraging to breed successfully in their second year, such a strategy, avoiding unnecessary migration, seems very sensible. Similar migratory strategies may eventually be documented in other long-lived species with delayed maturity and extensive migrations.

The Osprey was one of the species most severely stressed by organochlorine pesticides during the DDT era. Especially affected were the coastal populations of the northeastern states, such as those bordering on Long Island Sound, which were once among the densest populations of Ospreys known anywhere in the world. By the 1960s, the northeastern populations of Ospreys had crashed to near extinction, although a few pairs hung on in the region attempting, mostly unsuccessfully, to hatch eggs. Much of the decline was apparently due to direct mortality from dieldrin poisoning, but the surviving pairs were clearly also under heavy stress from DDE.

In an admirable effort to demonstrate that reproductive failure of the Long Island Sound population was in fact due to pesticide-stressed eggs, and also to enhance productivity of the Long Island Sound popula-

tion until pesticide levels might again subside to tolerable levels, Paul Spitzer and Stan Wiemeyer led a program in the late 1960s and early 1970s to substitute viable eggs from the still functional Osprey population of the Chesapeake Bay into the remaining Long Island Sound nests. This effort successfully boosted reproduction of the Long Island Sound birds through the crisis period, and with the more recent decline in levels of DDE and other pesticides in prey species of this region, the Ospreys are now showing a healthy increase on their own.

In addition to depending on control of environmental pollutants, overall conservation of the Osprey depends most of all on ensuring the basic productivity of its foraging habitat, and in many areas, ensuring that suitable nest sites are available. In past decades, coastal farmers of the eastern states often encouraged the establishment of breeding Ospreys near their homes by constructing artificial nests atop wagon wheels mounted on poles. Their rationale was that territorial Ospreys would protect domestic animals, such as chickens, from attack by other raptors. In areas where good fish supplies have existed and nest sites have been in short supply, such efforts have often enhanced Osprey numbers significantly. Nevertheless, expanded attempts to increase Osprey populations by such structures in more recent years have shown that these efforts will not accomplish very much in areas where fish populations are relatively low.

Recent population estimates for the lower United States indicate about eight thousand pairs of Ospreys concentrated in five main regions—the Atlantic Coast, Florida and the Gulf Coast, the Great Lakes, the northern Rocky Mountains, and the Pacific Northwest, with an additional eight hundred pairs in Baja California and the Gulf of California. Canada's Osprey population is apparently substantial, but population estimates are unavailable for most regions. Northern Quebec alone may hold two thousand pairs, and total numbers for the country may be many times this figure. Numbers in Alaska are relatively modest at about two hundred pairs, possibly because of strong competition from dense Bald Eagle populations. Overall, the species appears to be doing well, with recent declines seen in only a few areas, such as Florida Bay.

Eagles

Above: Many of the Bald Eagle nests of southern Florida in recent decades have been in giant black mangroves killed by Hurricane Donna of 1960. This awesome storm may also have benefited the eagles and other wildlife of the area by flushing large quantities of land-based nutrients into the bay and other estuarine areas. In more recent years, water diversion projects farther north and an absence of any major hurricanes have combined to deprive the region of much of the productivity that it had earlier. Left: The supremacy of the Bald Eagle is sometimes breached by lesser creatures. Around Osprey nests they are often forced into desperate barrel rolls to avoid the talons of their adversaries, and even crows sometimes drive them off with success.

Eagles

Bald Eagle
HALIAEETUS LEUCOCEPHALUS

ON A WINDLESS morning, the horizon of Florida Bay disappears in the distant haze, and the mangrove islands float motionless in a continuum of water and sky. Clouds in one realm have counterparts in the other, but which formations are real and which are reflection is difficult to determine.

Another realm lies hidden beneath the glassy surface of the bay, a shallow microcosm of soft marl muds and endless rank beds of turtle grass. This is the realm that powers the living world of the bay. Here marine plants combine dazzling light energy from the sun with carbon dioxide and other nutrients to form simple organic compounds – the basic foods that ultimately sustain the entire intricate web of interdependent organisms native to the region.

Long famed as a naturalist's paradise, Florida Bay nourishes a great variety of extraordinary creatures. Fins of nurse sharks, mullet, and porpoises crease the surface of the mangrove channels. Diamondback terrapins thrust their snouts into the air from the island lagoons. Strange *Cassiopeia* jellyfishes rest upside down on the soft mud bottom, displaying their flowerlike tentacles toward the surface. Overhead, scattered flocks of Roseate Spoonbills, White Ibis, and Brown Pelicans beat paths across the sky, while Reddish Egrets and other small herons stalk ceaselessly across the flats in pursuit of tiny killifishes. At night, essentially the entire North American populations of crocodiles and Great White Herons take over the shallows, waiting for larger fishes to move inshore to feed.

On the mangrove islands reside some of the largest colonies of nesting Ospreys and one of the most productive populations of Bald Eagles known for North America. As predators heavily dependent on waterbirds and large fishes, the eagles occupy a premier position in the food web of the bay, and reign as the crowning avian residents of the region. Here, perhaps more than anywhere else, this species seems to dominate its surroundings, matching in deeds what it claims by sublime appearances and truly earning its status as the national symbol of our country.

During the late 1960s and early 1970s, we often sought relief from university teaching duties in Tampa by weekend escapes to explore the wonders of Florida Bay. Launching our small skiff at first light from the marina at Flamingo, we left the modern world behind and entered a timeless world where the abundance of wildlife still seemed close to primeval. Our journeys most commonly took us out the old Homestead Canal to Cape Sable or out among the northwestern mangrove islands of the bay. But occasionally, we followed the tortuous channels through the Ten Thousand Islands north to Marco Island and beyond. Regardless of our route, we could count on unusual and memorable occurrences on most any day's boating. Many of these incidents involved the region's Bald Eagles, as they hunted their food and fought with other species over territory and prey.

The Bald Eagle is famous for its ability to force Ospreys to give up fish in midair, and several times during our boating days we had a chance to see this exciting piratic spectacle. Each time, the eagle used aggressive swooping dives to challenge an Osprey carrying prey high above us. Burdened with his prospective meal, the unfortunate Osprey was unable to distance himself from his tormentor and finally dropped the fish. The eagle, sensing victory, now peeled over into a vertical dive of feather-scorching speed to overtake and grab the fish before it hit the water. Few wildlife encounters can match the drama of these aerial thefts.

Less well known is that around Osprey nests, the

An enormous expanse of sky, sea, and sun, Florida Bay is a unique wilderness. The Bald Eagles of the Bay, many of them nesting on isolated mangrove islets, have long represented one of the most stable populations of this species in North America.

Young eagles do not normally attain fully white heads and tails until they are about six years old, and they do not commonly breed until fully adult in coloration. Such a prolonged maturation is common among the larger raptors and may in part be a reflection of the length of time it takes such birds to become fully skilled in foraging and other crucial activities.

A nestling eagle with a mullet awaits the return of its parents in a mangrove nest site of southern Florida. Mullet commonly swim close to the surface where they are vulnerable to Ospreys and Bald Eagles. Other prey taken frequently in this region include coots, various herons, and other waterbirds.

tables are often turned. Bald Eagles we watched intruding on nesting Ospreys in the bay had to summon all their acrobatic skills, including desperate sprints and barrel rolls, to avoid pummeling by this more agile species. Other inhabitants of the region, such as Common Crows, were also capable of driving off eagles that invaded their domains, so long as the eagles did not arrive with substantial initial advantages in altitude and speed.

The most thoroughly hostile greeting we have ever seen an eagle receive was bestowed on a bird that ventured too close to a nesting colony of Swallow-tailed Kites. This eagle, a resident of the northern Ten Thousand Islands, was mobbed by a whole flock of angry swooping assailants and left the area without delay. Despite a fully deserved reputation as a monarch of the skies, the Bald Eagle bows to lesser species on occasion.

On their own turf, the eagles assert full authority unchallenged. Characteristically choosing the tallest trees available, they make no effort to hide their nests from view and instead rely on their imposing size and demeanor to intimidate intruders. In the Florida Bay region, the tallest trees are almost always mangroves, sometimes living trees, sometimes skeletons left by hurricanes. But mangroves rarely grow very high, and the nests rarely are more than thirty feet from the ground. While still providing a commanding view over the surrounding terrain, such low nests do not compare with the towering tree nests used by the species in other regions.

Traditionally, nearly all the major mangrove islands of northwestern Florida Bay have each had a resident pair of nesting Bald Eagles as well as numerous pairs of Ospreys, while the islands farther south and east have had only sparser populations of these species. This spatial distribution has strongly suggested that productivity of the waters might be greatest where the nutrient-bearing freshwater runoff from the mainland and the Everglades meets the salt waters of the bay.

Sadly, despite inclusion of the entire region in Everglades National Park since 1947, the runoff from the glades no longer feeds the bay to the extent that it once did. The flow of water south has been increasingly diverted to the seas north of the park through a series of drainage canals. In addition, ever increasing amounts of Everglades water have been lost to domestic

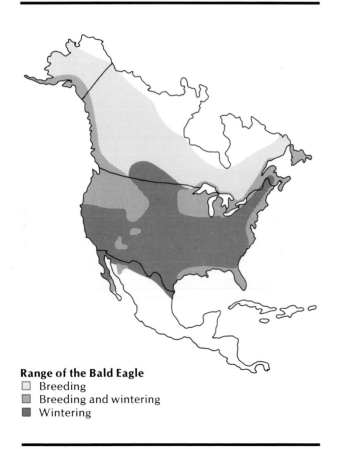

Range of the Bald Eagle
☐ Breeding
▨ Breeding and wintering
▰ Wintering

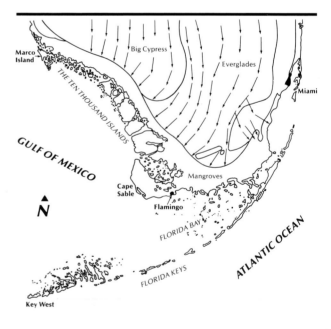

Southern Florida and Florida Bay
The arrows indicate the flow of surface water runoff, which no longer feeds the bay to the extent that it once did. The flow has been increasingly diverted to the seas north of the park, consumed by domestic and agricultural uses, and reserved in giant water conservation areas. The bay has been evolving from a highly productive estuary into a less fertile saltwater sea.

and agricultural uses of the human populations on the east and west coasts of the state. Finally, what waters have remained in the glades have been largely short-stopped in giant impoundments–the water conservation areas–that were finished in the 1960s. While the creation of these conservation areas very likely prevented the extirpation of the Everglade Kite in the short term, it has at the same time greatly constricted the very life blood of Florida Bay. The bay has been evolving from a highly productive estuary into a less fertile saltwater sea.

In part, the nutrient problems of Florida Bay may also be tied to the absence of any major hurricanes passing through the region in recent decades. Such storms, aside from their immediate detrimental effects on wildlife populations, periodically flush enormous amounts of nutrients into the bay from the mainland, and may be very important in sustaining the bay's productivity. While it may seem perverse to wish for hurricanes, they have been, and presumably still are, an important and natural component of the South Florida ecosystem. A direct hit by a major storm might now be the best thing that could happen for the overall ecological well-being of the region.

Regardless of just which causes have been most important, the evidence for progressive impoverishment of the wildlife of Florida Bay is strong. Intensive studies by George Powell, Jim Kushlan, Bill Robertson, and others indicate that many of the fish-eating birds of the bay, such as the Osprey, have been experiencing significant population losses in recent years. Some of these birds now have less than half the numbers of individuals that they did twenty years ago. The Bald Eagle population of the bay has held up much better than the populations of these other species, but concerns remain that it too may ultimately follow the others into decline.

Farther north in Florida, on the Kissimmee Prairie, in the central lakes region, and in wilderness areas near Gainesville, Bald Eagles have maintained substantial populations based on freshwater ecosystems, rather than on estuarine and saltwater conditions like those found in Florida Bay. Farther north still, on the Chesapeake Bay and in other regions of the northeastern and north-central states, the species has been making a dramatic comeback following the devastation wrought by the DDT era. Populations are also known to be increasing in certain regions of the western states, and have always appeared to be robust in the Pacific Northwest. The overall prospects for the Bald Eagle are not grim in the short term. The species has certainly been suffering local losses to housing developments and other forms of

human encroachment, but the total number of Bald Eagles in the United States and Canada is now estimated at a very healthy seventy thousand birds.

Bald Eagles precede most all other raptors of North America in breeding. Some pairs in the Florida population are known to begin egg laying as early as late October, and most have eggs no later than December or January. Early breeding in this population may be timed to allow adults a good food supply of wintering waterbirds for reproduction. Egg laying comes much later in more northerly populations, but even on the Chesapeake Bay commonly takes place in late February when nests are still buffeted by winter snowstorms. Alaskan Bald Eagles commonly commence incubation in April or May, a full half year after their Florida relatives.

Like most large raptors, Bald Eagles are not the most lively birds at their nests, though their noble appearance largely makes up for the leisurely pace of events. At nests we have watched from Alaska to various parts of Florida, the dominant spirit has always been one of lethargy, occasionally punctuated by periods of restrained activity when one or the other of the parent birds has arrived with a fish or waterbird in its talons. Feedings of chicks are conducted calmly and deliberately, with none of the frantic haste seen in many smaller raptors.

Hunting efforts of the species are spasmodic, and most individuals spend long periods perched, apparently waiting for promising foraging opportunities to come to them. Nevertheless, when the right opportunities arise, Bald Eagles do not hesitate to gear into frenzied efforts to seize victims. One adult we watched at a Florida nest commonly arrived nearly exhausted when he brought in prey, and sat panting heavily on a snag before taking the prey the rest of the way to the nest.

Renowned as fish-eaters, Bald Eagles are actually quite flexible in their diets, and like the Crested Caracara, are one of the few raptor species that commonly take turtles. In Florida, the diamondback terrapin often finishes its career in an eagle nest. Bald Eagles do not normally capture fish in the deep plunging dives characteristic of Ospreys, but generally snatch them right at the water surface in very shallow swoops. Birds and carrion also form very important parts of the diet, and in some regions the eagles turn heavily to mammals, such as rabbits, for food.

In California, Bald Eagles sometimes winter in the foraging range formerly used by the California Condor. During the mid-1980s, we occasionally had them come in to feed on calf carcasses put out for the condors. These Bald Eagles were much more sedate in behavior and much more tolerant of one another at carcasses than were the Golden Eagles feeding in the same region. The use of rangeland habitats by Bald Eagles, while surprising to those accustomed to seeing the species only in aquatic settings, is actually quite common, especially in the western states.

At distances too great for us to see details of head color, immature Bald Eagles were the species most easy to confuse with the California Condor. General tail and wing proportions of the two species are quite similar and contrast with the long-tailed appearance of the similar-sized Golden Eagle. Moreover, some immature Bald Eagles possess ragged white triangles on the under surfaces of the wings somewhat like those of condors. Only by counting the number of seconds it took distant birds to soar full circles in the sky could we reliably differentiate these two species. Bald Eagles normally took about twelve to fourteen seconds to complete a circle, while condors generally expended about sixteen seconds. These times were quite consistent and greatly exceeded the circling times of smaller raptors. Red-tailed Hawks, for example, usually circled in about eight seconds.

Perhaps the most impressive Bald Eagle spectacle to be seen today is the annual postbreeding gathering of thousands of individuals along the Chilkat River of southeastern Alaska. Drawn by the fall spawning runs of chum salmon, the eagles assemble to glean an easy living off a superabundant food supply. The salmon, their energies spent by the spawning process, die in windrows, and the eagles find it much easier to take them as carrion than alive. Wading into the shallows, they capture and haul their victims to shore on foot, then methodically rip them apart and consume them in an unhurried fashion.

With such an abundance of food, there is little need for intense aggression among the birds, though half-playful disputes erupt with some frequency. For the most part, the eagles perch amicably side by side on the gravel bars with no attempts at territorial defense. In favored locations, communal roosts often number many hundreds of birds. Similar, though smaller scale, gatherings of Bald Eagles are also known for certain winter trout-spawning areas along the Colorado River

in Arizona, just as gatherings of California Condors were once common for the salmon runs along the Columbia River in Oregon.

In 1982, after an enormous amount of heated debate, the most crucial parts of the Chilkat were set aside as a state Bald Eagle preserve. Previous to this step, controversy raged over alternative development plans for the area advocated by mining, lumbering, and fishing interests. Eventually, a consensus plan evolved which gave all interested parties, including the eagles, the prospect of long-term survival. In view of the huge numbers of eagles using the Chilkat, the development of a comprehensive preservation plan for this region was a major conservation achievement.

Another of the most gratifying chapters in Bald Eagle conservation was written by Charles Broley, a retired banker from Canada, who conducted a monumental study of the Bald Eagles of the central west coast of Florida. In 1939, at the age of fifty-eight, Broley moved to this state to begin a banding program of nestling eagles that extended into the late 1950s. Overall, he ringed more than 1,200 individuals, with a maximum of 150 in 1946. To do so, he was obliged to develop novel tree-climbing methods that allowed him to scramble up and around the overhung edges of some truly gigantic nests. Usually working alone, he learned how to encourage fully grown nestlings to disengage their talons from his flesh, and he sometimes was faced with long chases through dense scrub vegetation to retrieve youngsters that fledged prematurely on his approach. These efforts, together with his natural history studies at nests, greatly expanded knowledge of the species' habits, revealing, for example, that each summer many Florida eagles undertake a migration to the northeastern states and southern Canada.

A true naturalist who based his conclusions on experience in the field, Broley was the first to call attention to the declining fortunes of the Bald Eagle that began with the advent of DDT in 1947. His conservation efforts also led to the protection of many eyries and the virtual end of egg collecting of this species in the states. His achievements, attained entirely as a private citizen, will always stand as an inspiring example of what one highly motivated person can accomplish, given a measure of freedom and independence.

Golden Eagle

AQUILA CHRYSAETOS

CIRCLING HIGH ABOVE the line of cliffs from which he had fledged a few months earlier, the young California Condor awaited the return of his parents with food. It was late March 1980 and the youngster was not yet capable of foraging independently, though he was daily gaining experience in flight maneuvers, learning how air currents swept over the cliffs and how to land safely on points of rock buffeted by fickle crosswinds.

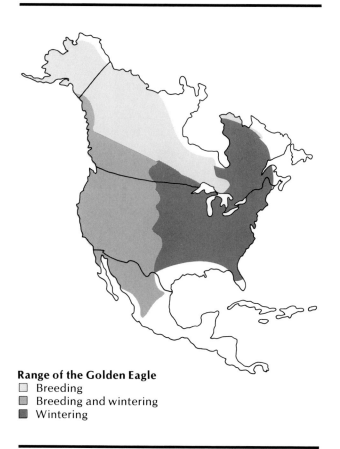

Range of the Golden Eagle
☐ Breeding
▨ Breeding and wintering
■ Wintering

Suddenly the leisurely circling of the condor was interrupted by the arrival of another large bird. In a searing stoop from distant crags to the south, an adult Golden Eagle came storming in to lock talons to the condor in midair. Despite being considerably smaller than the condor, the eagle had decidedly lethal intentions, and the two birds began a tumultuous free-fall toward the ground, breaking apart only moments before they would have crashed into the top of the cliff. The condor just barely fought off the attack and fled quickly down canyon out of reach of his assailant.

Undoubtedly, the condor's appreciation of his place in the universe had changed forever. He might still be the largest bird to sail the skies, but he knew now that he was not the fiercest. In watching this incident, we too gained a new appreciation of the natural world and who its avian rulers really are.

Golden Eagles are the most formidable of all raptor species in North America. Records exist for them even killing grown deer and pronghorn antelope, and they are known to kill foxes and coyotes with some frequency. The list of documented prey for this species includes most of the medium to large mammals on the continent, though, to be sure, many of the largest prey taken have been animals incapacitated by injury or hobbled by deep snow. Many of the largest prey have also been attacked under conditions of dire food stress, when no other prey were available.

Regardless, Golden Eagles certainly take larger prey on average than do any other North American raptors, and they normally dominate all others in disputes over food. In addition to terrorizing young condors, they are usually capable of intimidating adult condors, preventing them from gaining access to carrion under most conditions. The amount of crude violence they exhibit

Above: A young Golden Eagle, still weeks from fledging, exercises its wings at its nest in central Alaska. Right: In flight, adult Golden Eagles appear solid brown below, while immatures exhibit varying amounts of white on the wings and tail. Fully adult feathers are normally achieved at an age of about four to five years, but there is much variability, and some birds apparently retain some white in the tail throughout life.

Immature Golden Eagles contest possession of a calf carcass put out for California Condors. Normally only one eagle feeds at a carcass at a time, and others either wait or challenge the bird in possession in fights of extreme ferocity.

Dark-headed immature condors had an especially difficult time competing for food with Golden Eagles, though hungry adult condors were sometimes able to dislodge eagles from carcasses.

as they usurp and defend such food supplies is awesome. We have seen a number of eagles missing eyes and bearing other wounds, very likely resulting from battles with other eagles over prey.

Golden Eagles generally weigh about ten pounds and have a wingspread of six to seven feet. However, individuals vary considerably in size, and some birds reach thirteen pounds and have wingspreads close to eight feet. The most striking physical characteristics of the species are massive claws and legs that are feathered down to the toes. In coloration, all-aged birds are basically dark brown with a shaggy golden glaze to the back of the head and neck. Immatures are marked with a conspicuous white tail base and white patches on the undersides of their wings at the bases of the outer secondaries and inner primaries. These white patches are gradually lost with progressive molts until the birds finally achieve an overall brown coloration at about four to five years of age.

During the early 1980s, we spent many days in blinds overlooking calf carcasses that we had set out to attract condors in the foothills of California's southern San Joaquin Valley. However, for the most part we watched raven behavior and Golden Eagle behavior rather than condor behavior. The ravens fed in massed groups, while the eagles were loners, intolerant of any other birds on the carcasses while they fed, especially other eagles. When an eagle was feeding, all others usually waited, perched on the ground at some distance from the carcass. Normally it took each eagle about a half hour to forty-five minutes to fill its crop. Then it either took off on its own volition or was displaced by the next in line, sometimes in a flurry of battling as each bird went for the other with talons flashing.

There were enough eagles in the region that a carcass was sometimes attended almost continuously through an entire day. At times, we saw more than a dozen birds waiting their turn. It was often very difficult for condors to break into the loop to get food, and after waiting for a while, the condors attracted to the food commonly gave up and went off foraging elsewhere in apparent hopes of finding less thoroughly guarded food supplies.

Golden Eagles are indeed very fond of carrion, but in most regions they are primarily predators of medium-sized mammals, such as ground squirrels and rabbits. They also take considerable numbers of large birds. One population of the species studied by Yossi Leshem in Israel is heavily dependent on large lizards for prey and characteristically raises more young (often three per nest) than any other known Golden Eagle population in the world.

In addition, some Golden Eagles in Israel feed heavily on tortoises, which they kill by dropping and smashing on rocks from high in the air. At one nest studied by Leshem near Jerusalem, about a third of the diet was comprised of these creatures. As he pointed out in an account of the activities of this pair, tortoise predation by Golden Eagles is apparently a very ancient trait. It was even described by the Roman natural historian, Pliny, who attributed the death of the Greek poet Aeschylus to an eagle that apparently mistook his bald head for a rock and successfully aimed a tortoise at it. This tale just may have been stolen from the supermarket tabloids of ancient Athens, but Leshem's studies at least bring it into the realm of possibility. Clearly the Golden Eagle is a very adaptable species in its feeding habits, and is not to be underestimated in its capacity for unusual exploits.

Unfortunately, in some regions the appetite of the Golden Eagle for carrion has given the species a largely unfair reputation of being an important threat to sheep. Witnessed observations of eagles actually killing lambs are very rare, but nevertheless, sightings of them feeding on stillborn lambs have often been interpreted by ranchers to indicate predation. In the 1950s and 1960s, ranchers sponsored a massive slaughter of wintering eagles from airplanes in Texas, largely justified by the assumption that the eagles were a major menace. Walter Spofford, in studying this slaughter, estimated that a total of over twenty thousand eagles had been shot in the twenty years preceding 1964. Yet the many careful studies that have by now been conducted of eagle predation on livestock have generally shown that eagles take very few domestic animals and are rarely a significant source of their mortality. At the same time, eagles clearly offer benefits to ranchers in many areas by feeding heavily on the rabbits and ground squirrels that compete with their stock for forage.

Even granting that Golden Eagles may kill lambs on occasion, and forgetting for the moment that their rabbit killing is generally an economic assist for ranchers, it is difficult to believe that the expense of airplane campaigns to slaughter eagles might be cost-effective. The fact that no one has attempted to justify such campaigns with hard economic data suggests that there may really have been other motives involved.

What we may be dealing with here is a primordial human drive to do battle with wild creatures perceived as powerful and evil. Now that the grizzlies are gone and wolves have disappeared, it's up to the eagles, coyotes, and foxes to fill that need. After them, perhaps

In this canyon in the mountains of central Alaska, a pair of Golden Eagles raised a single youngster in the summer of 1968. The nest was placed in a cleft on the side of a rib of rock projecting from the canyon side immediately below an inactive wolf den. The youngster was fed an exclusive diet of ground squirrels.

Another Alaska Golden Eagle nest was located on an escarpment north of the Brooks Range far above the Arctic Circle. One of the most northerly breeding sites known for the species in the world, this nest also produced a single youngster on a diet of ground squirrels.

A Golden Eagle nest in southern Arizona was placed high in a cleft of a north-facing cliff. The nest was composed largely of yucca stalks and other debris, and the parent birds fed their two young a diet largely consisting of rabbits. The young were relatively peaceful in disposition, although they did challenge one another for prey on occasion.

weasels and muskrats. Unfortunately, the emotionalism surrounding the eagle-livestock issue has often precluded rational discussions, and human harassment of eagles may not cease completely until the frontier ethic itself has passed completely into history, if it ever does.

While some Golden Eagles are still shot and poisoned in the belief that they threaten livestock, many others have been lost to electrocution on power poles. Their wingspreads are sufficiently large that they are able to complete circuits between wires if as they land on one they brush another simultaneously. Intensive studies of this problem by Morley Nelson, Erv Boeker, and others have led to recommended changes in the design of power poles to make them safe for perching by large raptors. In some of the western states, rapid progress is being made in reducing such deaths by installation of these better-designed poles.

Golden Eagles are commonly regarded as birds of high mountains, but they are really much more typically birds of open country than of forested regions and are much more numerous nesting among low escarpments in the foothills of mountains than at high elevations. They characteristically place their nests on ledges of cliffs, although some populations nest in tall trees. The several active nests we have had a chance to observe in Alaska and Arizona were all cliff sites and were attended by adults that were thoroughly cautious about people. It is possible to find in some areas individual Golden Eagles that allow close approach, but the norm for the species is to be quite wary, far more so than the California Condor, for example.

The most interesting Golden Eagle nest we had a chance to observe was one we watched with Walter Spofford in Alaska in 1968. This nest was lodged in a cleft of a vertical flake of rock in a steep-sided ravine that cut into a hillside in the Alaska Range. Directly over the site was a den where wolves had gnawed on caribou bones, though we saw no wolves in the area when we watched the nest. The nest held a single chick, and we spent many days observing his development through the summer from a distant blind carefully concealed in brush. The chick was fed on a steady diet of arctic ground squirrels, and it was a delight to watch him slowly gaining his flight and prey-killing capacities, flapping his wings energetically as he stood in the nest, play-capturing already dead ground squirrels in the nest with stabs of his talons, and staring curiously at waterfowl on the ponds at the base of the ravine and at pikas on the slopes.

Another Golden Eagle nest we watched from a blind was situated on a rocky outcrop north of the Brooks Range on Alaska's North Slope. Our blind for this nest was a roofed-over pit sunk in a talus hillside, as there was no concealing vegetation in the area. One of the most northerly nests ever recorded for the species, it also held a single youngster developing vigorously on a steady diet of ground squirrels. The slopes of the outcrop were home for a large herd of Dall's sheep, but we saw no interactions between the eagles and sheep and found no evidence of lamb-predation at the nest.

At still another nest we watched closely, a site in Arizona, the primary prey was rabbits, and here two young competed for food on a giant platform of yucca stalks and other debris that the adults had evidently accumulated over a period of many years. Both young were fed good supplies of food and fledged successfully by early summer. They were on the wing much earlier in the year than the single youngsters in Alaska, who barely had enough time to begin flying before the return of cold weather in late summer and early fall. The Alaskan youngsters were likely still dependent on their parents through the migration period, as Golden Eagles of the far north are often known to migrate in family groups.

For many years Walter Spofford has been tracking a population of Golden Eagles that nests in northern New England and winters in the southeastern states. This is an extremely small population presumably because there are few large tracts of truly favorable hunting grounds left in the northeastern states. In fact, these eagles seem to be primarily dependent on bog habitats, feeding mainly on bitterns and herons, certainly an unusual diet that offers at most a marginal existence. Yet each year a number of Golden Eagles, presumably from this population and from eastern Canada, migrate south along the Appalachians to be seen by observers at Hawk Mountain and other lookouts, giving Easterners a chance to see this basically western species at close range. Despite relatively low productivity, the eastern population continues to hang on, demonstrating a surprising adaptability to the continuing landscape changes.

In the western states and western Canada and Alaska, Golden Eagles continue to survive in healthy populations despite persecution in some areas. The total numbers currently estimated for North America—about seventy thousand individuals—are very similar to the total numbers of Bald Eagles, and both species are known to be stable or increasing in many regions.

Falcons and Caracaras

Above: A male Gyrfalcon lands at his nest in an old rough-leg eyrie with a ptarmigan, only to quickly relinquish the prey to his mate arriving to feed the brood. Both adults were of the gray phase typical for the species in Alaska. Fledging of young began the following day. Right: Much more heavy-bodied than the Peregrine Falcon, the Gyrfalcon is not nearly as agile as that species, but is nevertheless impressively swift and powerful in flight.

Gyrfalcon
FALCO RUSTICOLUS

IT WAS LATE June of 1968 in the Alaska Range, still quite chilly. Temperatures were consistently plunging well below freezing overnight, greatly constricting the predawn flow of icy waters in the glacier-fed streams. But by afternoon, enough snow was again melting that we faced a challenge in crossing the torrents to get from one side of the valley to the other.

The day blustered with intermittent rain squalls, and we wondered if we had brought enough clothing. Nevertheless, the very exercise of climbing from the valley floor to the cliffs kept us quite warm, while the obviously fresh diggings of grizzly bears on all sides also helped keep our temperatures elevated. As we worked upwards through the lingering snow patches and thickets of willow scrub, it was impossible not to wonder who might be the first to run into one of these monsters. The terrain offered no refuge should a grizzly appear, and along our way were far too many swales and hollows where bears would be invisible until we blundered upon them. Outside parts of Alaska, Central Africa, and Amazonia, few land areas remain on the planet where the sensations of being a totally vulnerable prey species are still inescapable.

We had only once before seen a Gyrfalcon, a wintering, white-plumaged bird in upstate New York. But now the American Ornithologists' Union meetings in Fairbanks had gotten us to Alaska, and we joined a party led by Walter and Sally Spofford that was hiking to one of the few accessible eyries of this rugged northern species. With us were the wildlife artists Robert Verity Clem and John Henry Dick, and we were all keenly excited by the prospect of observing these birds at close range. The hike was a relatively long one, but we could see the nest cliff from the start and our progress was rapid.

We approached up the backside of a ridge which broke out into the nest cliff at its end. And as we finally crested the ridge at a point immediately opposite the nest cave, we quickly spotted one of the adult Gyrfalcons sitting on a barren knob about a hundred yards distant, a dramatic silhouette against the glaciers descending to the valley below. On seeing us, the bird soon took flight, then made a pass overhead to disappear in the distance.

During breaks in the persistent rain showers, we had time to view the remarkably harsh environment surrounding the site. Frigid snow patches and glaciers contrasted with dark talus slopes and rocky outcrops in all directions. The dwarfed plantlife of the region, just recovering from the winter, seemed to face enormous odds in just surviving. Yet as bitter as conditions seemed, they were absolutely lush in comparison to what the same scene must have looked like two months earlier when the Gyrfalcons had begun nesting. At that time, the entire region must have been white, and the only snow-free location would have been deep inside the cave that formed the eyrie itself.

Three well-grown young stood in the nest entrance, with only a few patches of natal down showing on their fast-developing feathers. The nesting cycle was nearing completion, and soon enough these youngsters would be on the wing learning just how ptarmigan and ground squirrels react to Gyrfalcon shadows. But outside of a few Rosy Finches and Snow Buntings, we saw few other birds in the immediate area. A very simple environment biologically, but one of astounding beauty and power, although very melancholy in mood on this sunless day.

In the days that followed, we had a chance to return to the eyrie to watch the nest closely. Unfortunately,

At her nest, a crevice in a crumbling cliff, a female Gyrfalcon lands amidst a frantic crescendo of screaming from her brood. Though close to fledging, these youngsters were still many weeks from true independence.

Lingering snow patches and fresh diggings of grizzly bears for peavine roots line the route to a Gyrfalcon eyrie in the mountains of central Alaska. Although the snow was disappearing fast by late June 1968, the landscape must have been almost entirely white when the Gyrfalcons began their nesting cycle several months earlier.

A fledgling Gyrfalcon awaits the return of his parents with food. On the wing in early July, this youngster still knew nothing of the process of capturing his own prey.

169

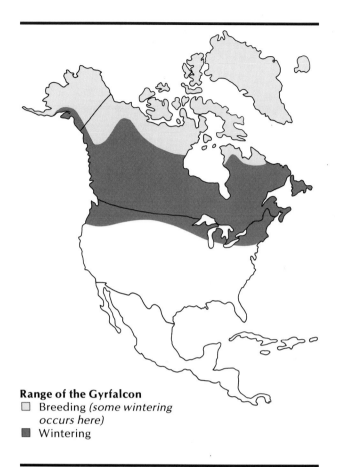

Range of the Gyrfalcon
☐ Breeding (some wintering occurs here)
■ Wintering

that it had secure protection from terrestrial predators, and we doubted that a grizzly would have much difficulty in scrambling to the entrance or that it might pass up an opportunity to dine on succulent young falcon flesh.

The eyrie was sufficiently accessible that ground squirrels, a frequent prey of the species, made repeated runs to the nest entrance to stare curiously at the young falcons from a few feet away. Their stares were met by even more curious stares from the falcons. Did they recognize each other for what their true relationship soon would be? There was no sign, and it appeared that the nestlings still knew food only as something that their parents brought in, not as something they would ever have to capture themselves.

Visits of the adults to the nest were not frequent or long-lasting, as the young were far beyond the stage where they needed brooding, and we had much more opportunity to watch the behavior of the youngsters than of the adults. The nestlings were quiet for the most part, but when an adult appeared in the area, they began a tireless screaming, which rose in a frenzied crescendo as the parent bird shot in to land on the nest ledge. The bedlam did not cease until the parent left on another foraging expedition and the chicks sensed that their prospects of further immediate food had disappeared.

sitting in the freezing, windy weather on a ledge just wide enough to accommodate a tiny blind led to one of the longest and most miserable bouts of flu we have ever experienced. Still, this was a small price to pay for the opportunity to see the world for a while through Gyrfalcon eyes.

Gyrfalcons come in a variety of color phases, usually classified as white, gray, and black, and for many years the birds of different phases were considered separate species of Gyrfalcons. However, it has by now become clear that the different color phases frequently interbreed and that they do not constitute separate species. Almost pure white birds are most common in northern Greenland and the eastern Arctic, while most Gyrfalcons in Alaska are gray-phased. Nevertheless, all phases can be found, at least to some extent, in all major arctic regions.

Both adults at the 1968 nest were of the gray phase. They were surprisingly confident in coming to the nest, despite the intrusion of a blind below them, and seemed not to recognize us as a major potential threat. We wondered if they might show a stronger response should a grizzly appear. Their nest was not so high on the cliff

Almost twenty years later, in July of 1987, we had another opportunity to watch nesting Gyrfalcons, this time on the North Slope of Alaska far above the Arctic Circle. One nest we observed from a blind was a sturdy old Rough-legged Hawk nest, and here gray-phased adults were feeding a brood of four young a diet primarily of ptarmigan. Like the adults at the nest of 1968, the adults at this nest were imperious in manner, paying scant attention to us or our blind. Not nearly as agile as a pair of Peregrine Falcons that were nesting about a mile away, they were, nevertheless, impressively swift in flight, especially as they dove on a nearby pair of Rough-legged Hawks that strayed too close to the nest.

The young Gyrfalcons, as they left the nest, were also remarkably bold, regarding our close approach with only a few signs of initial fear, then apparent boredom once they had concluded we meant them no harm. Their true attentions were focused on the skies as they awaited the return of their parents with food.

At two other Gyrfalcon nests of 1987, young were fully fledged by the time of our arrival and were covering respectable distances from the nest cliffs in their first exploratory flights out over the tundra. Not yet hunting on their own, they were still gaining the flight strength and agility that would ultimately give them the capacities to forage successfully. They spent most of their time perched, dealing with the clouds of lung-clogging mosquitoes that filled the air whenever the wind dropped below a moderate breeze, and watching Long-tailed Jaegers and Glaucous Gulls coursing over the rolling hills. From the nesting cliffs, the tundra was now in full flower, and far below, occasional moose and caribou browsed on willow and fireweed, while Dall's sheep kept to the steeper rocky slopes that allowed some refuge from attacks of wolves and other carnivores.

The Gyrfalcon is the largest of all the falcons and is closely related to the Prairie Falcon of the New World and the Saker Falcon of Asia. Like these species, it characteristically hunts in swift low flights, capturing prey by surprise, often right on the ground. In attack, the Gyrfalcon either immediately binds to the prey with its talons or delivers a stunning blow with its talons in passing, followed by a return to recover its insensate victim. The coup de grace is a quick bite to the neck at the base of the skull. The prey taken most commonly are terrestrial species such as ptarmigan and ground squirrels, but under conditions of scarcity of these prey, Gyrfalcons turn readily to other prey such as seabirds and hares. Nevertheless, overall breeding productivity varies quite closely with the availability of ptarmigan, and in years of ptarmigan scarcity, many pairs do not breed.

In winter, many Gyrfalcons remain in the Arctic as long as food supplies permit, but some individuals, especially juveniles, move farther south, reaching the northern states with some frequency in severe winters. On its southern wintering grounds, the species takes a great diversity of prey, ranging from other raptors to carrion.

Perhaps more than any other North American raptor, the Gyrfalcon gains security from detrimental human influences by the enormous logistic difficulties people face in penetrating its haunts. While the species is nowhere an abundant bird, the arctic grounds where it primarily occurs are still remote from civilization. The Gyrfalcon is not known to have suffered any significant impacts from the DDT era, and as far as information extends, it appears that its numbers are still as strong as they ever were.

Recent population estimates suggest that Alaska normally hosts perhaps five hundred pairs of Gyrfalcons, while Greenland may harbor as many as one thousand pairs. Many more occur across the Canadian Arctic, and in Iceland, where the Gyrfalcon is the national bird, there are normally about three hundred to four hundred pairs. The total population of this species, including both Old World and New World regions, may include as many as fifteen thousand to seventeen thousand pairs.

Falcons and Caracaras

Peregrine Falcon
FALCO PEREGRINUS

MUCH OF THE impressiveness of the Peregrine Falcon comes from the precipitous beauty of its native terrain and the size and power of the prey it is willing to challenge. Few birds, unless they are very large or very small or are species that never leave cover, are safe from this raptor, and peregrines are among the very few birds of prey known to regularly take swifts as victims. Capable of flying at tremendous speeds and executing

Viewed from the top of a peregrine nest cliff in central Alaska, the Tanana River stretches its many channels toward the distant Alaska Range.

Against the silt-choked Tanana River below, an adult female peregrine pauses before returning to her eggs.

The peregrine eyrie itself was nothing more than an overhung depression at the base of a band of rock, though it was well protected from access by terrestrial predators.

With a just-dispatched Green-winged Teal in one foot, an adult peregrine in Florida begins the process of plucking and disassembling.

In flight near their nests, the Alaskan peregrines were astonishingly swift and maneuverable, executing rapid changes in direction at top speed.

astonishingly agile maneuvers, the Peregrine Falcon is a true ruler of the air, fully worthy of its fame as a raptor of unequaled predatory abilities.

As a superlative long-winged predator of other birds, the Peregrine Falcon enjoys a nearly worldwide distribution, thriving in a great variety of settings from arctic tundra to tropical rain forests. In North America, the species is best known as an inhabitant of canyons and cliffs, often bordering on open country. From perches high above the surrounding terrain, it launches breathtaking stoops of incredible velocity as it attacks prey unfortunate enough to fly through its domain.

Although it takes birds of many sorts, the peregrine is perhaps best known as a predator of waterbirds. It was in its role as a slayer of ducks, befitting the old American name of Duck Hawk, that we became most familiar with the species.

During the late 1960s and early 1970s, we made frequent boat trips in south Florida, exploring the bays, keys, and canals of the tip of the peninsula, sometimes in a small skiff, sometimes in a canoe. Many of these trips were specifically in search of the wintering peregrines which concentrated in this region, undoubtedly attracted by the shoals of American Coots, Green-winged Teal, and Northern Pintails gathered in the shallow lakes and bays. The peregrines often perched in large dead mangrove snags bordering on open marshes or water. From such vantage points they were able to survey their surroundings for potential prey, waiting patiently for the proper set of circumstances to arise that would allow successful hunts.

Peregrines do not normally attack ducks that are sitting on the water. The ducks appear to know this and are extremely reluctant to take flight when a peregrine is in view. What might appear to be a vast larder of waterbirds for the peregrines is really largely out of their reach, and only when potential prey are in the air, especially when they are unaware of the peregrines, do they become vulnerable.

Even in flight, a duck can often outdistance a pursuing peregrine. Or if the peregrine is gaining, the duck can sometimes escape by diving into the water. We once watched this tactic employed by a Lesser Scaup fleeing a peregrine on Whitewater Bay. Clearly unable to outfly his assailant, the duck finally gained safety by simply folding his wings and dropping like a stone, raising a plume of spray as he hit the surface just ahead of his pursuer.

Our boat sometimes provided the crucial advantage that a peregrine needed to catch its prey off guard. As we moved through the waterways, we often flushed

waterfowl, who then became easy marks for attack because they concentrated their attention on escaping from us, only to place themselves in jeopardy from the rapidly reacting peregrines. Occasionally we even found peregrines that had gained a full appreciation of this wonderful duck-flushing quality of small boats and followed us high overhead for long distances, waiting for unsuspecting waterfowl to take to the air.

As fast as the peregrines are – their dives can reach two hundred miles per hour – they are not invincible and can often be eluded by their intended prey in level flight, where their speed is more commonly about fifty miles per hour. We sometimes watched a peregrine making numerous successive chases of ducks completely without success. One such bird we watched for several hours finally gave up and circled high into the sky, beginning short forays in midair to take what appeared to be dragonflies, eating his victims on the wing.

One particularly skilled adult peregrine of the winter of 1969–1970 foraged regularly along the shores of Bear Lake just off Florida Bay and gave us many exciting observations of its hunting capacities. This bird was nearly oblivious to our presence, and we were often

Range of the Peregrine Falcon
☐ Breeding *(some wintering occurs here)*
■ Wintering

able to watch it from distances of less than fifty feet without apparently disturbing it. Almost invariably, it used one of two different roost trees right on the shore of the lake, and we could count on finding the bird on one of these roosts if we got to the area soon enough after first light.

Our most memorable encounter with this bird occurred shortly after dawn of February 28, 1970. This was an especially cold morning with fresh winds out of the north, and just as we arrived, we were delighted to see the peregrine overtake and capture a Green-winged Teal, dispatching his prey with a bite to the neck as he gripped it in his talons and flew back to a perch in a nearby snag. There he began plucking the teal. Suddenly, for no apparent reason, he became very alert and soon took off, carrying the prey in one foot beyond a line of living mangroves several hundred yards to the west. There the peregrine inexplicably dropped the teal, although he soon returned to our vicinity, circling up and calling excitedly.

At last, we realized what was causing this puzzling behavior. An immature Bald Eagle came steaming across the lake from behind us and began coursing over the ground where the peregrine had dropped the teal. The eagle was obviously attempting to find the recently dispatched prey, while the peregrine cackled in dismay and harassed the eagle unmercifully. Unfortunately, about this time we drifted too close, and the eagle became aware of our presence and flew off into the distance, so we did not have a chance to see a natural conclusion to the incident. Nevertheless, the apparent attempt by the peregrine to hide its prey from the eagle was remarkable and suggested a degree of experience and sophistication in this bird that was far beyond normal raptor behavior.

The Bear Lake peregrine was also remarkable in another respect. He was an *anatum* peregrine, at that time a race of the species that was close to extinction in the eastern states, apparently due, at least in part, to the insidious eggshell-thinning effects of DDE. He and others of his kind, like a number of other bird- and fish-eating raptor species, were then suffering almost complete reproductive failure.

Fortunately, by the early 1970s, the effects of DDT and other organochlorine pesticides on birds of prey and other species were becoming well documented, and these pesticides were phased out of use in the United States and Canada. However, the eastern peregrines had been so thoroughly decimated that no viable breeding population was left. Recovery of the peregrine in this region could only be effected by a reestablishment program, and a highly successful effort to reintroduce the species into the wild from captivity was organized by Tom Cade and others through the 1970s and early 1980s. Because of this effort, the species is now largely out of danger in this part of North America.

Not all the peregrines wintering in Florida in the late 1960s and early 1970s were *anatum* peregrines. Many were arctic-breeding birds belonging to the race *tundrius*. As immatures, *tundrius* peregrines have very light sandy crowns to their heads, and as adults they characteristically show a very attractive light blue sheen to their crown, back, and wing feathers. Typical *anatum* peregrines from farther south have dark grayish-black helmets and upperparts.

Besides coming together on the wintering grounds, the *anatum* and *tundrius* races of the Peregrine Falcon also come together in the taiga of northern Canada and Alaska, and it was in this zone in central Alaska where we had our first chance to watch nesting peregrines. There, in 1968, Walter Spofford took us to a spectacular eyrie along a bend of the Tanana River. This was the last active peregrine nest in this region, as this population was also heavily stressed by pesticide contamination at the time. Here we were able to get an excellent appreciation of just what sort of habitat characteristics are favorable for the species. The peregrines were nesting high on a ledge of an escarpment overlooking a vast region of braided river flats, with the snow-crowned Alaska Range looming in the distance and an abundance of water and land birds in the near vicinity. The height of the cliffs and the unobstructed view gave the peregrines a crucial advantage over prey species in the area.

We have since seen peregrine eyries in a great many regions, ranging from Spain to Peru. Not all have been in regions with abundant waterbirds, but all have been in places with plentiful prey birds of one sort or another, and all have been characterized by topographic features that allowed the peregrines frequent opportunities to surprise their prey in vulnerable situations. Such places are not really all that widespread. Probably for this reason peregrines have never been and presumably never will be abundant birds, although they certainly achieve large enough populations in regions of relatively good habitat to qualify as locally common.

Among the most favorable nesting sites adopted by peregrines, especially by the reintroduced population in the eastern states, have been ledges on skyscrapers and giant bridges in the hearts of some of our largest cities. These human-built surrogates for cliff-canyon topography have proved highly attractive to these raptors, very likely because of the high populations of Rock

Doves and other urban birds inhabiting the surrounding city environments. Many of these nesting areas have also had the virtue of low populations of Great Horned Owls, which constitute a very significant threat to nesting success of Peregrine Falcons in many natural settings. Variants on the skyscraper theme include recent peregrine nests atop grain elevators in the prairie states and the traditional occupancy of abandoned lighthouses by peregrines in other parts of the world. Aside from the opposition of some pigeon fanciers, modern urban peregrines have enjoyed widespread support from city residents, and there are few sights to compare with a peregrine in hot pursuit of a luckless pigeon above the noisy traffic and bustle of our city streets.

Perhaps the North American region with the most impressive population of Peregrine Falcons today is the Grand Canyon of the Colorado River in Arizona. Recent surveys sponsored by the National Park Service have revealed a population here that may exceed 150 pairs. Nesting in spectacular cliffs ranging from black Precambrian schists to brilliant red Paleozoic shales, sandstones, and limestones, these peregrines enjoy an abundant food supply that includes everything from clouds of Violet-green Swallows, White-throated Swifts, and bats to shoals of waterfowl. Many of these species are ultimately dependent on the productivity of the Colorado River itself, which, as it continues to cut the cliffs and gorges of the region, simultaneously nourishes its inhabitants.

In the spring of 1989, we were most fortunate to be able to view these wonders at close range, as we joined the peregrine survey efforts in the canyon. By floating the many rapids of the Inner Gorge, we arrived each day at strategic observation points on sandy beaches and low bluffs. Here we scanned intently for glimpses of the falcons in late afternoon and early morning watches, before floating farther down canyon to the next set of observation points. We sighted peregrines throughout the canyon, though clearly we must also have missed seeing many individuals because of the steepness of the cliffs and our inability to examine more than a tiny fraction of the many escarpments from any viewpoint. The enormous scale on which the canyon is built dwarfs all efforts to explore it thoroughly or to arrive at a rigorously complete census of any of its inhabitants.

Our most memorable sighting of a peregrine in Grand Canyon came many years earlier, however. During the mid-1970s when we were surveying the southwestern states for Common Black Hawks and Zone-tailed Hawks, we once stopped off to watch the dawn unfold from the canyon's South Rim. Our intention was to enjoy the progression of colors as the sun touched formation after formation from its path across the sky. But as we first reached the rim, there, hanging motionless in the breeze only a few yards out and a few yards up, was an adult male peregrine in perfect feather. A few long seconds passed, and the bird then slowly tipped over in a long slanting dive that took him steadily downward toward the very Inner Gorge of the canyon, past innumerable layers of muted colors, past majestic peaks and amphitheaters, past ages of geological time, to the earliest Precambrian rocks nearly a mile below, and then finally out of sight. His journey, spanning the record of millions of years in the space of a few minutes, was silent and left us wondering if the bird could possibly have any knowledge of the geological epochs and succession of fossil life forms he had traversed. From the bones of almost contemporary mastodons, ground sloths, and condors, back to dinosaur footprints, to trilobites, and finally to primitive algal remains, a major part of the earth's history had passed before both the peregrine and us, and as separate branches of evolution we had all journeyed back to our common origins in the earliest life on the planet.

Falcons and Caracaras

Prairie Falcon
FALCO MEXICANUS

THE PRAIRIE FALCON is a highly mobile and aggressive raptor, with an overall tan coloration, black "armpits" visible in flight, a dark moustache, and long powerful wings. Coursing low over open terrain, with rapid wingbeats and swift, purposeful flight, it leaves its intended victims little time for escape maneuvers or retreat into cover, and it usually captures prey by surprise at close range rather than by extended pursuit. Prairie Falcons cover huge areas in their daily searching for food. Their kills depend more on chance encounters of vulnerable exposed prey than on thorough patient combing of the landscape.

With a range extending from northern Mexico to southern Canada and pretty much throughout the western states, the Prairie Falcon enjoys a wide distribution, but it is quite unevenly spread within this range. Recent estimates suggest a total breeding population for the species of perhaps about five thousand to six thousand pairs, mostly in the Rocky Mountain states and Pacific Coast states. However, many regions have not yet been carefully surveyed for this species, especially in northern Mexico, and this total may be substantially revised when more complete data become available.

A bird of the arid western canyons, grasslands, and deserts, the Prairie Falcon is very similar to the peregrine in size and general flying skills, but is much more inclined to come to the ground in hunting forays and is much more ready to take mammals as prey. Like the peregrine, the Prairie Falcon usually nests in high cliffs, though it is less restricted to regions with good waterfowl populations and often thrives in regions far from any sources of water whatsoever.

We have nowhere found Prairie Falcons to be more abundant than in certain regions of southern Califor-

Range of the Prairie Falcon
▨ Breeding and wintering

nia, where the last California Condors nested. Within one and one-half miles of an active condor nest in 1984, we found five successful pairs of prairies, and the condors suffered continual harassment from this species in many of their last nesting areas.

One condor pair of 1980 had an especially hard time dealing with prairies. This pair first appeared to be settling on a towering cliff with a number of excellent

The nesting cliff of a pair of Colorado Prairie Falcons towers above pinyon-juniper scrublands. Adults at this site were using an old raven nest as their eyrie.

The Snake River Birds of Prey Area in Idaho hosts greater densities of nesting raptors than any other region known in the world. Here Prairie Falcons average about three pairs per mile along the river. These high nesting densities are supported mainly by productive populations of Townsend's ground squirrels in the flatland regions adjoining the river.

On her Colorado nest cliff, an adult female Prairie Falcon called in alarm at intruders ranging from people to Golden Eagles.

Right: Very similar to the Peregrine Falcon in size and flying capacities, Prairie Falcons nevertheless concentrate much more heavily on mammals as prey. In most regions, the species takes ground squirrels as a staple, varied with a diversity of open-country birds.

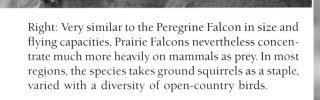

nest caves, but a pair of prairies moved into the same cliff and soon began diving aggressively on the condors. The condors immediately moved to another site about a mile away where they laid their egg. Unfortunately, another pair of prairies moved into this second cliff almost immediately thereafter and chose a pothole site just two hundred feet from the condor cave and directly facing it from across a narrow ravine. The condors had no choice but to persevere, but they had a terrible time through the reproductive cycle as they struggled to approach and leave their nest without being torn apart by the falcons.

On many occasions, a condor approaching this nest never even got close before it was forced to turn aside and flee down canyon, sometimes regurgitating mouthfuls of slimy food that cascaded to the ground as the condor attempted to lighten its load to escape the dives of its tormentors. Nevertheless, the condors always managed to get to their nest in the end, often by retreating to a safe distance, then sailing in very high over the nesting canyon and descending to their nest in long powerful stoops that the prairies could not deflect.

Despite the harassment, the condors succeeded in fledging their young, as did the prairies. And in the balance, the presence of the prairies nesting nearby may actually have been very beneficial to the condors' efforts. The falcons were also highly aggressive to other large species, such as Common Ravens and Golden Eagles, which constitute strong threats to condor eggs and chicks. By excluding these more menacing species from the vicinity, the falcons may have greatly reduced the chances of nest failure for the condors.

In any event, we were very grateful to the prairies, as they always spotted the condors returning to their nest far sooner than we did, and by their angry cackles alerted us to imminent action at the condor nest. Fortunately, the prairies never showed the slightest inclination to capture the young condor chick, even though the falcon nest faced the condor nest directly and the chick was often left unguarded and in full view of the falcons.

Two years later, when we were again studying the same condor pair nesting in the same canyon, we again watched an aggressive nearby pair of prairies defending the canyon from all intruders. In this year, however, the risks of this behavior to the prairies themselves finally became clear. A Golden Eagle passing through the region responded to one of the prairies in the midst of an attack by reaching out with one foot, snatching the falcon in midair, and killing it instantly.

The Prairie Falcons we watched in California fed very heavily on ground squirrels and commuted long distances from their nest canyons to their foraging grounds. Despite intensive poisoning campaigns, ground squirrels remain an abundant species in the grasslands of the state, perhaps mainly because they thrive best in regions that are heavily grazed and where the height of vegetation is relatively low.

Prairie Falcons were also common in southern Arizona, where we studied a number of raptor species in the late 1960s and early 1970s, and we finally had an opportunity to observe a relatively accessible pair in the Tucson Mountains in 1975. This pair had chosen a very well-protected cave that had evidently been used for many decades, possibly centuries, of nesting, as the hardened white excrement dripping from the entrance was many inches thick and advertised the nest from many miles away. With the help of Tom and Bill Mader and Rich Glinski from nearby Tucson, we set up the forty-foot-high tower blind we had earlier used in studying Swallow-tailed Kites in Florida, and this gave us a view directly into the falcon eyrie with its four young, as well as a spectacular view of the surrounding terrain.

Down below the escarpment on the flats stretching off to the horizon were the saguaro cacti and palo verdes characteristic of well-developed Sonoran Desert, with their associated Cactus Wrens, Gila Woodpeckers, and White-winged Doves. About the cliffs themselves flew Canyon Wrens and White-throated Swifts. Birds such as these formed most of the diet of the prairies during the days of observation, and the adults were highly successful in keeping their brood well fed. Nevertheless, in most regions Prairie Falcons tend to feed most heavily on mammals, and this emphasis was probably a critical factor in the much better survival of this species than the peregrine through the DDT era.

Our blind was especially well situated for observing the prey transfers between male and female adults. While the female did some hunting for the brood, she was more commonly in attendance in the nest vicinity, and stood ready to receive what the male had captured. She fed most of what he supplied to her hungry youngsters, but she also satisfied much of her own needs from the same source.

Food transfers between the adults usually took place in midair, with the female surging up from below to snatch the prey from her mate's talons in a quick roll of impressive skill and timing. The male also occasionally brought food to the nest when the female was off hunting, but he did not stay to rip it apart for the young. His primary role was clearly hunting, rather than tending the brood.

Above: Although the male Prairie Falcon sometimes brought prey directly to the site, he did not rip them apart for the young. Most commonly, he passed food to the female in the vicinity in an impressive aerial transfer. Right: Youngsters at the nest in Arizona were fed regularly and well by the female prairie.

One of the most remarkable concentrations of Prairie Falcons known is found in the Snake River Canyon of southwestern Idaho. Here, in 1972, Verland Ogden documented 101 pairs occupying a forty-five-mile stretch of river, and these pairs produced an astonishingly high average of 3.1 young per eyrie. In a more recent survey of eighty-one miles of the river, Mike Kochert and his colleagues found an almost unbelievable total of 215 pairs, or close to one pair every third of a mile. Such densities far surpass those achieved by any known nesting population of Peregrine Falcons.

Nevertheless, it is important to recognize that the foraging activities of the Snake River Prairie Falcons extend many miles away from the river, so that the actual home ranges of individual pairs are very large. Measurements of these home ranges have indicated an average size of about forty-six square miles, with some birds observed foraging as far as sixteen miles from their nests. Foraging ranges overlap broadly among adjacent pairs, and in practical terms it is unlikely, with ranges this large, that individuals could effectively defend exclusive foraging areas.

The Snake River Canyon is also a mecca for other raptor species, such as Golden Eagles and Red-tailed Hawks, and the overall density of nesting raptors here far exceeds the density known for nesting raptors in any other region of the world. Thankfully, much of the region has now been incorporated into a natural area set aside specifically for birds of prey and administered by the Bureau of Land Management. The area represents a very fortunate juxtaposition of extensive favorable cliffs for nesting and extensive open-country foraging grounds. The Prairie Falcons of this region are thriving primarily on an dense populations of Townsend's ground squirrels.

Much of the habitat occupied by the Prairie Falcon is arid, precipitous, and remote, giving considerable security from human influences. The dietary flexibility of the species further enhances its capacity to endure. Throughout its range, the Prairie Falcon remains a reasonably common species, and nothing indicates that it is having special difficulties in coping with the modern world.

Falcons and Caracaras

Aplomado Falcon
FALCO FEMORALIS

AT ONE TIME the Aplomado Falcon, a long-tailed, long-legged raptor with handsome black and chestnut bands across its breast and belly, bred with some regularity in southern Arizona, New Mexico, and Texas. However, several decades have passed since an active nest has been located north of the Mexican border, and the species has rarely even been seen in the United States in recent years. Despite much time spent in the Southwest, we have only once encountered an Aplomado Falcon in this region, a lone individual coursing over a wide reach of yucca grassland in southwestern New Mexico in early 1987.

In part, the virtual disappearance of the aplomado from the United States may have resulted from the over-enthusiastic activities of early egg collectors. But it is a reasonable surmise that habitat degradation and, more recently, DDE and dieldrin contamination have played more important roles. In the latter part of the nineteenth century, a combination of widespread drought and over-grazing devastated many of the lands just north of the Mexican border. Many of these regions have never fully recovered their former character, as has been particularly well documented for southern Arizona. Where aplomados still occur in Mexico and countries farther south, they are not restricted to virgin habitats, but they do appear to be restricted to regions with high prey densities and very specific habitat structures. The enormous habitat changes that occurred along the Mexican border around the turn of the last century may well have destroyed the potentials of many regions to support the species.

The name *aplomado* is derived from the Spanish word for "leadened," presumably referring to the gray coloration of the bird's back. Once thought to be a predator primarily of reptiles, rodents, and various insects, the species is actually a bird-feeder mainly as has been well established by recent intensive studies of Dean Hector in Mexico. It also takes insects with some frequency, but by weight, insects form only a minor part of the diet.

The means by which aplomados take birds include some unusual adaptations. In the spring of 1978, we joined Dean Hector in eastern Mexico to observe the hunting and nesting behavior of this species in some detail. We were greatly impressed with this falcon's specializations in dealing with its food supply and with the relationship of its hunting habits to its nesting habits.

Like other falcons, aplomados do not build their own nests, but instead occupy old nests of other species. The nests we saw in Veracruz were mainly former nests of Black-shouldered Kites and Roadside Hawks and were located in small groves of trees surrounded by largely open country. Around their nests, the aplomados were not exceptionally wary birds, and at one nest that we climbed to examine the nestlings, we found the female to be highly aggressive, cackling furiously and swooping in with reckless strafing runs, striking us repeatedly with her talons. Roughly the size and weight of a female Cooper's Hawk, she packed considerable power in her blows, and we kept our nest checks very brief to minimize the chances of injury, both to her and to us.

The nest of this female and her mate was placed in a small grove of acacias in the midst of a plowed cornfield and contained two chicks that were only several days old. Both were feathered in the white down typical of young nestling falcons, and both were free of the warble fly maggots that Dean Hector has sometimes found

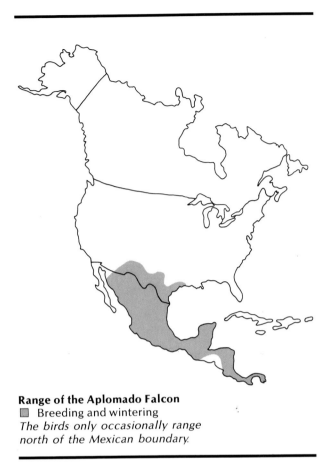

Range of the Aplomado Falcon
■ Breeding and wintering
The birds only occasionally range north of the Mexican boundary.

infesting young of this species. The nest itself was a dilapidated old twig platform with barely enough cup left to hold the chicks. A pair of Black-shouldered Kites, perhaps the original owners of the nest, were breeding simultaneously in an adjacent patch of thorn-scrub woodland only a few hundred yards away, but we saw no interactions between the kites and aplomados.

We spent several days watching the hunting behavior of this pair of aplomados. Generally, the female brooded and fed the young and was in attendance at the nest, while the male perched in nearby exposed snaggy trees, waiting for prey to move into the open somewhere in the surroundings. Almost all hunts took place within five hundred yards of the nest, and almost always, the male hunted in full view of the female, an important point as it soon developed.

Many of the male's forays were pursuits of flying insects. On these chases, he often followed an ascending path into the sky, followed at length by a return to his perch. During our observations, none of the insect prey were taken to the female at the nest.

On other occasions, the male pursued small birds that chanced to leave cover to fly across the open fields

In flight, the long tail of the aplomado is an excellent field mark for identification, distinguishing the species from other similar-sized falcons.

The Gray Ranch region of southwestern New Mexico was a former home for the Aplomado Falcon and represents one of the more promising regions for reintroduction of this species. The extensive grasslands on this ranch have not been subjected to the high levels of grazing that most other grasslands in the region have suffered.

A female aplomado lands at her nest site after an unsuccessful hunt.

The male aplomado brings a small bird to the female for feeding to the young.

185

near the nest. Some of these birds were migrants heading for more northerly regions. Others were local residents. The male grabbed some victims immediately in tail chases. Most of these he soon took to the nest in decapitated condition for presentation to the female.

But some intended victims managed to duck back into brush before the male could reach them. On several such occasions we saw the female aplomado leave her nest and young to join the male in a cooperative follow-up. While the male hovered in the air over the tree or bush in which the prospective victim had taken refuge, the female flew right into the bush and hopped from branch to branch, pursuing the prey on foot until the latter finally took flight into the open again where it was an easy mark for capture – a marvelous team effort.

The willingness of the falcons to enter the canopy of trees to chase after prey reminded us a bit of the behavior of Cooper's Hawks, and the long legs and very long tail of the aplomado show a strong resemblance to corresponding appendages of that species, perhaps aiding both raptors in balance at close quarters. It is also interesting that the female aplomado generally did the brush-beating, rather than the relatively small male, although at first sight the male might seem better adapted to working through the cluttered branches. However, we suspect that at least under some circumstances the male, with his greater agility, was perhaps a better choice to hover above, ready for the quick acceleration needed to capture the prey when it finally left cover.

In Dean Hector's overall studies of aplomados, the average success rate in capture attempts of birds was only 21 percent in solo hunts, as opposed to 45 percent in collaborative hunts of pair members. Further, the prey captured were often shared between the pair members. The enhanced success in hunting achieved by pairs may be one of the principal reasons that they commonly remain together in the nonbreeding season as well as the breeding season. Regardless of time of year, cooperative hunts are usually initiated by a sharp "chip" call, by which one bird alerts its mate to a hunting opportunity. The same chip call is given by breeding males when they return to their nesting areas with food for their mates and young.

Interestingly, even during pair hunts, female aplomados tended to capture much larger prey birds than did their mates, so the advantages of females leaving their nests to join their mates in hunting not only included enhanced capture rates but also increased chances of bringing down larger prey. In Dean Hector's overall observations, male Aplomado Falcons, which weigh approximately 64 percent of the weight of their mates, captured birds that averaged only 41 percent of the weight of the birds captured by females.

From what we saw of the hunting of the aplomado pairs, their habitat preferences now made a great deal of sense. The critical factors for breeding appear to be basically open country with an old stick nest of some raptor or corvid placed high in a tree or small grove, offering a good view of the surroundings. Also apparently essential are relatively high numbers of prey birds placing themselves in vulnerable positions in the surroundings. The abundant North American migrants, together with conspicuously high populations of resident species, appeared to offer excellent food resources for the Mexican aplomados.

Overall, the Mexican aplomados appeared to be adapting relatively well to the habitat changes in the region, and may in fact have even been benefiting from the conversion of scrublands to pasturelands. Presumably there may be some optimum balance between scrublands and pasturelands that maximizes prey supplies and hunting opportunities for the species, and long-term conservation of the aplomado in this region may well depend on determining what such a balance may consist of and working toward creating and maintaining it in selected areas.

In North America, the Aplomado Falcon was once known as a bird of yucca grasslands and Gulf Coast prairies, and the prevalence of winter records north of the Mexican border suggests that this population was resident year-round. Yucca grasslands and coastal prairies have by no means been wiped out in recent decades. However, in many regions continuous mesquite brush has invaded these habitats making them impractical for aplomados to hunt because they provide too much cover for prey. While it would be a very positive achievement to reestablish viable populations of the aplomado in the United States, and preliminary reintroduction efforts are currently underway in coastal prairie regions of southern Texas, the success of these efforts will probably depend importantly on finding specific release areas with prey supplies and habitat structure suiting the needs of the species.

Like other bird-feeding raptors, the aplomado has suffered from accumulation of DDE residues in its food supply. Dean Hector and Lloyd Kiff have documented alarmingly high levels of contamination and extraordinarily severe eggshell thinning in aplomados of coastal Mexico. Nevertheless, the highlands of northern Mexico and adjacent areas in Arizona and New Mexico are one of the few regions where the Peregrine Falcon

Commonly hunting as a team, Aplomado Falcon pairs characteristically watch for prey from conspicuous snags bordering on open country.

The eyrie of one pair was an abandoned nest, probably built by a Black-shouldered Kite, about twenty feet up in a huisache.

A female aplomado aggressively defends her nest from our approach, not hesitating to strike blows at close quarters.

187

managed to hang on through the DDT era without any programs to bolster wild populations. Peregrines are now increasing significantly in this region, as has been well documented by studies of Dave Ellis and Rich Glinski. Possibly this same region could also represent a relatively safe area for reestablishing the aplomado.

One of the most promising specific sites for aplomado reestablishment in this region is the Gray Ranch of southwestern New Mexico, recently purchased by the Nature Conservancy. This five-hundred-square-mile ranch includes a substantial basin of native grasslands, with apparently healthy populations of prey birds, such as Horned Larks and Meadowlarks. Potential nest sites for the aplomados are abundant here in old raven, Swainson's Hawk, and Red-tailed Hawk nests in the fingers of oak woodland working out into the more open grasslands and in the soaptree yuccas scattered in many areas. Moreover, aplomados were known to be common in this general region a century ago, and this ranch is one of the very few regions that survived the era of overgrazing in virtually intact condition. Because of its overall excellent condition, the Gray Ranch also represents a very promising site for reintroductions of a variety of other endangered mammals and birds that were earlier extirpated from the region, such as black-tailed prairie dogs and Thick-billed Parrots. It also represents a promising area for reintroduction of California Condors, as fossil remains indicate that these giant vultures roamed the region only a few thousand years ago.

Falcons and Caracaras

Merlin
FALCO COLUMBARIUS

THE SMALL FLOCK of migrant shorebirds working over the mudflat especially interested us, as one member of the flock was a species we had never seen before. It was a fall day in the early 1960s in the Tinicum Marshes of eastern Pennsylvania, and we were in the process of identifying our very first Stilt Sandpiper. With its image centered in the telescope at close range and with brilliant afternoon sunlight illuminating its feathers, we were easily able to confirm the bird's field marks. And just in time, it turned out. For suddenly, a Merlin appeared out of nowhere in the very center of the field of view and from the rear grabbed the very bird we had been scrutinizing before it had a chance to even consider flight. Without pausing, the Merlin carried off the sandpiper in its talons and disappeared in the distance. All this happened so quickly and unexpectedly, it took a few moments to be sure what species had made the kill. Regardless, we have rarely seen a prey capture by any raptor so vividly and closely, or had a first sighting of a new species terminated so abruptly.

As was obvious in this encounter, the flight of the Merlin is very direct, purposeful, and swift—much more so than the flight of the American Kestrel, the other small falcon of North America. Also obvious was the willingness of the Merlin to take prey on the ground, a trait also typical of Gyrfalcons and Prairie Falcons, but not normally seen in Peregrine Falcons or Aplomado Falcons, the other two North American falcons that focus on small or medium-sized birds as prey. While Merlins, like American Kestrels, also take considerable numbers of insects, the primary dietary emphasis of this falcon is clearly on avian species, especially those that occur in open country.

However, although most of our observations of hunting Merlins have been made in marshes and open fields, we have also seen them hunting with some frequency over forested habitats – in particular, the mature rainforests of eastern Puerto Rico. Here, during the early 1970s, we sometimes watched wintering individuals pursuing birds as large as Sharp-shinned Hawks that left the cover of the forest canopy. Merlins are also known to hunt over heavily wooded habitat in other regions, but although they sometimes perch within the canopy of trees, they rarely take prey in such locations. Presumably their relatively long wings would be at risk in pursuing prey within cover.

Merlins lack the bold facial markings found in most other North American falcons. Both sexes tend to be heavily streaked with brown underneath, while adult males have bluish-gray upperparts, and females and immatures have brownish upperparts. The tail is heavily banded in all ages and sexes, and lacks the rusty coloration found in American Kestrels.

For the most part, North American Merlins breed in Canada and Alaska, dipping down into the lower states only in the northwestern and north-central

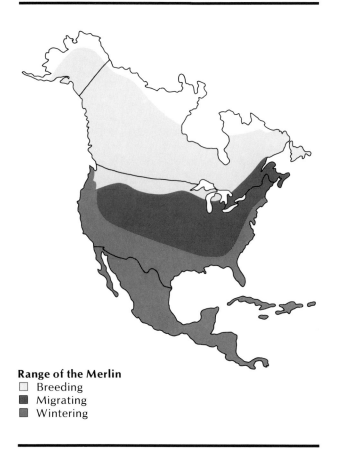

Range of the Merlin
☐ Breeding
◼ Migrating
◼ Wintering

regions. The species generally uses old stick nests of other relatively large birds, though in some regions it uses cliff ledges. When neither cliffs nor old stick nests are available, it is known to nest with frequency right on the ground. The one Merlin nest we had a chance to observe closely was an old Black-billed Magpie nest in a spruce grove surrounded by tundra vegetation high in the Alaska Range. This nest contained only two eggs and was not successful. Neither of the eggs hatched after full incubation.

We found this nest in 1968, at the height of the DDT era, and we were concerned that pesticide contamination might have been a factor in the failure. Merlins, because of their diet, were one of the species at potential risk, and the clutch size at the nest was unusually low, a potential sign of egg breakage and loss. To check the possibility of contamination with organochlorines, Jerry Swartz at the University of Alaska was able to arrange for analysis of the eggs after it was clear that they were inviable. The eggs did indeed prove to be highly contaminated, though whether their failure to hatch could be definitely attributed to this cause was uncertain. In any event, we were surprised to learn that even in a region as wild as this remote corner of Alaska, there was no real escape from contamination. Much of the problem presumably stemmed from the fact that the Merlins were feeding heavily on migrant birds and from the fact that the Merlins themselves were migratory.

Later in 1968, we visited another Merlin nesting territory with Jerry Swartz in the old gold-mining country of the mountains north of Fairbanks. No magpies bred in this region to offer stick nests for the Merlins, and this Merlin pair was one that habitually nested on the ground. However, we never found the actual nest site. By the time of our arrival, the brood had already fledged, and we found five young Merlins still with wisps of down on their heads perched atop spruces in the area. Jerry was in the process of starting a captive-breeding project with Merlins, and he was hoping to include young from this nest in the effort. Unfortunately, the young, though they had just left the nest and could not fly well, were able to stay just beyond our reach, even with a long-handled crab net. We got considerable exercise, but no success, in attempting to capture them.

We got even more exercise later in the day, when as we were hiking back to our vehicle we finally had a chance to experience the exact nightmare we had repeatedly envisioned in hiking to a Gyrfalcon nest earlier in that summer. For just as we got in sight of our vehicle, a full-grown grizzly bear suddenly appeared

Above: The male Merlin at the nest in Alaska was an efficient predator of small birds, although the nest held only two eggs, an unusually small clutch. Left: The nest site of a pair of Merlins in the mountains of central Alaska was an abandoned Black-billed Magpie nest in the top of a spruce bordering on open tundra.

Above: The female Merlin returns to the top of the nest tree after feeding on prey brought by the male. Right: A fledgling Merlin from a ground nest in the White Mountains of Alaska still exhibits wisps of down on his head. One of five young successfully raised by the pair, he was still limited in flight capacities but was able to make short journeys from treetop to treetop.

over a nearby hilltop running downhill at top speed directly toward us. A quick mental calculation, as we broke into a panic-stricken sprint ourselves, indicated that there was absolutely no way on earth that we could evade the bear. He was closing the distance to us rapidly, and there was not a scrap of nearby cover.

At moments like these, there is a strong tendency to give up and submit to the inevitable without a struggle. On sensing the futility of trying to escape, we soon stopped running and turned to face the overwhelming, oncoming threat. No time or even inclination for last profound thoughts. Just detached passive fascination with the certainty of our soon becoming bloody links in the arctic food web.

Unexpectedly, just as the bear was all but upon us, he too stopped running abruptly. For a moment he raised up and sniffed the air curiously, but then he immediately tore off in a new direction—away from us and down the valley. His departure was as rapid as his approach. Galloping over and through the dwarf willows and other brush as if they were no obstacles at all, he showed no signs of slowing down even as he finally disappeared over a last faraway hill.

Evidently, when we first saw the grizzly racing toward us, he was not actually aware of our presence, though there was no way for us to know this. Once he caught our scent, he was as frightened as we were and just as anxious to be somewhere else. The vision of that grizzly bounding down the valley, over rises and depressions, into the distance will always be linked in our minds with the futility of chasing fledgling Merlins from one side of a ravine to the other, in the fading hope that they might eventually tire enough to allow capture.

Breeding populations of the Merlin in the western United States and southern Canada have been experiencing an unprecedented increase in the 1970s and 1980s, an increase that apparently has been fueled in part by a recovery from the stresses of the pesticide era and in part by a remarkable spread of the species into urban environments, where it has been able to sustain exceptionally high productivity. Where this invasion has been studied most closely—by Lynn Oliphant and his associates in Saskatoon, Saskatchewan—it has apparently depended importantly on a just-previous invasion of the same urban areas by American Crows and Black-billed Magpies. Both these species build stick nests of requisite properties for later use by Merlins, and the recent advent of these nest sites has most likely been the crucial change opening up the city habitats for use by Merlins. The urban invasion of the crows and magpies has apparently been due primarily to maturation of ornamental spruce trees planted in residential areas; spruces are favored nesting places for these birds.

In the urban setting, the Merlins have found an excellent food supply, especially House Sparrows and Bohemian Waxwings, and they have suffered only infrequent losses to nest predators. As studied by Ian Warkentin and Paul Jones, the relatively high productivity of this population may in part be a function of the strong preferences of the Merlins for old crow nests high in dense conifers in which they are relatively inconspicuous to predators, but from which they are in an excellent position to launch attacks on vulnerable prey.

The urban invasion of Merlins parallels a recent invasion of urban areas in Scotland by European Sparrowhawks. But whereas the Merlin's invasion can be attributed in large measure to a change in nest availability, the sparrowhawk invasion apparently traces to other causes, as sparrowhawks build their own nests. Perhaps a progressively higher tolerance of our own species for raptors, evolving into interest and positive protection, has been an important component of the changes taking place. Perhaps also important has been the increasing sponsorship of small prey birds by feeding programs of urban residents. On a much more modest scale, we have noticed a local increase of nesting Cooper's Hawks in one region of Arizona where songbird feeding stations have greatly proliferated. In effect, these small-bird feeding stations have evolved into hawk-feeding stations—surely a much higher and more noble purpose than their original intent.

Falcons and Caracaras

American Kestrel
FALCO SPARVERIUS

MEANDERING MAINLY EAST to west across the border between southern New Mexico and Arizona, Skeleton Canyon is a rugged gorge of sculptured red rocks cut into the western flank of the parched Peloncillo Mountains. The sides of this narrow canyon are too devoid of moisture to allow more than a limited cover of grasses, yuccas, and thornscrub, while the canyon bottom itself boasts only a modest scattering of emory oaks and

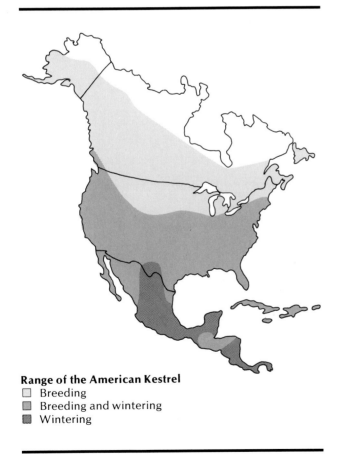

Range of the American Kestrel
- ☐ Breeding
- Breeding and wintering
- Wintering

sycamores nourished by an intermittently flowing stream. Despite considerable natural beauty, this is not a visually spectacular canyon on the scale of a Grand Canyon or a Zion Canyon. Nor is it a canyon blessed with a fauna and flora much different from what can be found in innumerable other dry canyons in the same general region.

It is, nevertheless, an extraordinary locality from the standpoint of turbulent human history. For it was here that the Clanton Gang, Curley Bill, Billy Grounds, and Zwing Hunt waylaid pack trains of Mexican smugglers in the early 1880s; and it was here, in late 1886, that the renowned Apache leader, Geronimo, together with his remnant band of warriors, made his final surrender to General Miles of the U.S. Army after decades of violent conflict. So many desperados, Indians, smugglers, and their beasts of burden met their ends in the canyon bottom that their lingering bleached bones gave rise to the modern name for the region.

The bones of Skeleton Canyon have long since disintegrated, and today the gorge has returned to the quietude it must once have enjoyed before Apaches and outlaws ever moved into the area. The occasional visitors to the canyon are now mostly unaware of the region's colorful past and find mainly lizards, snakes, grasshoppers, scorpions, and a host of other small creatures that have doubtless occupied the area for millennia. Ambushes and massacres are but a distant memory, and it has been many years since the hot summer air of the canyon has been stirred by anything more violent than the monotonous languid ratcheting of cicadas.

In this now thoroughly peaceful setting, we came to study one of the more pastoral of North America's raptors – the American Kestrel. Smaller than a Blue Jay

An American Kestrel hunts the open grasslands of the southern San Joaquin Valley of California.

An adult female kestrel prepares to enter the Skeleton Canyon nest in a dying sycamore. The uniform rufous ground color of her wings contrasted with the slaty-blue wings of her mate.

The male kestrel arrives at the nest entrance with a lizard. When it proved too large for the young to swallow, he carried it off for disposal elsewhere.

Skeleton Canyon of western New Mexico is a home for numerous pairs of American Kestrels and was once habitat for an assortment of human outlaws.

The male kestrel concentrated mainly on lizards as prey, while his mate brought mainly grasshoppers to the young.

Fledgling kestrels emerge from the nest. The entrance was a tight squeeze, giving good protection from predators but creating some problems in the fledging process.

and marked with bold patches of gray, white, black, and rufous on its head and neck, and with rufous on its back and tail, the kestrel is the most colorful and most diminutive diurnal raptor on our continent. It is also our most prolific raptor, commonly laying clutches of four to six eggs and producing more than one brood per year.

Kestrels were abundant in Skeleton Canyon, nesting in the many gnarled snags that line the main streambed and feeding on the great variety of small animals that inhabit the surrounding open areas. Less than a mile from the site of Geronimo's surrender, and almost exactly a century after that historic event, we spent a number of June days observing one particular nest in a natural cavity of a dying sycamore trunk. The site contained a vigorous brood of five young—four males and one female—and we had a chance to watch these youngsters make their first tentative explorations of the outside world.

Like the young of many other hole-nesting birds, young kestrels are relatively noisy, apparently deriving considerable security against predators from the nature of their nest sites. The entrance to the Skeleton Canyon nest was an especially tight squeeze for the birds, and doubtless would have prevented entry of most of the birds' potential enemies, such as raccoons and ring-tailed cats. From the protection of their nest hole, the young kestrels set up a clamor of anticipation each time they had any hints of the approach of one of their parents with food. Their tremulous triplet begging calls were easily audible from many yards away and continued for much of the day.

Both the male and female adults brought prey to the nest entrance, although the male sometimes passed prey to his mate in preference to bringing it in directly. Strangely, the male adult, despite his smaller size than the female, seemed to be concentrating on relatively large lizards, while the female brought in endless meals of grasshoppers. Other prey included nestling birds, mice, and cicadas; altogether a smorgasbord of small creatures, most of which were quickly eaten by the youngsters.

The nest entrance was only large enough for one youngster to occupy at a time, but once this youngster received a prey item, he disappeared below and his position at the entrance was relinquished to another, so that food distribution appeared to be relatively equal among the nestlings. Though we were curious as to how many young the nest held, we were reluctant to climb to the nest to make a direct inspection of the interior because the nest trunk was also being used by an active honeybee hive only a few feet away. Nevertheless, as time went by, we were able to recognize individual young by slight differences in facial feather patterns and to assess the makeup of the brood.

Differences in the amount of down on the youngsters' heads suggested significant age differences among the nestlings. However, the fledging process, which began June 8, seemed to infect all members of the brood more or less simultaneously, and their exits from the nest chamber followed one another rapidly. The first to leave the nest was one of the males, who struggled through the opening to perch on a broken branch base on top of the entrance at 8:22 in the morning. Soon after, his only sister exited in a similar way. Both began short explorations of the vicinity of the nest entrance, scrambling from branch to branch and fully stretching their wings and bobbing their tails for the first times.

The third youngster to exit, however, was a relatively young male still with a considerable amount of down on his head. Though obviously excited and anxious to leave, he apparently lacked the full confidence to do it properly. He soon got his wings outside the hole, but seemed reluctant to stand up on the nest lip, so he was trapped—unwilling to go the rest of the way out, yet unable to get back inside because his wings were caught awkwardly extended by the limited diameter of the entrance. This dilemma was no more frustrating to this bird than it was to the two youngsters left in the hole behind him. They now found their access to the outside and to food completely blocked. The impasse was only resolved when one of the males still inside the hole finally lifted the one stuck in the entrance up on his shoulders and forcibly launched him through the entrance to flutter uncertainly down into the branches below the hole.

The fledging process also seemed to excite the parent birds. They greatly increased their foraging rate, bringing twice as many prey to the nest on this day as they had on the previous day. The fledglings were indeed well attended through this crucial transition to outside existence.

Once the fledglings had left the hole, we were especially interested to observe how they handled the lizard prey that the adults were bringing them, as lizards are very tough-skinned animals that are difficult to dismember. Earlier we had once watched an adult kestrel giving up in attempting to rip apart a horned lizard it had captured, and during 1971 we watched numerous instances of young Cooper's Hawks at a nearby nest failing to rip apart lizards successfully and losing them over the side of the nest before managing to eat them.

Above: A nestling considers the prospect of fledging from a cavity in a cottonwood in southern Arizona. Right: Fledgling kestrels already show the distinctive sexual coloration differences characteristic of the species.

The young kestrels at the Skeleton Canyon nest, however, solved the lizard-ingestion problem in a very simple way – they swallowed the lizards whole and headfirst, including some comparatively large ones. Only once did we see the male adult bring a lizard so large that this was not possible, and he soon flew off with it, presumably to eat (or discard) it himself, after the youngsters failed to ingest it.

Another kestrel population that concentrates on lizards for food is one that occupies the island of Culebra, east of Puerto Rico. This is the densest population of kestrels we have ever encountered, and in a trip to this island in 1974, we were astounded by the fact that individuals of this species seemed to occupy every clump of trees in the semi-open scrub of the lowlands. Not only were kestrels remarkably common on this island, but they were also remarkably tame, often allowing approach to within ten or fifteen feet. Nesting mainly in the hollows of large Bucida trees, this population seemed to have found the very essence of optimal kestrel habitat.

Like the Red-tailed Hawk, the American Kestrel has evolved into a great variety of color forms in different regions. All races of the species, however, show a very distinctive difference in coloration between males and females. Males have conspicuous gray-blue wings, while the wings of females are basically rufous. The only other North American raptors exhibiting obvious sexual color differences are Northern Harriers, Everglade Kites, Hook-billed Kites, Merlins, Sharp-shinned Hawks, Ospreys, and Cooper's Hawks. In most of these species, the sexual differences are not nearly so marked as they are in the kestrel, nor are they found in juveniles as they are in the kestrel. The sexual dimorphism in color pattern in these species shows no obvious relationship with sexual size dimorphism, and no obvious simple behavioral or ecological characteristics bind these species together in ways that might explain why sexual differences in coloration might be adaptive for them and not for other species.

Another unusual feature of kestrel plumage is the presence of two dark spots on the back of the neck that look very much like eyes when the bird is viewed either from the rear or from the front when the head of the bird is bent over working on prey. The possible function of these "eyespots" has generated considerable speculation over the years, starting with an intriguing paper by William Clay over thirty years ago. Clay felt the spots might function mainly to deceive potential onlookers as to which way the kestrel is facing.

Do the spots actually function deceptively? Such an effect could inhibit attacks by potential predators – predators that the kestrel might be unaware of and would otherwise be vulnerable to. This is an attractive idea and one that we once tested in a haphazard way in the early 1970s with one such predator, the Cooper's Hawk. In studying nests of this accipiter in Arizona and New Mexico, we found that females almost invariably defended their nests by striking a climber from behind, rather than by frontal assault. This observation led first of all to our wearing a helmet when climbing nest trees. Later we painted conspicuous eyes on the back of the helmet to see if this might discourage attack. Unfortunately, there was no noticeable decline in the frequency of dives and blows, though it was hard to judge this in a rigorous way. Still, if kestrel eyespots might even only momentarily slow down other raptors attempting to capture these small falcons, this could be enough of an effect to have led to the evolution of this coloration. The kestrel's habit of bobbing its head serves to make the eye spots especially realistic and "owlish" in appearance, and we are quite willing to admit that our painted helmet was not nearly as professional a simulation. We still find the original suggestion of Clay as to the function of the eyespots to be the best explanation yet advanced.

The American Kestrel is a generally common species throughout its extensive range in North and South America and the West Indies. Missing only from the most arctic regions, it occupies a great variety of open and semi-open habitats, including many suburban and urban areas. It has adapted extremely well to disturbed areas and even nests frequently in cracks and crannies of buildings, and in bird boxes put out for its use and the use of other species. In fact, the kestrel rivals and may even surpass the Red-tailed Hawk for honors as the most abundant raptor on the continent.

Crested Caracara
POLYBORUS PLANCUS

THE CRESTED CARACARA just barely reaches the United States, mainly in the cattle-ranching country of south-central Florida and southern Texas, and in Sonoran Desert habitat of the Tohono O'Odham Indian Reservation of southwestern Arizona. Farther south, it is a widespread and common species in many regions of Central and South America and is even honored as the national bird of Mexico.

Medium-large in size, with long yellow legs, bright red naked cheeks, a conspicuous white throat and neck, and a handsomely barred black and white breast, the Crested Caracara is a striking raptor with a curious blend of disparate characteristics. Half-falcon and half-vulture, half-aerial and half-terrestrial, it seemingly combines the major features of several avian groups in one species. However, it is clearly a member of the Falconidae and is most closely related to such species as the Gyrfalcon and Peregrine Falcon among the North American raptors.

For us, the caracara will always be linked with the cabbage palm hammock prairies of Florida stretching to the west and north of Lake Okeechobee. These prairies, especially those bordering the Kissimmee River and Fisheating Creek, are among the most picturesque regions of the state, and during the two years we made this region our home in the late 1970s, we were pleased to discover as neighbors not only a sizable population of caracaras but also a great diversity of other wildlife species, all living in apparent harmony with traditional cattle-grazing operations. Burrowing Owls, Meadowlarks, Sandhill Cranes, various herons and ibis, Bald Eagles, Black Vultures, Turkey Vultures, and Red-tailed Hawks were common in open areas, while Wild Turkeys, Barred Owls, Red-shouldered Hawks, Pileated Woodpeckers, and Red-bellied Woodpeckers abounded in the adjacent hammocks and cypress swamps.

We saw Crested Caracaras most commonly in relatively open areas where they found much of their food on foot, striding along much in the manner of the Secretary Bird of Africa. The diet of this species is quite varied and ranges from carrion to all sorts of invertebrates and vertebrates. It is a truly opportunistic generalist capable of taking advantage of ephemeral abundances of practically any animal food supplies it can manage to locate and capture.

Despite its strikingly conspicuous appearance, the Crested Caracara is not always the easiest bird to find. In part, this results from the fact that the bird often forages on foot, obscured from distant view by vegetation. In part, it apparently results from the skill with which the species has come to exploit the ecology of our own species. In many areas, caracaras have learned that they can make an easy living by foraging along the highways at daybreak, reaping the bounty of rabbits, armadillos, possums, and other vertebrates flattened by vehicles overnight. Since few people are out cruising the highways at first light, and since caracaras have mostly fed to repletion and retreated to favored roosts in the cabbage palms by the time that traffic really begins to build up, the birds are usually out of view when most observers would have a chance to see them. It is surprising how much more "common" the caracara suddenly becomes once you become aware of this daily pattern and start looking for the species at the proper time of day.

One pair we watched with some frequency in 1979 made regular dawn patrols of a stretch of several miles of state highway 27 west of Lake Okeechobee. Stroking rapidly along with strong wingbeats, heads down, they had first choice of the assortment of overnight traffic victims. Local Turkey Vultures and Black Vultures were

With its head thrown back completely upside down, an adult caracara gives the peculiar rattling cry thought to be the source of the bird's name.

Commonly foraging along highways at first light, Crested Caracaras feed heavily on armadillos, possums, and coons that have met destruction overnight. At these windfalls of fresh food, caracaras normally dominate other scavengers such as Black Vultures and Turkey Vultures.

Caracaras reveal their ecological affinities to vultures by a lack of feathering to the regions surrounding their bills. They normally travel in pairs at all times of year.

Crested Caracaras characteristically nest in the tops of cabbage palms. Unlike their close relatives the falcons, but like their distant relatives the kites and hawks, they build substantial nests of twigs.

When the nesting grove of a pair of Crested Caracaras was first discovered near Fisheating Creek, the ground in the vicinity was strewn with the fresh remains of turtles that the pair had apparently been eating. Later in the breeding cycle, the pair fed mainly on carrion.

happy to feast on these victims as well, but because of their dependence on good soaring conditions, both these species normally began foraging later in the day. Their choices by this time were limited to leftovers from the caracaras and to more recently killed prey.

During 1979, we lived on the prairie between Moore Haven and Fisheating Creek and maintained a feeding station of road-killed mammals out by our backyard chicken coop so that we could enjoy the company of the local scavengers. Black Vultures and Turkey Vultures were regular visitors, as were a pair of caracaras that true to form would arrive just at first light to see what the Snyders might have unaccountably discarded overnight. At these morning feasts, the caracaras normally dominated the other common scavengers in head-on confrontations, strutting erect about the carcasses and controlling the situation quite thoroughly.

During the spring these caracaras had a brood to feed, and we sometimes watched an adult ripping small strips of meat from a carcass, laying them in a neat pile on the ground. When the pile had grown to the size of a small apple, the bird would carefully pick it up as a mass in its bill and head straight back to the nest about a mile distant, returning for another load soon afterwards.

In time, the caracara pair also brought their brood of two fledglings to the carcass dump, but four individuals are as many caracaras as we have ever seen together at one time. Occasionally, other observers have seen larger groups, but such occurrences are so unusual, at least in Florida, that when Rod Chandler of the National Audubon Society recently encountered a group of fifty caracaras on the Kissimmee Prairie, it was the first time in his entire long life as an outdoorsman in the region that he had seen more than a single family group together.

In 1978, we had an opportunity to observe the nesting activities of a pair of caracaras in a cabbage palm hammock near Fisheating Creek. When we first discovered the nest, the ground in the vicinity was littered with the shells of turtles that the pair had apparently brought in and fed upon earlier. At the nest itself, however, the only food fed to the young through the rest of the breeding cycle was unrecognizable pieces of meat, apparently carrion.

From the blind we constructed in a nearby cabbage palm, we found the caracaras to be quite tolerant of our presence. They provisioned their young with great frequency, apparently having an excellent food supply to exploit in the region. On one day we recorded no less than fifteen feeding trips of the adults to the nest,

Range of the Crested Caracara
Breeding and wintering

and the nestlings appeared to be receiving as much food as they could possibly consume.

At intervals during the nestling period, we weighed and measured the young to track their development, and found that as they matured they became quite difficult to handle, attacking us with both their bills and talons. Such behavior is also typical of falcons, their close relatives, but is not normally observed in hawks, eagles, and kites, which characteristically defend themselves with their talons only.

Around the nest, the adults sometimes gave a startling display that is quite unlike anything we have seen in other North American raptors, though it is very reminiscent of displays given by European White Storks at their nests. In this display, the bird throws its head so far back that the top of its head touches its back and the head is upside down. Simultaneously, the bird gives a rattling cry lasting a second or so, a cry thought by some to be the source of the name *caracara*. What specific meaning this display might have is unknown.

The most intriguing caracara nesting sites we have ever seen were on the Kissimmee Prairie, and were not in fact active nests, but "ghosts" of nests more than fifty

Above: Fledgling caracaras have streaked rather than barred underparts and lack their parents' bright red faces. Right: Crested Caracara nest trees of the 1920s on the Kissimmee Prairie drew the attention of an obsessive egg collector from Gainesville, Charles Doe. These trees stand today with his trademark ladders of nails marching up the trunks. Rod Chandler of the National Audubon Society inspects the condition of one of the trunks.

years old that had long since fallen. In late 1979, we became aware from conversations with Joe Howell that one of the Kissimmee Prairie egg collectors of the 1920s, a recluse from Gainesville named Charles Doe, usually climbed to nests by a very individual method. Instead of using climbing spikes, he pounded steps of nails up trees that held the nests. On learning this, we asked Rod Chandler of Okeechobee if he recalled ever having seen such trees on the prairie. Rod didn't respond immediately, but several days later he phoned us to say that he had relocated a couple of such trees that he had remembered from his youth in the 1930s and had often wondered about.

The trees were cabbage palms, and when we went to see them, we found that the nail scars and in some cases the actual nails, giant rusty spikes, could still be seen marching up the trunks. The nail scars and nails in 1979 stopped short of the crowns of the cabbage palms by about fifteen feet, indicating the relatively modest amount of growth that the palms had put on in the previous five decades. Charles Doe was a rabid collector of the eggs of all birds, but he had a special fondness for the eggs of Sandhill Cranes and Crested Caracaras. In these nail-scarred palms we have little doubt we were looking at the signs of his past depredations on caracaras, as this is the one species that characteristically nests in cabbage palms, and there are still many caracaras in the region.

The extreme diversity of foods acceptable to the caracara has allowed the species to coexist in good numbers with people in many areas. Nevertheless, its continued existence in the United States may depend largely on the survival of ranching as a livelihood in Florida and Texas. The species seems to be limited primarily to cattle country and cannot be expected to survive continuing conversion of the ranchlands to citrus orchards and housing developments. Like the Everglade Kite, the Crested Caracara faces a relatively uncertain future if the human population of our southern states continues to increase at the rate it has been.

The Florida caracara population has been recently estimated by Jim Layne to consist of only about 150 pairs and perhaps 150 to two hundred immatures. Relatively little of its range is in any officially protected status. With Disney World and associated developments just to the north and rapidly expanding retirement communities in many locations near Lake Okeechobee, the prospects of this population seem precarious. Only the recently acquired 6,500-acre sanctuary of the National Audubon Society on the Kissimmee Prairie presently offers any secure hopes of preserving a central Florida prairie ecosystem in perpetuity. This sanctuary, a most significant achievement resulting largely from the persistent efforts of Rod Chandler, is nevertheless much too small by itself to sustain a viable caracara population, let alone viable populations of many other species. Only a single caracara pair is known to use the sanctuary as it presently exists.

We find it difficult to overstate the values of expanding the Kissimmee Prairie sanctuary so that it does become large enough to sustain viable populations of such species as caracaras. Another bird that could benefit greatly from such a sanctuary is the Florida Sandhill Crane. Still another is a species of raptor that has been missing from our fauna for some two hundred years – the King Vulture. Populations of this bird still occur in Central and South America, and the species evidently occurred in central Florida up until the time of the American Revolution, as was described in an extraordinary firsthand account by the early American naturalist, William Bartram. Florida's King Vultures may have disappeared largely because local Indian tribes eagerly sought these birds as a source of ceremonial feathers and because the birds apparently were very easy to approach and kill. Bartram's account of this species – he called it the Painted Vulture – is one of the most fascinating descriptions of early natural history in the New World. Though it has been discounted by some authors, we find it compelling in detail and scarcely to be doubted.

Given adequate protection from human depredations and given adequate amounts of suitable habitat, it seems quite plausible that the King Vulture could be reestablished in Florida, and in much the same habitats used presently by caracaras. The overall populations of scavenging birds on the Kissimmee Prairie are presently robust, and the region represents a potential long-term stronghold for such birds if it can be sufficiently protected before it is too late. Preservation of a truly viable prairie ecosystem for these and other species need not entail actual purchase of vast acreages if land use can be dedicated to practices no more intensive than traditional ranching by conservation easements or other equivalent means. Nevertheless, it would be prudent and important to acquire large areas to be managed strictly for wildlife as core parts of such a preserve.

Like all other raptors of North America, the Crested Caracara cannot survive in the absence of the particular habitats to which it is adapted. This does not mean that this species, any more than any other raptor, needs to "monopolize" habitats to the exclusion of all human activities. But unless our species can become sensitive to the requirements of these birds and make deliberate efforts to accommodate their needs in a long-term, self-sustaining way, we will surely lose them one by one and face a progressively more depressing and less stable world in the future.

The recoveries of the Peregrine Falcon, Bald Eagle, and Osprey from severely stressed population levels only a few decades ago, and the prospective recovery of the California Condor from an even worse condition just a few years ago, give hope that we can manage to preserve all our raptorial birds if enough efforts are made on their behalf. That these efforts are worth making, we take as self-evident. None of these species should be considered "expendable," and all deserve our enduring commitment to their survival. The prehistoric cave painters of the world had their symbolic priorities right, as did the ancient Egyptians, the Peruvian Incas, and many a motorcycle gang of our more recent past. Raptors are among the most magnificent of all living organisms and will always bring excitement and pleasure to our lives. May they fly forever.

Precautions in Observing Raptors

WHILE WE WISH to encourage the study of raptorial birds, both as an intrinsically rewarding activity and as an essential and important part of ensuring their conservation, we also want to emphasize that birds of prey deserve special treatment in field observations because of their general scarcity and sensitivity to disturbance. Careless or poorly conceived efforts to study these birds can result in much more harm than good.

Although some raptors are quite tolerant of nearby human activities, most tend to be quite wary, no doubt because a long history of human harassment has favored the survival of individuals with considerable fear of our species. Certain raptors, such as the Golden Eagle and the Ferruginous Hawk, are extraordinarily difficult to work with at close range, especially in regions where they have been heavily persecuted. Unless an observer takes appropriate precautions, attempts to study these birds closely can quickly lead to regrettable consequences such as nest desertions. To promote their survival, most raptors are protected by both state and federal regulations, and permits are required for many kinds of intensive studies.

In some raptors, individuals vary greatly in their wariness depending on whether they are at their nests or in feeding areas. Everglade Kites, for example, are usually quite approachable and safely observable on their foraging grounds—yet they tend to be extremely sensitive around nests. In conducting reproductive studies of this species, we have found that it is rare to encounter pairs that tolerate blinds anywhere nearby, even in late breeding stages. To get undisturbed nesting observations, it is usually necessary to work with telescopes from distances of several hundred yards.

California Condors behave rather differently, exhibiting great reluctance to flush from their nests and more curiosity than alarm with respect to human approach in many circumstances. We have sometimes had condors fly in from afar to circle low over our heads, obviously inspecting us closely (perhaps to discover if any amongst us might be in failing health?). We have seen them similarly inspect groups of cattle on the open range. This curiosity has always made the species highly vulnerable to shooting and other forms of human molestation, and may well have been an important factor in the species' decline. Nevertheless, around carcasses on the foraging grounds, California Condors, like other vultures, tend to be very cautious and slow to land, quickly flushing if approached even at a great distance.

Other raptors exhibit different peculiarities in their reactions to human disturbance, and it is very important for an observer to have some knowledge of the usual patterns of a species' responsiveness to people before attempting close observations. Nevertheless, it is also quite true that although there are typical patterns for species, particular individuals may differ greatly from others of the same species in their sensitivity. On very rare occasions we have even found relatively approachable individuals in the Golden Eagle, perhaps the most wary species of all. By the same token, we have sometimes found unusually skittish individuals in species that are normally quite approachable. Many species exhibit tremendous differences in approachability depending on where in their range you are observing them. When the individual characteristics of raptors encountered in the field are unknown, it is always best to treat these birds as potentially very sensitive to disturbance.

In many respects, migration concentration points provide the safest and most enjoyable circumstances under which to observe raptors. At strategic overlooks, such as Hawk Mountain in Pennsylvania, Cape May Point in New Jersey, Point Pelee in Ontario, Derby Hill in New York, and the Goshute Mountains in Nevada, it is sometimes possible to view thousands of raptors at very close range in a single day during appropriate times of the year, and the presence of numerous observers in no way threatens the security or behavior of the birds as they stream past. Observations at migration lookouts represent an ideal way to gain a first appreciation of raptors and to gain initial skills in their identification.

Observations at raptor nests should be made only with the utmost of caution, and only after an observer has had considerable field experience working with raptors in other contexts and has gained considerable sensitivity to their behavior. Blinds are almost always a necessity for nest observations and as a rule should be placed at fair distances and entered only during darkness. The disturbance involved in building blinds can itself represent a significant stress. Construction should be carried out in stages, always checking that the birds are accepting progressive developments. For some especially wary species, even distant blinds are likely to cause the birds to desert their nests if built during the early part of the breeding cycle, and you simply cannot work safely with such species unless you establish blinds during the nonbreeding season or late in the breeding cycle, keeping the blinds very well hidden and inconspicuous. Observing nesting raptors successfully calls for close attention to their behavior and a willingness to break off operations if signs of stress become evident.

Observers pose special risks for species nesting in extremely hot or cold environments. In such environments, eggs or small chicks left uncovered can perish very quickly, and close parental attendance at the nest is essential for chick or egg survival. For such species, observers must take great care not to disrupt normal patterns of parental attendance at nests.

Other risks to be avoided in working with nesting raptors involve inadvertent advertisement of the nests to other predators. It is essential to avoid making trails leading to nests and to refrain from building blinds that are conspicuous and call attention to the location of nests.

While these precautions may seem difficult to fulfill in some cases, they are important and necessary to minimize the chances of harmful consequences developing from observations and studies of these birds.

Suggested Further Readings

THE LITERATURE ON North American raptors is much too extensive for a thorough treatment here. In the following list of references, we seek mainly to acquaint readers with materials that will document and amplify what we have presented in the written accounts and will introduce a diversity of significant raptor studies not discussed in the text. While not all-encompassing, these references will serve as an efficient entry into the general raptor literature and into the literature on individual North American raptor species.

As initial readings we highly recommend the natural history accounts of North American raptors given by various authors in Palmer's *Handbook of North American Birds*, volumes 4 and 5, and given in Bent's *Life Histories of North American Birds of Prey*. For a general account of raptor biology, the preeminent work is Newton's *Population Ecology of Raptors*. The literature on individual species is quite uneven in depth. Certain species, like the Short-tailed Hawk, Gray Hawk, Common Black Hawk, Aplomado Falcon, and Hook-billed Kite, have received very little study. For other species, like the Golden Eagle, the Osprey, and the Peregrine Falcon, the literature is vast and worldwide. For these species, we list only a small sampling of published accounts and limit ourselves to English language publications. Readers seeking extensive information on particular species should consult both the general references and the references listed under individual species.

GENERAL REFERENCES

Beebe, F. L. 1974. *Field studies of the falconiformes of British Columbia*. British Columbia Provincial Museum Occasional Papers No. 17.

Bendire, C. E. 1892. *Life histories of North American birds*. U.S. Nat. Mus. Spec. Bull. 1.

Bent, A. C. 1937–1938. *Life histories of North American birds of prey*, Parts 1 and 2. Smithsonian Institution United States National Museum Bulletins 167 and 170.

Broun, M. 1949. *Hawks aloft: the story of Hawk Mountain*. Dodd, Mead Company, New York.

Brown, L., and D. Amadon. 1968. *Eagles, hawks, and falcons of the world*. McGraw-Hill, New York.

Cade, T. J. 1982. *The falcons of the world*. Cornell University Press, Ithaca, New York.

Chancellor, R. D. (ed.). 1977. *World conference on birds of prey, Vienna, 1–3 October 1975, report of proceedings*. International Council for Bird Preservation.

Clark, W. S. 1987. *A field guide to hawks of North America*. Houghton Mifflin, Boston, Massachusetts.

Craighead, J. J., and F. C. Craighead, Jr. 1956. *Hawks, owls, and wildlife*. Stackpole, Harrisburg, Pennsylvania.

Cramp, S., and K. E. L. Simmons (eds.). 1980. *Handbook of the birds of Europe, the Middle East, and North Africa; the birds of the western Palearctic*, Vol. 2, *Hawks to bustards*. Oxford University Press, New York.

Dunne, P., D. Sibley, and C. Sutton. 1987. *Hawks in flight*. Houghton Miflin, Boston, Massachusetts.

Garcelon, D. K., and G. W. Roemer (eds.). 1988. *Proceedings of the international symposium on raptor reintroduction, 1985*. Institute for Wildlife Studies, Arcata, California.

Hamerstrom, F. N., Jr., B. E. Harrell, and R. R. Olendorff (eds.). 1974. *Management of raptors. Proc. Conf. Raptor Conserv. Tech., Fort Collins, Colorado, 22–24 March, 1973*. Raptor Res. Rep. No. 2.

Ladd, W. N., and P. F. Schempf (eds.). 1982. *A symposium and workshop on raptor management and biology in Alaska and western Canada*. U.S. Fish Wildl. Serv., Anchorage, Alaska.

Millsap, B. 1981. *Distributional status of falconiforms in west-central Arizona: with notes on ecology, reproductive success, and management*. U.S.D.I. Bur. Land Manage. Tech. Note 355.

Murphy, J. R., C. M. White, and B. E. Harrell (eds.). 1975. *Population studies of raptors. Proc. Conf. Raptor Conserv. Tech., Fort Collins, Colorado, 22–24 March, 1973*. Raptor Res. Rep. No. 3.

National Wildlife Federation. 1988. *Proceedings of the Southwest raptor management symnposium and workshop*. National Wildlife Federation Scientific and Technical Series No. 11.

National Wildlife Federation. 1989. *Proceedings of the western raptor management symposium and workshop*. National Wildlife Federation Scientific and Technical Series No. 12.

National Wildlife Federation. 1989. *Proceedings of the northeast raptor management symnposium and workshop*. National Wildlife Federation Scientific and Technical Series No. 13.

Newton, I. 1979. *Population ecology of raptors*. Poyser, Berkhamsted, England.

Newton, I. (ed.). 1990. *Birds of Prey*. Facts On File, New York.

Newton, I., and R. D. Chancellor (eds.). 1985. *Conservation studies on raptors.* ICBP Technical Publication No. 5.

Olendorff, R. R. 1971. *Falconiform reproduction; a review.* Part 1, *The pre-nestling period.* Raptor Res. Rep. No. 1.

Olendorff, R. R. 1973. *The ecology of nesting birds of prey of northeastern Colorado.* Technical Report No. 211, Grassland Biome, U.S. International Biological Program.

Olendorff, R., and S. Olendorff. 1968–1970. *An extensive bibliography of falconry, eagles, hawks, falcons.* Parts 1–3, published privately.

Palmer, R. S. (ed.). 1988. *Handbook of North American birds,* Vols. 4 and 5, *Diurnal raptors,* Parts 1 and 2. Yale University Press, New Haven, Connecticut.

Senner, S. E., C. M. White, and J. R. Parrish. 1986. *Raptor conservation in the next 50 years, proceedings of a conference held at Hawk Mountain Sanctuary, Kempton, Pennsylvania, U.S.A. on 14 October, 1984.* Raptor Res. Rep. No. 5.

Wilbur, S. R., and J. A. Jackson (eds.). 1983. *Vulture biology and management.* University of California Press, Berkeley.

REFERENCES TO INDIVIDUAL SPECIES

CALIFORNIA CONDOR

Emslie, S. D. 1987. Age and diet of fossil California Condors in Grand Canyon, Arizona. *Science* 237:768–770.

Finley, W. L. 1906–1910. Life history of the California Condor. *Condor* 8:135–142; 10:5–10, 59–65; 12:5–11.

Harris, H. 1941. The annals of *Gymnogyps* to 1900. *Condor* 43:3–55.

Janssen, D. L., J. E. Oosterhuis, J. L. Allen, M. P. Anderson, D. G. Kelts, and S. N. Wiemeyer. 1986. Lead poisoning in free-ranging California Condors. *J. Am. Vet. Med. Assoc.* 155:1052–1056.

Kiff, L. 1983. An historical perspective on the condor. *Outdoor California* 44:5–6, 34–37.

Koford, C. B. 1953. *The California Condor.* Nat. Audubon Soc. Res. Rep. 4.

Miller, A. H., I. McMillan, and E. McMillan. 1965. *The current status and welfare of the California Condor.* Nat. Audubon Soc. Res. Rep. 6.

Snyder, N. F. R. 1983. California Condor reproduction, past and present. *Bird Conserv.* 1:67–86.

Snyder, N. F. R., and J. A. Hamber. 1985. Replacement-clutching and annual nesting of California Condors. *Condor* 87:374–378.

Snyder, N. F. R., and E. V. Johnson. 1985. Photographic censusing of the 1982–1983 California Condor population. *Condor* 87:1–13.

Snyder, N. F. R., E. V. Johnson, and D. A. Clendenen. 1987. Primary molt of California Condors. *Condor* 89:468–485.

Snyder, N. F. R., R. R. Ramey, and F. C. Sibley. 1986. Nest-site biology of the California Condor. *Condor* 88:228–241.

Snyder, N. F. R., and H. A. Snyder. 1989. Biology and conservation of the California Condor. *Current Ornithology* 6:175–267.

Verner, J. 1978. *California Condors: status of the recovery effort.* U. S. Forest Service Gen. Tech. Rep. PSW-28.

Wallace, M. P., and S. A. Temple. 1987. Releasing captive-reared Andean Condors to the wild. *J. Wildl. Manage.* 51:541–550.

Wilbur, S. R. 1978. *The California Condor, 1966–76: a look at its past and future.* N. Am. Fauna 72.

TURKEY VULTURE

Arad, Z., U. Midtgard, and M. H. Bernstein. 1989. Thermoregulation in Turkey Vultures: vascular anatomy, arteriovenous heat exchange, and behavior. *Condor* 91:505–514.

Audubon, J. J. 1826. Account of the habits of the Turkey Buzzard *Vultur aura* particularly with the view of exploding the opinion generally entertained of its extraordinary powers of smelling. *Edinb. New Phil. J.* 2:172–184.

Clark, R. G., and R. D. Ohmart. 1985. Spread-winged posture of Turkey Vultures: single or multiple function? *Condor* 87:350–355.

Coles, V. 1944. Nesting of the Turkey Vulture in Ohio caves. *Auk* 61:219–228.

Davis, D. 1979. Morning and evening roosts of Turkey Vultures at Malheur Refuge, Oregon. *West. Birds* 10:125–130.

Houston, D. C. 1985. Evolutionary ecology of Afrotropical and Neotropical vultures in forests. Pp. 856–864 in *Neotropical ornithology,* M. Foster (ed.), Ornithological Monographs No. 36.

Houston, D. C. 1986. Scavenging efficiency of Turkey Vultures in a tropical forest. *Condor* 88:318–323.

Houston, D. C. 1988. Competition for food between Neotropical vultures in forest. *Ibis* 130:402–417.

Houston, D. C. 1988. Digestive efficiency and hunting behavior in cats, dogs, and vultures. *J. Zool. Lond.* 216:603–605.

Owre, O. T., and P. O. Northington. 1961. Indication of the sense of smell in the Turkey Vulture, *Cathartes aura* (Linnaeus), from feeding tests. *Am. Midl. Nat.* 66:200–205.

Stager, K. E. 1964. *The role of olfaction in food location by the Turkey Vulture.* Contrib. Sci. (Los Angeles) 81.

Work, T. H., and A. S. Wool. 1942. The nest life of the Turkey Vulture. *Condor* 44:149–159.

BLACK VULTURE

Brown, W. H. 1976. Winter population trends in the Black and Turkey Vultures. *Am. Birds* 30:909–912.

Coleman, J. S. 1985. Home range, habitat use, behavior, and morphology of the Gettysburg vultures. M.S. thesis, Virginia Polytechnic Institute and State University, Blacksburg.

Kahl, M. P., Jr. 1963. Thermoregulation in the Wood Stork, with special reference to the role of the legs. *Physiol. Zool.* 36:141–151.

Ligon, J. D. 1967. *Relationships of the cathartid vultures.* Occas. Pap. Mus. Zool. Univ. Mich. 651.

Parmalee, P. W. 1954. The vultures: their movements, economic status, and control in Texas. *Auk* 71:443–453.

Parmalee, P., and B. Parmalee. 1967. Results of banding studies of Black Vultures in eastern North America. *Condor* 69:146–155.

Rabenold, P. P. 1986. Family associations in communally roosting Black Vultures. *Auk* 103:32–41.

Rabenold, P. P. 1987. Recruitment to food in Black Vultures: evidence for following from communal roosts. *Anim. Behav.* 35:1775–1785.

Rabenold, P. P. 1987. Roost attendance and aggression in Black Vultures. *Auk* 104:647–653.

Stewart, P. 1978. Behavioral interactions and niche separation in Black and Turkey Vultures. *Living Bird* 17:79–84.

Thomas, E. S. 1928. Nesting of the Black Vulture in Hocking County, Ohio. *Ohio State Mus. Sci. Bull.* 1:29–35.

EVERGLADE (SNAIL) KITE

Beissinger, S. R. 1986. Demography, environmental uncertainty, and the evolution of mate desertion in the Snail Kite. *Ecology* 67:1445–1459.

Beissinger, S. R., 1990. Alternative foods of a diet specialist, the Snail Kite. *Auk* 107:327–333.

Beissinger, S. R., and N. F. R. Snyder. 1987. Mate desertion in the Snail Kite. *Anim. Behav.* 35:477–487.

Beissinger, S. R., and J. E. Takekawa. 1983. Habitat use and dispersal of snail Kites in Florida during drought conditions. *Fla. Field Nat.* 11:89–106.

Chandler, R., and J. M. Anderson. 1974. Notes on Everglade Kite reproduction. *Am. Birds* 28:856–858.

Nicholson, D. J. 1926. Nesting habits of the Everglade Kite in Florida. *Auk* 43:62–67.

Snyder, N. F. R., S. R. Beissinger, and R. E. Chandler. 1989. Reproduction and demography of the Florida Everglade (Snail) Kite. *Condor* 91:300–316.

Snyder, N. F. R., S. R. Beissinger, and M. R. Fuller. 1989. Solar radio-transmitters on Snail Kites in Florida. *J. Field Ornithol.* 60:171–177.

Snyder, N. F. R., and H. W. Kale, II. 1983. Mollusc predation by Snail Kites in Colombia. *Auk* 100:93–97.

Snyder, N. F. R., J. C. Ogden, J. D. Bittner, and G. A. Grau. 1984. Larval dermestid beetles feeding on nestling Snail Kites, Wood Storks, and Great Blue Herons. *Condor* 86:170–174.

Snyder, N. F. R., and H. A. Snyder. 1969. A comparative study of mollusc predation by Limpkins, Everglade Kites, and Boat-tailed Grackles. *Living Bird* 8:177–233.

Snyder, N. F. R., and H. A. Snyder. 1970. Feeding territories in the Everglade Kite. *Condor* 72:492–493.

Snyder, N. F. R., and H. A. Snyder. 1971. Defenses of the Florida apple snail (*Pomacea paludosa*). *Behaviour* 40:175–215.

Sykes, P. W., Jr. 1983. Recent population trend of the Snail Kite in Florida and its relationship to water levels. *J. Field Ornithol.* 54:237–246.

Takekawa, J. E., and S. R. Beissinger. 1989. Cyclic drought, dispersal, and the conservation of the Snail Kite in Florida: lessons in critical habitat. *Conservation Biology* 3:302–311.

HOOK-BILLED KITE

Delnicki, D. 1978. Second occurrence and first successful nesting record of the Hook-billed Kite in the United States. *Auk* 95:427.

Fleetwood, R. J., and J. L. Hamilton. 1967. Occurrence and nesting of the Hook-billed Kite (*Chondrohierax uncinatus*) in Texas. *Auk* 84:598–601.

Paulson, D. R. 1983. Flocking in the Hook-billed Kite. *Auk* 100:749– 750.

Smith, T. B. 1982. Nests and young of two rare raptors from Mexico. *Biotropica* 14:79–80.

Smith, T. B., and S. A. Temple. 1982. Feeding habits and bill polymorphism in Hook-billed Kites. *Auk* 99:197–207.

Smith, T. B., and S. A. Temple. 1982. Grenada Hook-billed Kite: recent status and life history notes. *Condor* 84:131.

Voous, K. H. 1969. Predation potential in birds of prey from Surinam. *Ardea* 57:117–148.

BLACK-SHOULDERED (WHITE-TAILED) KITE

Dixon, J. B., R. E. Dixon, and J. E. Dixon. 1957. Natural history of the White-tailed Kite in San Diego County, California. *Condor* 59: 156–165.

Eisenmann, E. 1971. Range expansion and population increase in North and Middle America of the White-tailed Kite (*Elanus leucurus*). *Am. Birds* 25:529–536.

Gatz, T. A., M. D. Jakle, R. L. Glinski, and G. Monson. 1985. First nesting records and current status of the Black-shouldered Kite in Arizona. *West. Birds* 16:57–61.

Hawbecker, A. C. 1942. A life history study of the White-tailed Kite. *Condor* 44:267–275.

Larson, D. 1980. Increase in the White-tailed Kite populations of California and Texas, 1944–1978. *Am. Birds* 34:689–690.

Mendelsohn, J. M. 1981. A study of the Black-shouldered Kite (*Elanus caeruleus*). Ph.D. dissertation, University of Natal, Pietermaritzburg, South Africa.

Moore, R. T., and A. Barr. 1941. Habits of the White-tailed Kite. *Auk* 58:453–462.

Pickwell, G. B. 1930. The White-tailed Kite. *Condor* 32:221–239.

Pickwell, G. B. 1932. Requiem for the White-tailed Kites of Santa Clara Valley. *Condor* 34:44–45.

Pruett-Jones, S. G., M. A. Pruett-Jones, and R. L. Knight. 1980. The White-tailed Kite in North and Middle America: current status and recent population changes. *Am. Birds* 34:682–688.

Stendell, R. C., and P. Meyers. 1973. White-tailed Kite predation on a fluctuating vole population. *Condor* 75:359–360.

Waian, L. 1976. A resurgence of kites. *Nat. Hist.* 85(9):40–47.

Waian, L. B., and R. E. Stendell. 1970. The White-tailed Kite in California with observations of the Santa Barbara population. *Calif. Fish Game* 56:188–198.

Warner, J. S., and R. L. Rudd. 1975. Hunting by the White-tailed Kites (*Elanus leucurus*). *Condor* 77:226–230.

Watson, F. G. 1940. A behavior study of the White-tailed Kite. *Condor* 42:295–304.

MISSISSIPPI KITE

Fitch, H. S. 1963. Observations on the Mississippi Kite in southwestern Kansas. *Univ. Kansas Publ., Mus. Nat. Hist.* 12:503–519.

Glinski, R. L., and R. D. Ohmart. 1983. Breeding ecology of the Mississippi Kite. *Condor* 85:200–207.

Hunter, W. C., R. D. Ohmart, and B. W. Anderson. 1988. Use of exotic saltcedar (*Tamarix chinensis*) by birds in arid riparian systems. *Condor* 90:113–123.

Parker, J. W. 1974. The breeding biology of the Mississippi Kite in the Great Plains. Ph.D. dissertation, University of Kansas, Lawrence.

Parker, J. W., and J. C. Ogden. 1979. The recent history and status of the Mississippi Kite. *Am. Birds* 33:119–129.

Robinson, T. W. 1965. *Introduction, spread, and areal extent of saltcedar* (Tamarix) *in the western states.* U.S. Geological Survey, Prof. Pap. 491-A. Gov. Printing Office, Washington, D.C.

Sutton, G. M. 1939. The Mississippi Kite in spring. *Condor* 41:41–53

Sutton, G. M. 1944. The kites of the genus *Ictinia*. *Wilson Bull.* 56:3–8.

AMERICAN SWALLOW-TAILED KITE

Cely, J. E., and J. A. Sorrow. 1990. *The American Swallow-tailed Kite in South Carolina.* South Carolina Wildlife and

Marine Resources Department, Nongame and Heritage Trust Publications No. 1.

Green, R. O., Jr., N. D. Reed, and M. H. Wright, Jr. 1972. Swallow-tailed Kite. *Nat. Geog.* 142:496–505.

Lemke, T. O. 1979. Fruit-eating behavior of Swallow-tailed Kites (*Elanoides forficatus*) in Colombia. *Condor* 81:207–208.

Lohrer, C. E., and F. E. Lohrer. 1984. Persistent predation by American Swallow-tailed Kites on Eastern Kingbirds. *Fla. Field Nat.* 12:42–43.

Millsap, B. A. 1987. Summer concentration of American Swallow-tailed Kites at Lake Okeechobee, Florida, with comments on post-breeding movements. *Fla. Field Nat.* 15:85–92.

Skutch, A. F. 1965. Life history notes on two tropical American kites. *Condor* 67:235–246.

Snyder, N. F. R. 1974. Breeding biology of Swallow-tailed Kites in Florida. *Living Bird* 13:73–97.

Sutton, I. D. 1955. Nesting of the Swallow-tailed Kite. *Everglades Natural History* 3:72–84.

Wright, M., R. Green, and N. Reed. 1971. The swallowtails of Royal Palm. *Audubon* 73:40–49.

NORTHERN HARRIER (MARSH HAWK, HARRIER, HEN HARRIER)

Balfour, E. 1957. Observations on the breeding biology of the Hen Harrier in Orkney. *Bird Notes* 27:177–183, 216–224.

Balfour, E., and C. J. Cadbury. 1979. Polygyny, spacing and sex ratio among Hen Harriers *Circus cyaneus* in Orkney, Scotland. *Ornis. Scand.* 10:133–141.

Bildstein, K. L. 1978. *Behavioral ecology of Red-tailed Hawks* (Buteo jamaicensis)*, Rough-legged Hawks* (Buteo lagopus)*, Northern Harriers* (Circus cyaneus)*, and American Kestrels* (Falco sparverius) *in south central Ohio.* Ohio Biol. Surv., Biol. Notes No. 18.

Bildstein, K. L. 1979. Fluctuations in the numbers of Northern Harriers (*Circus cyaneus hudsonius*) at communal roosts in south central Ohio. *Raptor Res.* 13:40–46.

Bildstein, K. L., W. S. Clark, D. L. Evans, M. Field, L. Soucy, and E. Henckel. 1984. Sex and age differences in fall migration of Northern Harriers. *J. Field Ornithol.* 55:143–150.

Breckenridge, W. J. 1935. An ecological study of some Minnesota Marsh Hawks. *Condor* 37:268–276.

Collopy, N. W., and K. L. Bildstein. 1987. Foraging behavior of Northern Harriers in southeastern salt and freshwater marshes. *Auk* 104:11–16.

Errington, P. L., and W. J. Breckenridge. 1936. Food habits of Marsh Hawks in the glaciated prairie region of north-central United States. *Amer. Midl. Nat.* 7:831–848.

Hamerstrom, F. 1986. *Harrier, hawk of the marshes.* Smithsonian Institution Press, Washington, D.C.

Picozzi, N. 1978. Dispersion, breeding and prey of the Hen Harrier (*Circus cyaneus*) in Glen Dye, Kincardineshire. *Ibis* 120:498–509.

Rice, W. R. 1982. Acoustical location of prey by the Marsh Hawk: adaptation to concealed prey. *Auk* 99:403–413.

Schipper, W. J. A. 1973. A comparison of prey selection in sympatric harriers, *Circus* in Western Europe. *Le Gerfaut* 63:17–120.

Schipper, W. J. A. 1977. Hunting in three European harriers (*Circus*) during the breeding season. *Ardea* 65:53–72.

Schipper, W. J. A. 1978. A comparison of breeding ecology in three European harriers (*Circus*). *Ardea* 66:77–102.

Schipper, W. J. A., L. S. Buurma, and P. H. Bossenbroek. 1975. Comparative study of hunting behaviour of wintering Hen Harriers *Circus cyaneus* and Marsh Harriers *Circus aeruginosus*. *Ardea* 63:1–29.

Simmons, R. 1988. Honest advertising, sexual selection, courtship displays, and body condition of polygynous male Harriers. *Auk* 104:11–16.

Watson, A. D. 1977. *The Hen Harrier.* Poyser, Berkhamsted, England.

NORTHERN GOSHAWK

Eng, R. L., and G. W. Gullion. 1962. The predation of Goshawks upon Ruffed Grouse on the Cloquet Forest Research Center, Minnesota. *Wilson Bull.* 74:227–242.

Goslow, G. E., Jr. 1971. The attack and strike of some North American raptors. *Auk* 88:815–827.

Kenward, R. E. 1976. The effect of predation by Goshawks *Accipiter gentilis* on Wood-pigeon *Columba palumbus* populations. Ph.D. dissertation, University of Oxford, England.

Kenward, R. E. 1979. Winter predation by Goshawks in lowland Britain. *Brit. Birds* 72:64–73.

Kenward, R. E. 1982. Goshawk hunting behaviour, and range size as a function of food and habitat availability. *J. Anim. Ecol.* 51:69–80.

Kenward, R. E., and I. M. Lindsay. 1981. *Understanding the Goshawk.* International Association for Falconry and Conservation of Birds of Prey.

Marquiss, M., and I. Newton. 1982. The Goshawk in Britain. *Brit. Birds* 75:243–260.

Meng, H. 1959. Food habits of nesting Cooper's Hawks and Goshawks in New York and Pennsylvania. *Wilson Bull.* 71:169–174.

Mueller, H. C., D. D. Berger, and G. Allez. 1977. The periodic invasions of Goshawks. *Auk* 94:652–653.

Opdam, P. 1975. Inter- and intraspecific differentiation with respect to feeding ecology in two sympatric species of the genus *Accipiter*. *Ardea* 63:30–54.

Reynolds, R. T., and E. C. Meslow. 1984. Partitioning of food and niche characteristics of coexisting *Accipiter* during breeding. *Auk* 101:761–779.

Schnell, J. H. 1958. Nesting behavior and food habits of Goshawks in the Sierra Nevada of California. *Condor* 60:377–403.

Wattel, J. 1973. *Geographic differentiation in the genus Accipiter.* Publ. Nuttall Ornith. Club, No. 13.

Wimberger, P. H. 1984. The use of green plant material in bird nests to avoid ectoparasites. *Auk* 101:615–618.

COOPER'S HAWK

Cade, T. J., J. L. Lincer, C. M. White, D. G. Roseneau, and L. G. Swartz. 1971. DDE residues and egg shell changes in Alaskan falcons and hawks. *Science* 172:955–957.

Fitch, H. S., B. Glading, and V. House. 1946. Observations on Cooper's Hawk nesting and predation. *California Fish and Game* 32:144–154.

Hennesy, S. P. 1978. Ecological relationships of accipiters in northern Utah with special emphasis on the effects of human disturbance. M.S. thesis, Utah State University, Logan.

Hickey, J. J., and D. W. Anderson. 1968. Chlorinated hydrocarbons and eggshell changes in raptorial and fish-eating birds. *Science* 162:271–273.

Janik, C. A., and J. Mosher. 1982. Breeding biology of raptors in the central Appalachians. *Raptor Res.* 16:18–24.

Meng. H. 1951. The Cooper's Hawk. Ph.D. dissertation, Cornell University, Ithaca, New York.

Moore, K. R., and C. J. Henny. 1983. Nest site characteristics of three coexisting accipiter hawks in northeastern Oregon. *Raptor Res.* 17:65–76.

Porter, R. D., and S. N. Wiemeyer. 1969. Dieldrin and DDT: effects on Sparrow Hawk eggshells and reproduction. *Science* 165:199–200.

Ratcliffe, D. A. 1967. Decrease in eggshell weight in certain birds of prey. *Nature* 215:208–210.

Reynolds, R. T. 1979. Food and habitat partitioning in the groups of coexisting *Accipiter*. Ph.D. dissertation, Oregon State University, Corvallis.

Reynolds, R. T., E. C. Meslow, and H. M. Wight. 1982. Nesting habitat of coexisting *Accipiter* in Oregon. *J. Wildl. Manage.* 46:124–138.

Roberts, J. O. L. 1967. Iris colour and age of Sharp-shinned Hawks. *Ontario Bird Banding* 3:95–106.

Snyder, H. A., and N. F. R. Snyder. 1974. Increased mortality of Cooper's Hawks accustomed to man. *Condor* 76:215–216.

Snyder, N. F. R., and H. A. Snyder. 1973. Experimental study of feeding rates of nesting Cooper's Hawks. *Condor* 75:461–463.

Snyder, N. F. R., and H. A. Snyder. 1974. Function of eye coloration in North American accipiters. *Condor* 76:219–222.

Snyder, N. and H. Snyder. 1974. Can the Cooper's Hawk survive? *Nat. Geog.* 145:433–442.

Snyder, N. F. R., and H. A. Snyder. 1979. Biology of North American accipiters in Arizona and New Mexico. *National Geographic Society Research Reports, 1970 projects*, pp. 487–491.

Snyder, N. F. R., H. A. Snyder, J. L. Lincer, and R. T. Reynolds. 1973. Organochlorines, heavy metals, and the biology of North American accipiters. *BioScience* 23:300–305.

SHARP-SHINNED HAWK

Amadon, D. 1975. Why are female birds of prey larger than males? *Raptor Res.* 9:1–11.

Andersson, M., and R. A. Norberg. 1981. Evolution of reversed sexual size dimorphism and role partitioning among predatory birds, with a size scaling of flight performance. *Biol. J. Linn. Soc.* 15:105–130.

Clark, W. S. 1984. Field identification of *Accipiters* in North America. *Birding* 16:151–263.

Clarke, R. G. 1984. The Sharp-shinned Hawk (*Accipiter striatus vieillot*) in interior Alaska. M.S. thesis, University of Alaska, Fairbanks.

Delannoy, C. A., and A. Cruz. 1988. Breeding biology of the Puerto Rican Sharp-shinned Hawk (*Accipiter striatus venator*). Auk 105: 649–662.

Marquiss, M., and I. Newton. 1982. A radio-tracking study of the ranging behaviour and dispersion of European Sparrowhawks *Accipiter nisus*. *J. Anim. Ecol.* 51:111–133.

Mueller, H. C., D. D. Berger, and G. Allez. 1979. The identification of North American accipiters. *Am. Birds* 33:226–240.

Newton, I. 1986. *The Sparrowhawk*. Poyser, Calton, England.

Platt, J. B. 1973. Habitat and time utilization of a pair of nesting Sharp-shinned Hawks (*Accipiter striatus velox*). M.S. thesis, Brigham Young University, Provo, Utah.

Reynolds, R. T. 1972. Sexual dimorphism in *Accipiter* hawks: a new hypothesis. *Condor* 74:191–197.

Snyder, N. F. R., and J. W. Wiley. 1976. *Sexual size dimorphism in hawks and owls of North America*. Ornithological Monographs No. 20.

Storer, R. W. 1952. Variation in the resident Sharp-shinned Hawks of Mexico. *Condor* 54:283–287.

Storer, R. W. 1966. Sexual dimorphism and food habits in three North American accipiters. *Auk* 83:423–436.

RED-TAILED HAWK

Fitch, H. S., F. Swenson, and D. F. Tillotson. 1946. Behavior and food habits of the Red-tailed Hawk. *Condor* 48:205–237.

Howell, J., B. Smith, J. B. Holt, Jr., and D. R. Osborne. 1978. Habitat structure and productivity in Red-tailed Hawks. *Bird-Banding* 49:162–171.

Janes, S. W. 1984. Influences of territory composition and interspecific competition on Red-tailed Hawk reproductive success. *Ecology* 65:862–870.

Johnson, S. J. 1973. Post-fledging activity of Red-tailed Hawks. *Raptor Res.* 7:43–48.

Knight, R. L., and A. W. Erickson. 1976. High incidence of snakes in the diet of nesting Red-tailed Hawks. *Raptor Res.* 10:108–111.

Luttich, S. N., L. B. Keith, and J. D. Stephenson. 1971. Population dynamics of the Red-tailed Hawk (*Buteo jamaicensis*) at Rochester, Alberta. *Auk* 88:75–87.

Luttich, S., D. H. Rusch, E. C. Meslow, and L. B. Keith. 1970. Ecology of Red-tailed Hawk predation in Alberta. *Ecology* 51:190–203.

McInvaille, W. B., Jr., and L. B. Keith. 1974. Predator-prey relations and breeding ecology of the Great Horned Owl and Red-tailed Hawk in central Alberta. *Can. Field-Nat.* 88:1–20.

Mindell, D. P. 1983. Harlan's Hawk (*Buteo jamaicensis harlani*): a valid subspecies. *Auk* 100:161–169.

Schmutz, J. K., S. M. Schmutz, and D. A. Boag. 1980. Coexistence of three species of hawks (*Buteo* spp.) in the prairie-parkland ecotone. *Can. J. Zool.* 58:1075–1089.

Snyder, N. F. R., J. W. Wiley, and C. B. Kepler. 1987. *The parrots of Luquillo, biology and conservation of the Puerto Rican Parrot*. Western Foundation of Vertebrate Zoology, Los Angeles, California.

BROAD-WINGED HAWK

Burns, F. L. 1911. A monograph of the Broad-winged Hawk (*Buteo platypterus*). *Wilson Bull.* 23:139–320

Crocoll, S. T., and J. W. Parker. 1989. The breeding biology of Broad-winged and Red-shouldered Hawks in western New York. *J. Raptor Res.* 23:125–139.

Fitch, H. S. 1974. Observations on the food and nesting of the Broad-winged Hawk (*Buteo platypterus*) in northeastern Kansas. *Condor* 76:331–333.

Fuller, M. 1979. Spatiotemporal relationships of four sympatric raptor species. Ph.D. dissertation, University of Minnesota, Minneapolis.

Harwood, M. 1973. *The view from Hawk Mountain*. Scribner's, New York.

Matray, P. F. 1974. Broad-winged Hawk nesting and ecology. *Auk* 91:307–324.

Rosenfield, R. N. 1984. Nesting biology of Broad-winged Hawks in Wisconsin. *Raptor Res.* 18:6–9.

Rusch, D. H., and P. Doerr. 1972. Broad-winged Hawk nesting and food habits. *Auk* 89:139–145.

Titus, K., and J. A. Mosher. 1981. Nest-site habitat selected by woodland hawks in the central Appalachians. *Auk* 98:270–281.

RED-SHOULDERED HAWK

Bednarz, J. C., and J. J. Dinsmore. 1981. Status, habitat use, and management of Red-shouldered Hawks in Iowa. *J. Wildl. Manage.* 45:236–241.

Brown, W. H. 1971. Winter population trends in the Red-shouldered Hawk. *Am. Birds* 25:813–817.

Campbell, C. A. 1975. Ecology and reproduction of Red-shouldered Hawks in the Waterloo region, southern Ontario. *Raptor Res.* 9:12–17.

Dixon, J. B. 1928. Life history of the Red-bellied Hawk. *Condor* 30:228–236.

Henny, C. J., F. C. Schmid, E. M. Martin, and L. L. Hood. 1973. Territorial behavior, pesticides, and the population ecology of Red-shouldered Hawks in central Maryland, 1943–1971. *Ecology* 54:545–554.

Kimmel, V. L., and L. H. Fredrickson. 1981. Nesting ecology of the Red-shouldered Hawk in southeastern Missouri. *Trans. Mo. Acad. Sci.* 15:21–27.

McCrary, M. D. 1981. Space and habitat utilization by Red-shouldered Hawks (*Buteo lineatus elegans*) in southern California. M.S. thesis, California State University, Long Beach.

Nicholson, D. J. 1930. Habits of the Florida Red-shouldered Hawk. *Wilson Bull.* 42:32–35.

Portnoy, J. W., and W. E. Dodge. 1979. Red-shouldered Hawk nesting ecology and behavior. *Wilson Bull.* 91:104–117.

Stewart, R. E. 1949. Ecology of a nesting Red-shouldered Hawk population. *Wilson Bull.* 61:26–35.

Wiley, J. W. 1975. The nesting and reproductive success of Red-tailed Hawks and Red-shouldered Hawks in Orange County, California, 1973. *Condor* 77:133–139.

Wiley, J. W., and B. N. Wiley. 1981. Breeding season ecology and behavior of Ridgway's Hawk (*Buteo ridgwayi*). *Condor* 83:132–151.

GRAY HAWK (MEXICAN GOSHAWK)

Amadon, D., and A. R. Phillips. 1939. Notes on the Mexican Goshawk. *Auk* 56:183–184.

Knopf, F. L., R. R. Johnson, T. Rich, F. B. Samson, and R. C. Szaro. 1988. Conservation of riparian ecosystems in the United States. *Wilson Bull.* 100:272–284.

Millsap, B. A. 1986. Biosystematics of the Gray Hawk, *Buteo nitidus* (Latham). M.S. thesis, George Mason University, Fairfax, Virginia.

Stensrude, C. 1965. Observations on a pair of Gray Hawks in southern Arizona. *Condor* 67:319–321.

Sutton, G. 1953. Gray Hawk. *Wilson Bull.* 65:5–7.

Zimmerman, D. A. 1965. The Gray Hawk in the Southwest. *Aud. Field Notes* 19:475–477.

SHORT-TAILED HAWK

Brandt, H. W. 1924. The nesting of the Short-tailed Hawk. *Auk* 41:59–64.

Moore, J. C., L. A. Stimson, and W. B. Robertson. 1953. Observations of the Short-tailed Hawk in Florida. *Auk* 70:470–478.

Nicholson, D. J. 1951. Notes on the very rare Short-tailed Hawk. *Fla. Nat.* 24:32–33.

Ogden, J. C. 1973. Field identification of difficult birds: I. Short-tailed Hawk. *Fla. Field Nat.* 1:30–33.

Ogden, J. C. 1974. The Short-tailed Hawk in Florida: I. Migration, habitat, hunting techniques, and food habits. *Auk* 91:95–110.

Ogden, J. C. 1978. Rare Short-tailed Hawk. Pp. 55–57 in *Rare and endangered biota of Florida*, Vol. 2, *Birds*, H. W. Kale, III., (ed.), University Presses of Florida, Gainesville.

Pennock, C. J. 1890. Notes on the nesting of *Buteo brachyurus* at St. Marks, Florida. *Auk* 7:56–57.

SWAINSON'S HAWK

Bechard, M. J. 1980. Factors affecting nest productivity of Swainson's Hawk (*Buteo swainsoni*) in southeastern Washington. Ph.D. dissertation, Washington State University, Pullman.

Bechard, M. J. 1982. Effect of vegetative cover on foraging site selection by Swainson's Hawk. *Condor* 84:153–159.

Bechard, M. J. 1983. Food supply and the occurrence of brood reduction in Swainson's Hawk. *Wilson Bull.* 95:233–242

Bednarz, J. C. 1988. A comparative study of the breeding ecology of Harris' and Swainson's Hawks in southeastern New Mexico. *Condor* 90:311–323.

Gilmer, D. S., and R. E. Stewart. 1984. Swainson's Hawk nesting ecology in North Dakota. *Condor* 86:12–18.

Johnson, C. G., L. A. Nickerson, and M. J. Bechard. 1987. Grasshopper consumption and summer flocks of non-breeding Swainson's Hawks. *Condor* 89:676–678.

Kerlinger, P. 1989. *Flight strategies of migrating hawks.* University of Chicago Press, Chicago, Illinois.

Kirkley, J. S., and J. A. Gessaman. 1990. Water economy of nestling Swainson's Hawks. *Condor* 92:29–44.

Risebrough, R. W., R. W. Schlorff, P. H. Bloom, and E. E. Littrell. 1989. Investigations of the decline of Swainson's Hawk in California. *J. Raptor Res.* 23:63–71.

Schmutz, J. K. 1984. Ferruginous and Swainson's Hawk abundance and distribution in relation to land use in southeastern Alberta. *J. Wildl. Manage.* 48:1180–1187.

Schmutz, J. K., R. W. Fyfe, D. A. Moore, and A. R. Smith. 1984. Artificial nests for Ferruginous and Swainson's Hawks. *J. Wildl. Manage.* 48:1009–1013.

Skutch, A. F. 1945. The migration of Swainson's and Broad-winged Hawks through Costa Rica. *Northwest Sci.* 19:80–89.

Smith, N. G. 1985. Some uncertain aspects of migration by Swainson's Hawks (*Buteo swainsoni*) and Turkey Vultures (*Cathartes aura*). *Proc. North American Hawk Migration Conf. No. 4*, Rochester, New York.

Smith, N. G., D. L. Goldstein, and G. A. Bartholomew. 1986. Is long-distance migration possible for soaring hawks using only stored fat? *Auk* 106:607–611.

ROUGH-LEGGED HAWK

Bechard, M. J., and C. S. Houston. 1984. Probable identity of purported Rough-legged Hawk nests in the western U.S. and Canada. *Condor* 86:348–352.

Cade, T. J. 1955. Variation of the Common Rough-legged Hawk in North America. *Condor* 57:313–346.

Hagen, Y. 1969. Norwegian studies on the reproduction of birds of prey and owls in relation to micro-rodent population fluctuations. *Fauna* 22:73–126.

Schnell, G. D. 1967. Population fluctuations, spatial distributions, and food habits of Rough-legged Hawks in Illinois. *Kansas Ornith. Soc. Bull.* 18:21–28.

Schnell, G. D. 1968. Differential habitat utilization by wintering Rough-legged and Red-tailed Hawks. *Condor* 70:373–377.

Schnell, G. D. 1969. Communal roosts of wintering Rough-legged Hawks (*Buteo lagopus*). *Auk* 86:682–690.

Sutton, G. M., and D. F. Parmalee. 1956. The Rough-legged Hawk in the American Arctic. *Arctic* 9:202–207.

Watson, J. W. 1984. Rough-legged Hawk winter ecology in southeastern Idaho. M.S. thesis, Montana State University, Bozeman.

White, C. M., and T. J. Cade. 1971. Cliff-nesting raptors and ravens along the Colville River in Arctic Alaska. *Living Bird* 10:107–150.

FERRUGINOUS (FERRUGINOUS ROUGH-LEGGED) HAWK

Blair, C. L., and F. Schitoskey, Jr. 1982. Breeding biology and diet of the Ferruginous Hawk in South Dakota. *Wilson Bull.* 94:46–54.

Gilmer, D. S., and R. E. Stewart. 1983. Ferruginous Hawk populations and habitat use in North Dakota. *J. Wildl. Manage.* 47:146–157.

Paulson, D. R. 1973. Predator polymorphism and apostatic selection. *Evolution* 27:269–277.

Preston, C. R. 1980. Differential perch site selection by color morphs of the Red-tailed Hawk (*Buteo jamaicensis*). *Auk* 97:782–789.

Schmutz, S. M., and J. K. Schmutz. 1981. Inheritance of color phases of Ferruginous Hawks. *Condor* 83:187–189.

Smith, D. G., and J. R. Murphy. 1978. Biology of the Ferruginous Hawk in central Utah. *Sociobiology* 3:79–95.

Smith, D. G., J. R. Murphy, and N. D. Woffinden. 1981. Relationship between jackrabbit abundance and Ferruginous Hawk reproduction. *Condor* 83:52–56.

Steenhof, K., and M. N. Kochert. 1985. Dietary shifts of sympatric buteos during a prey decline. *Oecologia* 66:6–16.

Wakeley, J. S. 1974. Activity periods, hunting methods, and efficiency of the Ferruginous Hawk. *Raptor Res.* 8:67–72.

Wakeley, J. S. 1978. Activity budgets, energy expenditures, and energy intakes of nesting Ferruginous Hawks. *Auk* 95:667–676.

Wakeley, J. S. 1978. Hunting methods and factors affecting their use by Ferruginous Hawks. *Condor* 80:327–333.

Wakeley, J. S. 1978. Factors affecting the use of hunting sites by Ferruginous Hawks. *Condor* 80:316–326.

White, C. M., and T. L. Thurow. 1985. Reproduction of Ferruginous Hawks exposed to controlled disturbance. *Condor* 87:14–22.

Woffinden, N. D., and J. R. Murphy. 1977. Population dynamics of the Ferruginous Hawk during a prey decline. *Great Basin Nat.* 37:411–425.

WHITE-TAILED HAWK

Farquhar, C. C. 1986. Ecology and breeding behavior of the White-tailed Hawk on the northern coastal prairies of Texas. Ph.D. dissertation, Texas A and M University, College Station.

Howell, T. R. 1971. An ecological study of the birds of the lowland pine savanna and adjacent rain forest in northeastern Nicaraugua. *Living Bird* 10:185–242.

Mader, W. J. 1981. Notes on nesting raptors in the Llanos of Venezuela. *Condor* 83:48–51.

Morrison, M. L. 1978. Breeding characteristics, eggshell thinning, and population trends of White-tailed Hawks in Texas. *Bull. Texas Ornithol. Soc.* 11:35–40.

Stevenson, J. O., and L. H. Meitzen. 1946. Behavior and food habits of Sennett's White-tailed Hawk in Texas. *Wilson Bull.* 58:198–205.

Tewes, M. E. 1984. Opportunistic feeding by White-tailed Hawks at prescribed burns. *Wilson Bull.* 96:135–136.

ZONE-TAILED HAWK

Matteson, S., and J. Riley. 1981. Distribution and reproductive success of Zone-tailed Hawks in west Texas. *Wilson Bull.* 93:282–284.

Mueller, H. C. 1972. Zone-tailed Hawk and Turkey Vulture: mimicry or aerodynamics? *Condor* 74:221–222.

Snyder, H. A., and R. Glinski. 1978. *Report on the breeding raptors of the Coronado National Forest.* Coronado National Forest, Tucson, Arizona.

Willis, E. 1963. Is the Zone-tailed Hawk a mimic of the Turkey Vulture? *Condor* 65:313–317.

Zimmerman, D. A. 1976. Comments on the feeding habits and vulture mimicry of the Zone-tailed Hawk. *Condor* 78:420–421.

COMMON BLACK HAWK

Mader, W. J. 1982. Ecology and breeding habits of the Savanna Hawk in the Llanos of Venezuela. *Condor* 84:261–271.

Murphy, J. 1978. Management considerations for some western hawks. *Trans. North Am. Wildl. and Nat. Resour. Conf.* 43:241–251.

Schnell, J. H. 1976. *The behavior and ecology of the Black-hawks (Buteogallus anthracinus) in Aravaipa Canyon (Graham/Pinal Counties, Arizona).* Progress Rep. to Defenders of Wildl. and U.S. Dept. Interior. Bur. Land Manage.

Schnell, J. H. 1979. *Habitat management series for unique or endangered species. Rep. 18. Black-hawk (Buteogallus anthracinus).* U.S. Dept. Interior, Bur. Land Manage., Denver, Colorado.

BAY-WINGED (HARRIS') HAWK

Bednarz, J. C. 1987. Pair and group reproductive success, polyandry, and cooperative breeding in Harris' Hawk. *Auk* 104:393–404.

Bednarz, J. C. 1987. Successive nesting and autumnal breeding in Harris' Hawks. *Auk* 104:85–96.

Bednarz, J. C. 1988. Cooperative hunting in Harris' Hawks (*Parabuteo unicinctus*). *Science* 239:1525–1527.

Bednarz, J. C., and J. D. Ligon. 1988. A study of the ecological bases of cooperative breeding in the Harris' Hawk. *Ecology* 69:1176–1187.

Dawson, J. W. 1988. The cooperative breeding system of the Harris' Hawk in Arizona. M.S. thesis, University of Arizona, Tucson.

Dawson, J. W., and R. W. Mannan. 1989. A comparison of two methods of estimating group size in Harris' Hawks. *Auk* 107:480–483.

Griffin, C. R. 1976. A preliminary comparison of Texas and Arizona Harris' Hawk (*Parabuteo unicinctus*) populations. *Raptor Res.* 10:50–54.

Hastings, J. R., and R. M. Turner. 1965. *The changing mile*. University of Arizona Press, Tucson.

Mader, W. J. 1975. Biology of the Harris' Hawk in southern Arizona. *Living Bird* 14:59–85.

Mader, W. J. 1975. Extra adults at Harris' Hawk nests. *Condor* 77:482–485.

Mader, W. J. 1978. A comparative nesting study of Red-tailed and Harris' Hawks in southern Arizona. *Auk* 95:327–337.

Mader, W. J. 1979. Breeding behavior of a polyandrous trio of Harris' Hawks in southern Arizona. *Auk* 96:776–788.

Whaley, W. H. 1986. Population ecology of the Harris' Hawk in Arizona. *Raptor Res.* 20:1–15.

OSPREY

Ames, P. L., and G. S. Mersereau. 1964. Some factors in the decline of the Osprey in Connecticut. *Auk* 81:173–185.

Gerrard, J. M., D. W. A. Whitfield, and W. J. Mader. 1976. Osprey–Bald Eagle relationships in Saskatchewan. *Blue Jay* 34:240–246.

Jamison, I., N. Seymour, and R. P. Bancroft. 1982. Use of two habitats related to changes in prey availability in a population of Ospreys in northeastern Nova Scotia. *Wilson Bull.* 94:557–564.

Knight, C. W. R. 1932. The nest life of the Osprey. *Nat. Geog.* 62:247–260.

Ogden, J. C. (ed.). 1977. *Transactions of the North American Osprey research conference*. U.S. Natl. Park Serv. Proc. Ser. No. 2.

Poole, A. 1979. Sibling aggression among nestling Ospreys in Florida Bay. *Auk* 96:415–417.

Prevost, Y. 1979. Osprey–Bald Eagle interactions at a common foraging site. *Auk* 96:413–414.

Reese, J. G. 1977. Reproductive success of Ospreys in central Chesapeake Bay. *Auk* 94:202–221.

Spitzer, P. R. 1978. Osprey egg and nestling transfers: their value as ecological experiments and as management procedures. Pp. 171–182 in *Endangered birds: management techniques for preserving threatened species*, S. A. Temple (ed.), University of Wisconsin Press, Madison.

Spitzer, P., and A. Poole. 1980. Coastal Ospreys between N.Y. City and Boston: a decade of reproductive recovery. *Am. Birds* 34:234–241.

Swenson, J. E. 1979. The relationship between prey species ecology and dive success in Ospreys. *Auk* 96:408–412.

Ueoka, M. L., and J. R. Koplin. 1973. Foraging behavior of Ospreys in northwestern California. *Raptor Res.* 7:32–38.

Wiemeyer, S. N., P. R. Spitzer, W. C. Krantz, T. G. Lamont, and E. Cromartie. 1975. Effects of environmental pollutants on Connecticut and Maryland Ospreys. *J. Wildl. Manage.* 39:124–139.

BALD EAGLE

Bird, D. M. (chief ed.). 1983. *Biology and management of Bald Eagles and Ospreys*. Harpell Press, Ste. Anne de Bellevue, Quebec, Canada.

Broley, C. L. 1947. Migration and nesting of Florida Bald Eagles. *Wilson Bull.* 59:3–20.

Broley, C. L. 1950. The plight of the Florida Bald Eagle. *Audubon Mag.* 52:43–49.

Broley, M. J. 1952. *Eagle Man*. Pellegrini and Cudahay, New York.

Gerrard, J. M., and G. R. Bartolotti. 1988. *The Bald Eagle, haunts and habits of a wilderness monarch*. Smithsonian Institution Press, Washington, D.C.

Grier, J. W. 1982. Ban of DDT and subsequent recovery of reproduction in Bald Eagles. *Science* 218:1232–1234.

Hansen, A. J., and J. I. Hodges. 1985. High rates of nonbreeding adult Bald Eagles in southeastern Alaska. *J. Wildl. Manage.* 49:454–458.

Herrick, F. H. 1924. Life history of the Bald Eagle. *Auk* 41:89–105, 213–231, 389–422, and 517–541.

Herrick, F. H. 1934. *The American Eagle*. D. Appleton-Century, New York.

Imler, R. H., and E. R. Kalmbach. 1955. *The Bald Eagle and its economic status*. U.S.D.I. Fish Wildl. Serv. Circ. 30.

Lincer, J. L., W. S. Clark, and M. N. LeFranc, Jr. 1979. *Working bibliography of the Bald Eagle*. National Wildlife Federation Scientific and Technical Series No. 2.

Love, J. A. 1983. *The return of the Sea Eagle*. Cambridge University Press, Cambridge, England.

Platt, J. B. 1976. Bald Eagles wintering in a Utah desert. *Am. Birds* 30:783–788.

Powell, G. V. N., R. D. Bjork, J. C. Ogden, R. T. Paul, A. H. Powell, and W. B. Robertson, Jr. 1989. Population trends in some Florida Bay wading birds. *Wilson Bull.* 101:436–457.

Rearden, J. 1984. The Chilkat miracle. *Audubon* 86:40–54.

Sherrod, S. K., C. M. White, and F. S. L. Williamson. 1976. Biology of the Bald Eagle in Amchitka island, Alaska. *Living Bird* 15:143–182.

Sprunt, A., IV, W. B. Robertson, Jr., S. Postupalsky, R. J. Hensel, C. E. Knoder, and F. J. Ligas. 1973. Comparative productivity of six Bald Eagle populations. *Trans. N. Amer. Wildl. and Nat. Res. Conf.* 38:96–106.

Stalmaster, M. 1987. *The Bald Eagle*. Universe, New York.

GOLDEN EAGLE

Arnold, L. W. 1954. *The Golden Eagle and its economic status*. U.S.D.I. Fish Wildl. Serv. Circ. 27.

Boeker, E. L., and P. R. Nickerson. 1975. Raptor electrocutions. *Wildl. Soc. Bull.* 3:79–81.

Boeker, E. L., and T. D. Ray. 1971. Golden Eagle population studies in the Southwest. *Condor* 73:463–467.

Collopy, M. W. 1984. Parental care and feeding ecology of Golden Eagles. *Auk* 101:753–760.

Ellis, D. H. 1979. *Development of behavior in the Golden Eagle*. Wildl. Monogr. No. 70.

Gordon, S. 1927. *Days with the Golden Eagle*. Williams and Norgate, London.

LeFranc, M. N., Jr., and W. S. Clark. 1983. *Working bibliography of the Golden Eagle and the genus* Aquila. National Wildlife Federation Scientific and Technical Series No. 7.

Leshem, Y. 1979–1980. Golden Eagles in our backyard. *Israel Land and Nature* 5:70–75.

McGahan, J. 1967. Quantified estimates of predation by a Golden Eagle population. *J. Wildl. Manage.* 31:496–501.

McGahan, J. 1968. Ecology of the Golden Eagle. *Auk* 85:1–12.

Nelson, M. W., and P. Nelson. 1976. Power lines and birds of prey. *Idaho Wildl. Rev.* 28:3–7.

Olendorff, R. R. 1975. *Golden Eagle Country*. Alfred A. Knopf, New York.

Olendorff, R. R., A. D. Miller, and R. N. Lehman. 1981. *Suggested practices for raptor protection on power lines, the state of the art in 1981*. Raptor Research Rep. No. 4.

Spofford, W. R. 1964. *The Golden Eagle in the Trans-Pecos and Edwards Plateau of Texas.* Audubon Conserv. Report No. 1, National Audubon Society, New York.

Spofford, W. R. 1971. The breeding status of the Golden Eagle in the Appalachians. *Am. Birds* 25:3–7.

Wiley, R. W., and E. G. Bolen. 1971. Eagle-livestock relationships: livestock carcass census and wound characteristics. *Southwest Nat.* 16:151–169.

GYRFALCON

Bengston, S. A. 1971. Hunting methods and choice of prey of Gyrfalcons *Falco rusticolus* at Myvatn in northeast Iceland. *Ibis* 113:468–476.

Bente, P. J. 1981. Nesting behavior and hunting activity of the Gyrfalcon, *Falco rusticolus*, in southcentral Alaska. M.S. thesis, University of Alaska, Fairbanks.

Burnham, W. A., and W. G. Mattox. 1984. Biology of the Peregrine and Gyrfalcon in Greenland. *Meddr. Groland.* 14:1–30.

Cade, T. J. 1960. Ecology of the peregrine and Gyrfalcon populations in Alaska. *Univ. Calif. Publ. Zool.* 63:151–290.

Jenkins, M. A. 1978. Gyrfalcon nesting behavior from hatching to fledging. *Auk* 95:122–127.

Platt, J. B. 1976. Gyrfalcon nest site selection and winter activity in the western Canadian Arctic. *Can. Field-Nat.* 90:338–345.

Platt, J. B. 1977. The breeding behavior of wild and captive Gyrfalcons in relation to their environment and human disturbance. Ph.D. dissertation, Cornell University, Ithaca, New York.

White, C. M., and R. B. Weeden. 1966. Hunting methods of Gyrfalcons and behavior of their prey (ptarmigan). *Condor* 68:517–519.

Wrege, P., and T. J. Cade. 1977. Courtship behavior of the large falcons in captivity. *Raptor Res.* 11:1–27.

PEREGRINE FALCON (DUCK HAWK)

Beebe, F. L. 1960. The marine peregrines of the northwest Pacific Coast. *Condor* 62:154–189.

Bond, R. M. 1946. The peregrine population of western North America. *Condor* 48:101–116.

Cade, T. J., J. H. Enderson, C. G. Thelander, and C. M. White (eds.). 1988. *Peregrine Falcon populations, their management and recovery.* Peregrine Fund, Boise, Idaho.

Cade, T. J., C. M. White, and J. R. Haugh. 1968. Peregrines and pesticides in Alaska. *Condor* 70:170–178.

Enderson, J. H. 1965. A breeding and migration survey of the Peregrine Falcon. *Wilson Bull.* 77:327–339.

Herbert, R. A., and K. G. S. Herbert. 1965. Behavior of Peregrine Falcons in the New York City region. *Auk* 82:62–94.

Hickey, J. J. 1942. Eastern populations of the Duck Hawk. *Auk* 59:176–204.

Hickey, J. J. (ed.). 1969. *Peregrine Falcon populations, their biology and decline.* University of Wisconsin Press, Madison.

Mearns, R., and I. Newton. 1984. Turnover and dispersal in a peregrine *Falco peregrinus* population. *Ibis* 126:347–355.

Nelson, R. W. 1977. Behavioral ecology of coastal peregrines (*Falco peregrinus*). Ph.D. dissertation, University of Calgary, Calgary, Alberta, Canada.

Peakall, D. B., and L. F. Kiff. 1979. Eggshell thinning and DDE residue levels among Peregrine Falcons: a global perspective. *Ibis* 121:200–204.

Porter, R. D., M. A. Jenkins, and A. L. Gaski. 1987. *Working bibliography of the Peregrine Falcon.* National Wildlife Federation Scientific and Technical Series No. 9.

Ratcliffe, D. A. 1980. *The Peregrine Falcon.* Poyser, Calton, England.

Roalkvam, R. 1985. How effective are hunting peregrines? *Raptor Res.* 19:27–29.

Sherrod, S. K. 1983. *Behavior of fledgling peregrines.* The Peregrine Fund, Ithaca, New York.

White, C. M. 1968. Diagnosis and relationships of the North American tundra-inhabiting Peregrine Falcons. *Auk* 85:179–191.

PRAIRIE FALCON

Boyce, D. A., Jr., R. L. Garrett, and B. J. Walton. 1986. Distribution and density of Prairie Falcons nesting in California during the 1970s. *Raptor Res.* 20:71–74.

Enderson, J. H. 1964. A study of the Prairie Falcon in the central Rocky Mountain region. *Auk* 81:332–352.

Enderson, J. H., and P. H. Wrege. 1973. DDE residues and eggshell thickness in Prairie Falcons. *J. Wildl. Manage.* 37:476–478.

Fyfe, R. 1972. Breeding behavior of captive and wild Prairie and Peregrine Falcons. *Raptor Res.* 6 (suppl. C):43–52.

Fyfe, R. W., J. Campbell, B. Hayson, and K. Hodson. 1969. Regional population declines and organochlorine insecticides in Canadian Prairie Falcons. *Can. Field-Nat.* 83:191–200.

Ogden, V. T., and M. Hornocker. 1977. Nesting density and success of Prairie Falcons in southwestern Idaho. *J. Wildl. Manage.* 41:1–11.

Porter, R. D., and C. M. White. 1973. The Peregrine Falcon in Utah; emphasizing ecology and competition with the Prairie Falcon. *Brigham Young Univ. Sci. Bull.* 18:1–74.

Steenhof, K., M. N. Kochert, and M. Q. Moritsch. 1984. Dispersal and migration of southwestern Idaho raptors. *J. Field Ornithol.* 55:357–368.

U.S. Department of Interior. 1979. *Snake River birds of prey special research report.* Bureau of Land Management, Boise, Idaho.

APLOMADO FALCON

Bendire, C. E. 1887. Notes on a collection of birds' nests and eggs from southern Arizona territory. *Proc. U.S. Nat. Mus.* 11:551–558.

Brooks, A. 1933. Some notes on the birds of Brownsville, Texas. *Auk* 50:59–63.

Hector, D. P. 1980. Our rare falcon of the desert grassland. *Birding* 12:92–102.

Hector, D. P. 1981. The habitat, diet, and foraging behavior of the Aplomado Falcon, *Falco femoralis* (Temminck). M.S. thesis, Oklahoma State University, Stillwater.

Hector, D. P. 1985. The diet of the Aplomado Falcon (*Falco femoralis*) in eastern Mexico. *Condor* 87:336–342.

Hector, D. P. 1986. Cooperative hunting and its relationship to foraging success and prey sizes in an avian predator. *Ethology* 73:247–257.

Hector, D. P. 1987. The decline of the Aplomado Falcon in the United States. *Am. Birds* 41:381–389.

Kiff, L. F., D. B. Peakall, and D. P. Hector. 1981. Eggshell thinning and organochlorine residues in the Bat and Aplomado Falcons in Mexico. *Proc. XVII Int. Ornithol. Cong., 1978,* pp. 949–952.

Ligon, J. S. 1961. *New Mexico birds and where to find them.* University of New Mexico Press, Albuquerque.

MERLIN (PIGEON HAWK)

Bibby, C. J. 1986. Merlins in Wales: site occupancy and breeding in relation to vegetation. *J. Appl. Ecol.* 23:1–12.

Craighead, J. J., and F. C. Craighead. 1940. Nesting Pigeon Hawks. *Wilson Bull.* 52:241–248.

Feldsine, J. W., and L. W. Oliphant. 1985. Breeding behavior of the Merlin: the courtship period. *Raptor Res.* 19:60–67.

Laing, K. 1985. Food habits and breeding biology of Merlins in Denali National Park, Alaska. *Raptor Res.* 19:42–51.

Newton, I., E. R. Meek, and B. Little. 1986. Population and breeding of Northumbrian Merlins. *Brit. Birds* 79:155–170.

Oliphant, L. W., and E. A. Haug. 1985. Productivity, population density, and rate of increase in an expanding Merlin population. *Raptor Res.* 19:56–59.

Oliphant, L. W., and S. McTaggart. 1977. Prey utilized by urban Merlins. *Can. Field-Nat.* 91:190–192.

Oliphant, L. W., and W. J. P. Thompson. 1978. Recent breeding success of Richardson's Merlin in Saskatchewan. *Raptor Res.* 12:35–39.

Page, G., and D. F. Whitacre. 1975. Raptor predation on wintering shorebirds. *Condor* 77:73–83.

Rowan, W. 1921–1922. Observations on the breeding habits of the Merlin. *Brit. Birds* 15:122–129, 194–202, 222–231, 246–253.

Warkentin, I. G., and P. C. James. 1988. Nest-site selection by urban Merlins. *Condor* 90:734–738.

Wiklund, C. G. 1979. Increased breeding success for Merlins nesting among colonies of Fieldfares *Turdus pilaris*. *Ibis* 121:109–111.

AMERICAN KESTREL (SPARROW HAWK)

Balgooyen, T. G. 1976. Behavior and ecology of the American Kestrel in the Sierra Nevada of California. *Univ. Calif. Publ. Zool.* 103:1–83.

Bird, D. M., and R. Bowman (eds.). 1987. *The ancestral kestrel.* Raptor Res. Rep. No. 6.

Cade, T. J. 1955. Experiments on winter territoriality of the American Kestrel. *Wilson Bull.* 67:5–17.

Clay, W. M. 1953. Protective coloration in the American Sparrow Hawk. *Wilson Bull.* 65:129–134.

Collopy, M. W. 1973. Predatory efficiency of American Kestrels wintering in northwestern California. *Raptor Res.* 7:25–31.

Enderson, J. H. 1960. A population study of the Sparrow Hawk in east-central Illinois. *Wilson Bull.* 72:222–231.

Hamerstrom, F., F. N. Hamerstrom, and J. Hart. 1973. Nest boxes: an effective management tool for Kestrels. *J. Wildl. Manage.* 37:400–403.

Lincer, J. 1975. DDE-induced eggshell thinning in the American Kestrel: a comparison of the field situation with laboratory studies. *J. Appl. Ecol.* 12:781–793.

Smallwood, J. A. 1988. A mechanism of sexual segregation by habitat in American Kestrels (*Falco sparverius*) wintering in south-central Florida. *Auk* 105:36–46.

Sparrowe, R. D. 1972. Prey-catching behavior in the Sparrow Hawk. *J. Wildl. Manage.* 36:297–308.

Toland, B. R. 1987. The effect of vegetative cover on foraging strategies, hunting success and nesting distribution of American Kestrels in central Missouri. *Raptor Res.* 21:14–20.

Willoughby, E. J., and T. J. Cade. 1964. Breeding behavior of the American Kestrel. *Living Bird* 3:75–96.

CRESTED (AUDUBON'S) CARACARA

Bartram, W. 1791. *Travels through North and South Carolina, Georgia, East and West Florida.* James and Johnson, Philadelphia, Pennsylvania.

Glazener, W. C. 1964. Notes on the feeding habits of the Caracara in south Texas. *Condor* 66:162.

Harper, F. 1936. The *Vultur sacra* of William Bartram. *Auk* 53:381–392.

Layne, J. N. 1978. Threatened Audubon's Caracara. Pp. 34–35 in *Rare and endangered biota of Florida*, Vol. 2, Birds, H. W. Kale, III., (ed.), University Presses of Florida, Gainesville.

Nicholson, D. J. 1928. The Audubon Caracara of Florida. *Oologist* 45:2–8.

Schroder, H. H. 1947. Caracara of the Florida prairies. *Nat. Hist.* 56:84–85.

Sutton, G. M. 1951. *Mexican birds: first impressions.* University of Oklahoma Press, Norman.

Wallace, M. P., and S. A. Temple. 1987. Competitive interactions within and between species in a guild of avian scavengers. *Auk* 104:290–295.

Whitacre, D., D. Ukrain, and G. Falxa. 1982. Notes on the hunting behavior and diet of the Crested Caracara in northeastern Chiapas and Tabasco, Mexico. *Wilson Bull.* 94:565–566.

Index

About the Authors

NOEL AND HELEN SNYDER are best known for their important roles in the efforts to prevent the extinction of two critically endangered species of birds, the Puerto Rican Parrot and the California Condor, but their contributions to zoological research and conservation have also involved many other species. Following graduate studies at Cornell University, they were based in Florida from 1967 to 1972, where Noel taught at the University of South Florida and where they carried on studies of Everglade Kites and Limpkins and the snails these species feed upon. Their Florida research also included a detailed study of the nesting biology of Swallow-tailed Kites. At the same time they pursued summer field research on the breeding biology of Cooper's Hawks, Sharp-shinned Hawks, and Northern Goshawks in Arizona and New Mexico, giving special attention to the effects of pesticides on these birds.

From 1972 through 1976 they conducted intensive studies of the Puerto Rican Parrot for the U. S. Fish and Wildlife Service and the U. S. Forest Service, and were successful in reversing the rapid decline of this highly endangered species. Their efforts on behalf of the Puerto Rican Parrot are summarized in *The Parrots of Luquillo, Natural History and Conservation of the Puerto Rican Parrot*, coauthored with James Wiley and Cameron Kepler, and published by the Western Foundation of Vertebrate Zoology.

In the mid-1970s, Helen carried on investigations into the status, distribution, and biology of Common Black Hawks and Zone-tailed Hawks in the Southwest, in collaboration with Rich Glinski. And in the late 1970s, the Snyders returned to Florida to resume field studies of the Everglade Kite, this time with efforts focused on gaining an understanding of the demography and reproductive biology of the species.

From 1980 through 1986, they participated in a cooperative campaign of the U. S. Fish and Wildlife Service and many other organizations to rescue the California Condor from almost certain extinction. Their contributions to this program centered on reproduction, censusing, and mortality studies, and on efforts to form a viable captive population, and are summarized in a review entitled "Biology and Conservation of the California Condor," which appeared in *Current Ornithology*, volume 6. For exhaustive efforts on behalf of the condor and the Puerto Rican Parrot, Noel was awarded the prestigious Brewster Medal of the American Ornithologists' Union in 1989, and a Distinguished Achievement Award by the Society for Conservation Biology.

Since 1986, the Snyders have been engaged in an effort to restore the Thick-billed Parrot to the wild in Arizona, a collaborative program of the Arizona Game and Fish Department with the U. S. Fish and Wildlife Service, the U. S. Forest Service, and Wildlife Preservation Trust International.